Seeking Truth

365 DAYS
IN THE WISDOM AND
POETIC BOOKS OF THE BIBLE

JENNIFER HAYES YATES

Interior images and author photo by Genesis Shalom Harrington

Edited by Josiah Lee Yates

Formatting by Jen Henderson of Wild Words Formatting

jenniferhyates.com

Introduction

"What is truth?"

These were words spoken by Pilate in response to a profound statement from Jesus:

"Everyone on the side of truth listens to me" (John 18:37b-38a).

Do you ever find yourself wondering exactly what the truth is in a situation? Have you read posts on social media from two different sides of an issue and struggled to know which one is actually right?

In an age in which information is so readily available yet so easily adjustable, we have to be discerning to know what is right and true. Jesus made it clear that He is truth (John 14:6a). And He is the Word made flesh (John 1:14a).

Therefore, in His Word, we can find truth—not just words that declare truth, but words that, when read prayerfully under the leadership of the Spirit of truth (John 15:26), will guide us into truth (John 16:13).

And I don't know about you, but I need truth in my life. I need to know the truth about my relationships, my purpose and calling, my worship, and my sin.

When I first started spending quality time with God, I began reading a psalm every day. I love the Psalms because through them we can express all of our emotions—whether positive or negative—and then turn our hearts to worship God. By expressing our feelings truthfully in worship, we are less likely to express them negatively throughout our day.

Then I began to read a chapter of Proverbs daily, and in them I found wisdom for making daily decisions. The truths contained in the book of Proverbs gave me a godly way of thinking that was both practical and applicable.

As I ventured into Ecclesiastes, I was confused at first. The writer seemed to be so negative and fatalistic. But I realized he was really being honest. In these words, I began to see God reveal our purpose for living which stood in stark contrast to the world's view—a truth that I could appreciate.

As a lover of poetry and language, Song of Songs quickly drew me in to the beauty of romantic love, the truth about dating and marriage, and an image of the love of God for His people.

And then there is Job. No matter how much I appreciated the ancient verse, I couldn't wrap my head around God's drawing Job into this challenge with Satan. It just didn't seem fair or consistent with God's character. But as my son pointed out, I could hardly write a devotional on the wisdom and poetry books of the Bible and leave Job out.

So, I have done an in-depth study of the Book of Job, and guess what? I have a new favorite book of the Bible. Nowhere else do we find such raw honesty and startling truth. I saved Job for the end because the principles found there seemed to wrap up the heart of this book.

I pray that starting your day in the truth to be gleaned in these poetic books will create in you a desire for more of God and His Word. Let His truth establish in you a firm foundation of worship, wisdom, purpose, passion, and a godly response to pain.

As women of God, let's be on the side of truth.

"Send forth your light and your truth, let them
guide me; let them bring me to your holy mountain,
to the place where you dwell" (Psalm 43:3).

How to Use This Book

One of the mainstays of my daily time with the Lord has been a devotional book. I have always enjoyed reading short commentaries on Scripture as a way to focus my heart before I dive into my prayer and Bible study time.

I can still recall the first devotional I read after deciding to follow Jesus. *Faith's Checkbook* by Charles Haddon Spurgeon remains my favorite devotional reading of all time.

Because a devotional book is intended to be a brief daily reading on a Scripture, how we approach each one depends upon the individual. I would like to make a few suggestions for how to use this book.

I intentionally left off the date so that the devotional can be started on any day of the year. Each day begins with a Scripture, followed by the devotion. At the end, there are references to the Scriptures noted in the reading and some additional verses.

If you are short on time, you may prefer to just read the Scripture and the devotion that follows. For those who want to add more insight, I suggest reading the context of the verse at the top (perhaps the entire chapter), plus the additional Scriptures noted at the bottom of each page.

If you prefer a more in-depth approach to the devotional, I recommend doing all of the above, while also journaling your thoughts and reflections from each day. This approach allows you to think about what God wants to communicate and how that might impact your daily life.

However you choose to use this book, my prayer is that the Holy Spirit will use these words to guide you to His truth.

DAY 1

*"Blessed is the man who does not walk in
the counsel of the wicked or stand in the way of
sinners or sit in the seat of mockers" (Psalm 1:1).*

We all need answers at some point in life. The world has much to offer us in the way of advice. We can search online and find the answer to any question, tune in to multiple "counselors" on every afternoon television channel, or simply seek guidance on social media.

At first, we may just go along with the culture around us. After all, we don't want to make waves. Then we can get comfortable enough in the world's way to hang out there. But if we stay too long immersed in what is counter to God's Word, we eventually will settle right in with those who mock God.

This progression shows us how easy it is to fall into the world's way of thinking. But seeking the world's counsel will not lead us to truth. God calls us to a biblical worldview, where everything is held up to the standard of His Word.

According to our culture, "Truth is relative." But Jesus said He *is* the truth. The world tells us to look out for number one. Jesus said the first will be last and the last will be first. The world tells us to follow our hearts. Jesus said to follow Him.

If we're not careful, we will start living by the world's standards instead of God's. The only way to live rightly in the world is to live in the Word. We must start our day with time in God's presence, seeking Him, meditating on His truth, and allowing His Word to be our guide in all we say and do.

Otherwise, we'll be like chaff that the wind just blows away (Psalm 1:4).

Our culture, characterized by social media, sound bites, and meme theology, will lead us away from truth. The progression is gradual and subtle. Let's be women who seek truth daily in the Word of God.

For further reading: Matthew 5:44, Mark 9:35, John 14:6, James 4:4

DAY 2

"But his delight is in the law of the LORD,
and on his law he meditates day and night. He is like
a tree planted by streams of water..." (Psalm 1:2-3a).

The lane that leads to our home is lined with pecan trees that have held their ground for over a century. Some of them have rotted from the inside, eventually succumbing to the wind and rains; but most of them are still flourishing, producing tasty pecans every fall that our family enjoys.

We can choose to walk with the world, but we will end up like those trees that didn't last. But blessed—happy, fortunate, characterized by God's favor—are those who delight in God's Word. Going along with the world may seem easier than staying in the Word, but the blessings of God far outweigh the curse of sin. God's Word is full of truth, wisdom, instruction, and encouragement that will feed our spirits and bring us life.

If we find the Bible difficult to understand, we can ask the Holy Spirit to teach us. If we feel we don't have time to spend in the Word, we can take a break from TV or social media and ask God to give us a hunger and thirst for Him.

If we find reading the Bible boring, we can start with a short book, such as Ephesians, and think about one verse at a time and how to apply its principles in our daily lives. We can try journaling our thoughts on each section of Scripture or praying God's Word back to Him.

Those who delight in God and His Word have a beautiful promise! We will be like a tree planted by the water—fruitful, prospering, beautiful, and blessed. We will bear fruit that will last: love, joy, peace, patience, kindness, goodness, faithfulness, gentleness, and self-control. We will be full of life, thriving, bringing shade to others, having roots that go way down deep in the love and security of Christ. And we will never wither, always drinking in the life-giving water of Jesus, planted right by the streams of His grace.

For further reading: Psalm 92:12-14, Proverbs 11:28, Galatians 5:22-23, Ephesians 3:14-19

DAY 3

*"He is like a tree planted by streams of water,
which yields its fruit in season and whose leaf does
not wither. Whatever he does prospers" (Psalm 1:3).*

There's something to be said for being steady in every season. We all go through different seasons of life from youth to marriage, raising kids and graduating kids, empty nest, retirement, old age. We also go through different seasons in ministry, times of sickness or grief, times of prosperity and times of need, or perhaps seasons of preparation for what is to come.

Knowing that we will indeed go through different seasons in life, how can we navigate the ups and downs with peace, stability, and faithfulness?

Trees go through all of the seasons. I look forward each year to our pecan trees once again bursting with green in the spring. They are so barren and dull all winter. But the funny thing is that even in the spring, most of them are still bearing fruit from the previous season. All through the winter, when the trees no longer look pretty, they are still full of fruit.

What about me? When things aren't looking all that pretty in my life, am I still bearing fruit? During the transitions and the setbacks am I still trusting God and walking in the Spirit? Am I still prepared to share God's love and truth with someone? During the times of sickness or grief, do I still believe that God is with me?

The tree in Psalm 1 yields its fruit in season. The reason the tree is able to bear fruit in the appropriate season is because it's planted by the stream night and day, like a woman of God rooted and grounded in the Lord and in His Word.

If we want to be steady, bearing fruit no matter what season we are in, we need to stay close to Jesus and drink deeply of His life-giving Word both night and day, in and out of season.

For further reading: Joshua 1:8, John 15:16, Colossians 1:10, 2 Timothy 4:2

DAY 4

"For the LORD watches over the way of the righteous,
but the way of the wicked will perish" (Psalm 1:6).

Sometimes life seems very black or white, in or out, right or left. And sometimes we feel it's all gray, and we're not sure what's what.

While it's true there are areas of our lives that aren't crystal clear, one thing we can be sure of is the truth of this verse. God very clearly offers us two choices in life: the way of the righteous and the way of the wicked.

Most of us would not consider ourselves to be wicked, but the truth is that there are only two paths in life. We are either on the Lord's side or Satan's side. If we haven't made the choice to surrender our lives to God through accepting the sacrifice of Jesus for our sins, then we are by default choosing to follow the enemy.

The way of the righteous simply means the path of following Christ. He has become our righteousness. By Jesus' death on the cross, He paid the debt (death) that we owed for our sin, taking our place, our blame, our shame all upon Himself.

He exchanged his righteousness for our sinfulness, thereby making us right with God. That's what it means to take the way of the righteous. Because we have chosen to follow Jesus, the Lord watches over our way forevermore. We are promised eternal life—forever in the presence of all that is good and right.

Not choosing to follow Jesus, however, puts us on the path of the wicked. By not choosing the free gift of Christ, we are choosing to take the path that leads to death.

Despite our good intentions, our actual choices are what determine our path and, therefore, our destination. Choose the way of truth and righteousness by holding everything up to the standard of God's Word. Jesus is the way, the truth, and the life

For further reading: Deuteronomy 30:19, John 3:16, Romans 6:23, 10:9-10

DAY 5

"The One enthroned in heaven laughs; the Lord scoffs at them"
(Psalm 2:4).

Every time a new leader comes to power, people rebel. It's amazing that with all God has to offer—salvation, eternal life, peace, hope, love, and joy—people still choose to rebel against the Lord.

We see a perfect example of this in Acts 4. As the apostles continued to proclaim the truth that Jesus is the Son of God and that He had risen from the dead, the religious leaders rebelled. Many disciples were imprisoned during this time, including Peter and John. They were released only because the leaders feared the people who were praising God for the miracles, but they were told "not to speak or teach at all in the name of Jesus" (Acts 4:18).

What is it about the name of Jesus that makes people rebel? Could it be that, just as these religious leaders felt threatened by the authority of Jesus, many today feel threatened by the One who wants to lead them? Although God's heart for us is good, many don't want anyone on the throne of their hearts but themselves. We live in a culture in which *self* rules. We want to be the master of our own destiny. We want to be our own boss and live by our own standards. And God will let us.

We all have been given free will and have the opportunity to choose whom we will follow—self or the Savior. But regardless of our choices, God stays in control. He can't be manipulated, thwarted, or dethroned. We can rebel against Him and choose to run our own lives, but God still reigns over all, and He knows what is best for us.

Jesus is King whether we acknowledge Him or not. We may think we rule ourselves, but the truth is that we cannot control our destinies. God is sovereign. And in His love and mercy, He has graciously extended to each of us the opportunity to submit to Him and His authority over us. When we submit to His loving rule in our lives, we walk in the peace and contentment that come from being in His will. His authority is perfect because He is faithful and true.

For further reading: Joshua 24:15, Acts 4, Romans 13:1, Philippians 2:10-11, Colossians 1:16

DAY 6

"But you are a shield around me, O LORD;
you bestow glory on me and lift up my head" (Psalm 3:3).

David wrote this psalm as he fled from his own son Absalom, who wanted to kill him and usurp the throne. Even as God blessed David, David still battled the enemy; and so will we.

When we choose to follow Jesus, we gain a powerful enemy. At times we may feel overwhelmed by the battle. The good news is that Jesus is the greater One. When David felt surrounded by the foes that rose up against him, he remembered that God was on his side. David declared that the Lord was a shield around him. The Lord would protect him from his enemies, and God will do the same for us.

In Ephesians 6, we read that our battle is not against flesh and blood. We first must realize that our enemy is Satan, and he has already been defeated. He has great power, but he has no authority in the life of a believer apart from what God allows. As we suit up in the armor of God, we lift up our shield of faith, which protects us from the darts of the enemy. Satan's fiery darts are his lies and deception. Our shield is our faith in God's ability to protect us.

I love the fact that David said the Lord would bestow glory on him and lift up his head. In other words, even though some, including his own son, were out to get him, David would still be honored by God, and that was what really mattered to him.

When you feel that you are surrounded by foes, remember the Lord is on your side. He is the lifter of your head. When the world looks down on you or even mocks you for following God, He will be your shield. The Lord will bring deliverance. Walk in His Spirit, where there is love and joy and peace. You can lie down and sleep without fear or anxiety, because the Lord of hosts is on your side.

Choose wisely to follow God, and you will rest in the blessing of being on the right side of the fight.

For further reading: 2 Samuel 15:13-17:22, Ephesians 6, 1 John 4:4

DAY 7

"Know that the LORD has set apart the godly for himself;
the LORD will hear when I call to him" (Psalm 4:3).

No matter what we are facing in life, we have a God who is bigger. He spoke the universe into being. There's no problem too big or too small for our God. When our hearts are devoted to God, He delights in our prayers.

We like to think that we can choose our own way in life and then call on God when we are in trouble, but God doesn't work that way. If we choose to be our own master and live on our own terms, the Lord will let us. But He isn't obligated to answer our prayers.

The Word tells us that if we cherish sin, we allow that sin to mar our relationship with God. To cherish sin means that we delight in it. We are all sinners, but as followers of Jesus, we should be convicted and repent of sin. If we cherish sin and stay in it, refusing to repent, then we are not living for God. If we *are* living for God, we hate sin just as He does. We may struggle with a sin, but we are working with God to overcome it.

The danger here in Psalm 4 is for those who "love delusions and seek false gods" (2b). There are those who believe that as long as they go to church or do right things, God is obligated to answer their prayers. The word translated "delusions" is actually "emptiness" or "vanity."[1]

In other words, these are people who chase after what is false, rather than seeking God's truth in His Word. But God has "set apart the godly for himself." The godly are those who are faithful and seek God. When we live our lives surrendered to God and His ways, we can be sure that He hears our prayers. We may not always understand how God works, but we can know He works for our good.

Whatever you are facing today, know that the Lord has set apart the godly for himself. Choose God and His ways over the world and your own way. You will find that whatever answer He gives, you can "lie down and sleep in peace" (Psalm 4:8).

For further reading: Psalm 66:18, Isaiah 59:1-2, Romans 8:28, 1 Peter 3:12

DAY 8

*"In the morning, O LORD, you hear my voice; in the morning
I lay my requests before you and wait in expectation" (Psalm 5:3).*

You may not be a morning person, and that's okay. I used to hate to get up early, but once I made a commitment to seek God first every morning, I began to experience His presence in a way that made me hungry for more.

The decision came after an especially trying time. I was a believer, but I was miserable, overwhelmed, and struggling with sin. I wanted to do the right thing, but I couldn't seem to make godly decisions. I finally got desperate enough that I cried out to God for help, and that is when God began to show me that I was not seeking Him first.

I still loved God. I still went to church. I still talked about God and prayed. But I was not completely surrendered to the Lord. I wanted to do things my way, and my way wasn't working.

God has created us with a need for Him. We need Him desperately, in every area of our lives. The only way to truly be at peace is to live our lives completely surrendered to Him. And He wants to be first.

God won't settle for second place in our lives. He's a jealous God. He commands that we have no other gods before Him. He wants our hearts.

Just as the Israelites were commanded to give God the first fruits of all their labor, we should give Him the first fruits of our day. David knew that if he started his day with God, he could wait in expectation, knowing that God would take care of him and meet his needs.

The Lord is calling each of us into His presence where His mercies are new every morning. He desires to bless us with His joy and peace, and He is faithful. Won't you make a commitment right now to start every day with Him?

Even if it's just a few moments, decide now that you will seek Him first every day for the rest of your life. That's a decision you will never regret.

For further reading: Exodus 20:3, Lamentations 3:23, Matthew 6:33, Mark 1:35

DAY 9

"My soul is in anguish. How long, O LORD, how long?" (Psalm 6:3).

Have you ever asked that question? Believers are not immune from suffering. In fact, we've been promised suffering in this world.

"I have told you these things, so that in me you may have peace. In this world you will have trouble. But take heart! I have overcome the world" (John 16:33).

Sometimes the pain can seem overwhelming, but we are not overcome. No, we are the overcomers. Sometimes the greatest witness to an unbelieving world is for a Christian to go through great suffering with peace. Inside we may be crying, "How long, Lord?" But just like David, we know where to turn. There may be trouble in the world, but there is healing and grace in Jesus.

Jesus suffered in this world, too. He was rejected, criticized, mocked, and bullied. He suffered grief, heartache, and frustration. He was wrongfully arrested, convicted without a fair trial, beaten, and executed for crimes he didn't commit. And we are called to follow in His steps.

You may think that's a little much to ask. Why follow Him if it means we will suffer and be persecuted? The truth is that we will suffer in this world either way. This world has already been corrupted by sin and death. No one is immune. The rain falls on the righteous and the unrighteous. But the sinner suffers without the peace and joy of knowing Jesus.

The difference is that with our faith in Christ, we are able to walk through pain and suffering with hope as the anchor of our soul. We have the hope of healing, salvation, and deliverance through Jesus Christ.

So if you are currently asking, "How long, O Lord?" just know that no matter how long this time of suffering may be, if you are in Christ, you can dwell in the secret place with Him where there is peace. Soak up His presence, spend time in His Word, and trust in His promises.

For the Lord has heard your cry for mercy. Help is on the way.

For further reading: Matthew 5:45, John 16:33, Hebrews 6:19, 1 Peter 2:21

DAY 10

"O Lord my God, I take refuge in you;
save and deliver me from all who pursue me" (Psalm 7:1).

If you are doing any good thing for God, you can bet the enemy is pursuing you. Not only that, but he knows exactly how to tempt you. The devil will do all in his power to get you to turn from God, go astray, ruin your witness, not believe God, or walk in fear so you won't do great things for God. You are a threat to his kingdom.

But God is your refuge. One of the best ways to defeat the devil is to keep doing good. David refused to do evil, even when the enemy was close on his heels. He trusted God to bring justice and prove his innocence and his integrity.

When the enemy uses people against us, sometimes it's hard not to retaliate or try to prove that we are right. But being right is highly overrated. It's better to *do* what is right than to *be* right. When we continue to do the right thing over and over, even when we are faced with adversity, God will show Himself strong on our behalf.

David reminded himself that the one who had done evil against him would have to give an account to God for the wrong he had done. But if David also did wrong, he too would have to stand before God. Therefore, David decided to trust God and continue to do the right thing. He sought God for help rather than trying to solve the problem in his own power. He chose to thank God and sing praises to Him for His righteousness rather than to complain about his enemy.

Our right response to attacks from the enemy is to do as David did and trust God, seeking His help and praising Him for who He is. We can choose to let our focus be on God and His goodness and the righteous choices that He wants us to make. The enemy will seek to distract us from the work we are doing for the Lord. Instead, let's commit to keep doing the right thing and giving God the glory for being our Deliverer in times of trouble.

For further reading: Genesis 4:7, 1 Corinthians 10:13, 2 Thessalonians 3:13, 1 Peter 5:8

DAY 11

"From the lips of children and infants you have ordained praise because of your enemies, to silence the foe and the avenger"
(Psalm 8:2).

Do you ever stop to just look around at the beauty of God's creation? His handiwork can be seen in the sun, moon, and stars; the mountains, oceans, and rivers; the birds, bees, and butterflies; the grass, flowers, and trees. Yet nowhere in all creation is His glory seen more than in the faces of the people He created. We alone are created in the image of God. We alone were created to know Him, serve Him, love Him, and live with Him forever.

In all of His glory, God had little need for you and me. Yet He made us just a little lower than the angels and crowned us with glory and honor (Psalm 8:5). Jesus came to die for you and me to make a way for us to know Him.

Even though we have an enemy while we are here on earth, the very praise from our lips silences the enemy, because we are God's beloved. We are the ones He died for. We are the ones who will inherit the earth.

We have been made ruler over the works of God's hands; we are stewards of all He has provided for us—the land, animals, and resources of earth. All these things were given that we might use them to benefit mankind. We are responsible for how we steward all that God has allowed us to use—our time, gifts, talents, resources, and our very bodies.

Do we consider all that we are and all that we have as gifts from God?

"You are not your own; you were bought at a price. Therefore honor God with your body" (1 Corinthians 6:19b-20). All we are and all we have are gifts from God that can be used to honor Him.

Today let all you say and do bring Him glory. Let the praises from your lips silence the enemy. You were bought at a great price—the blood of His Son.

Walk in that truth today.

For further reading: Genesis 1:28, Matthew 5:5, James 1:17

DAY 12

"Those who know your name will trust in you, for you, LORD, have never forsaken those who seek you" (Psalm 9:10).

The Lord's name is representative of His character. To know His name means to understand who God is. We know Him only because He has chosen to reveal Himself to us through His Son.

"Now this is eternal life: that they may know you, the only true God, and Jesus Christ, whom you have sent" (John 17:3).

To know His name is to know Jesus, the One whom God has sent. Before Jesus came to earth, God was a mystery. He dwelled between the cherubim on the mercy seat in the holy of holies in the temple. His presence was separated from the people by a thick curtain. Only the high priest could enter behind the curtain and only one day a year—on the Jewish Day of Atonement.

When Jesus died on the cross, that curtain was torn in two from top to bottom, signifying the removal of the barrier between us and God.

"Therefore, brothers, since we have confidence to enter the Most Holy Place by the blood of Jesus, by a new and living way opened for us through the curtain, that is, his body, and since we have a great priest over the house of God, let us draw near to God with a sincere heart in full assurance of faith" (Hebrews 10:19-22a).

The more we know God as revealed to us through His Word, the more we will love and trust Him. Seek God first every day, spending quality time in the Word. As you read the Bible, highlight, take notes, journal your thoughts, think about how the Word applies to you and your current situation or what God may be speaking to you. The more we interact with the Word, the more we will understand God's character. As we know Him and trust Him, we will be able to rest in the assurance that He will never forsake those who seek Him.

What are you seeking today? What is your number one priority? Seek the Lord and trust in His name.

For further reading: Luke 23:45, Hebrews 11:6, James 4:8

DAY 13

"In his pride the wicked does not seek him;
in all his thoughts there is no room for God" (Psalm 10:4).

Sometimes it can be difficult to let our light shine in a world that is increasingly hostile to God. From the erosion of marriage and the murder of innocent babies to the rise of secular humanism, it's easy to see that in many people's thoughts "there is no room for God." Often it seems that God is standing far off and doesn't see. The wicked sometimes seem to prosper.

"But you, O God, do see trouble and grief; you consider it to take it in hand" (Psalm 10:14).

But God *does* see. Every person on earth will be called to account for his sin. For the Christian, there will be redemption. For the lost, there will be only judgment.

Just as God was with Joseph throughout his life, He is with those who seek Him. Joseph was hated and sold into slavery by his own brothers, accused of sexual misconduct by his boss's wife, and thrown into prison where he was forgotten. "But while Joseph was there in the prison, the LORD was with him; he showed him kindness and granted him favor in the eyes of the prison warden" (Genesis 39:20b-21).

God raised him up from the prison and used him to save a nation from starvation, leading to the salvation of his entire family, including his brothers. When his brothers realized all that had happened, they came before him, begging to just be his slaves.

"But Joseph said to them, 'Don't be afraid. Am I in the place of God? You intended to harm me, but God intended it for good to accomplish what is now being done, the saving of many lives'" (Genesis 50:19-20).

In all the evil around Joseph, he chose to maintain his integrity and shine his light. We too can be examples of love and faithfulness, even among those who have no thought for God. Who knows if our example might open their eyes to truth?

For further reading: Genesis 39-50, Proverbs 15:3, Jeremiah 16:17, Romans 8:28, Hebrews 4:13

DAY 14

"The LORD is in his holy temple;
the LORD is on his heavenly throne" (Psalm 11:4).

If we choose to dwell on all the evil going on in the world around us, we will have much to fear. Pandemics, racism, terrorism, persecution of Christians, and the dwindling away of godly values can all leave us afraid of what is to come.

David knew what it was like to be surrounded by the enemy, but he also knew where to look for comfort. The enemy may be shooting from the shadows, but Jesus is the Light. The foundations may be crumbling, but Jesus is the Rock.

In other words, no matter what is going on around us, as long as we are in Christ, we have no reason to fear. Nothing takes God by surprise. The evening news is not news to God. He knows all things and He is in control of all things.

David declared that the Lord is in His holy temple. He is still on the throne. Nothing can defeat Him.

What can the righteous do?

Don't take the advice of the wicked to flee. Find refuge in the Lord. Seek His face, pray, worship, and meditate on His Word. God has told us over and over in His Word: Do not fear! Others may fear, but we trust in God.

As we look to the Lord and trust in Him, He sees us. He sees our hearts. He hears our prayers. He is on the side of those who love Him and fear Him.

"If God is for us, who can be against us? He who did not spare his own Son, but gave him up for us all—how will he not also, along with him, graciously give us all things?" (Romans 8:31b-32).

Don't be shaken by all that is going on in the world around you. Put your trust in the One who holds all of heaven and earth in His hands. His throne is not shaken. He is a firm foundation in whom we can trust.

For further reading: Isaiah 41:10, 59:10, 2 Corinthians 4:16-18, Hebrews 12:28

DAY 15

"And the words of the LORD are flawless, like silver refined in a furnace of clay, purified seven times" (Psalm 12:6).

Anybody can write a book, start a blog, or create a podcast–I am living proof of that fact. But it doesn't mean they have truth for your life. Truth comes from God's Word.

That said, lots of people can tell you what's in God's Word and be totally wrong, myself included. So if you get your theology from Facebook or Instagram, you might want to pay attention.

David described a similar time when no one spoke truth—either by lying or flattering with deception. But God heard the cries of the oppressed and spoke His Words.

And His Words are always truth—flawless, like silver refined in a furnace, purified seven times.

In others words, God's Word has been tested and comes out perfect every time.

We never need to doubt the veracity of God's holy Word. He is God and He cannot lie. We need to test everything we hear to see whether it is truth or not. If it lines up with God's Word, we need to stand on that truth and not doubt. But if it contradicts God's truth, we need to reject it as lies from the enemy.

The only way to know truth is to stay in the Word of God. Make time for regular Bible study. Meet with others and discuss God's Word. Take notes during sermons, and then look up each passage and study it for yourself.

Don't be caught off guard and fall for cultural lies and deception. God's Word is truth for all time.

For further reading: John 8:44-45, 17:17, Acts 17:11, 2 Timothy 3:16-17, Hebrews 4:12

DAY 16

"I will sing to the LORD, for he has been good to me" (Psalm 13:6).

If you've ever lost a loved one, you know the pain of grief so deep and raw that it seems your heart will never be whole again. David knew that pain all too well. He cried out to God, admitting in his humanness that he felt forgotten, that God had hidden His face from him. Whether David was dealing with grief over loss, the pain of illness, or a broken relationship, we really don't know. But the sorrow in his heart was deep and painful, to the point that he felt close to death (Psalm 13:3).

But David knew where to turn. He could have cursed God. He could have turned to people for help. He could have given up on life altogether. But David knew the heart of God. He knew that if he cried out to God, His love would not fail.

Sometimes we go through things in life so painful we aren't sure our hearts can take it. When the grief is so raw that we can barely catch our breath, God is there. He's in the rainbow that travels across the sky. He's in the deer that leaps across the field. He's there in the face of a friend who shows up unexpectedly. He's in the voice of a loved one who calls to say I love you.

God is there even in the long, sleepless nights when all we can do is whisper a prayer or hum a chorus in our heads. He's there in the waiting room when the news is not what we hoped for. God is there even when we think we've given up, because He never gives up on us.

God is there. Because He is Immanuel—God with us.

When our hearts are hurting, He is the gentle, healing salve that soothes the pain and brings us a spirit of calm and rest. Go to the Lord as David did. Trust in His unfailing love. It's okay to let your heart rejoice in Him, even when you are in pain.

Sometimes the most beautiful songs are born out of our brokenness.

For further reading: Isaiah 61:1, Jeremiah 8:22, Matthew 1:23, 1 Thessalonians 4:13

DAY 17

"The fool says in his heart, 'There is no God'" (Psalm 14:1).

You know the saying, "There are no atheists in foxholes"? It's easy to say there is no God when all is going well in one's life, but few people faced with death ignore God. Only a fool will ignore the evidence all around and claim there is no God.

Many people today live as if there is no God. Like those David describes in this psalm, they are corrupt and their deeds are vile. They live as if they will give an account to no one.

But the truth is that none of us are righteous in God's eyes apart from Jesus. We have all become corrupted by sin. We all need a Savior. From the atheist to the Spirit-filled Christian, we all stand evenly at the foot of the cross in need of the blood of Jesus.

The atheist may be a fool for not believing the truth about God, but we are all fools without the wisdom of God. Those who do not acknowledge the existence of God are in a very dangerous place, especially if they are seeking to bring harm to God's people.

From the cross, Jesus prayed, "Father, forgive them, for they do not know what they are doing" (Luke 23:34). Does God love the fool, the atheist, the one who doesn't believe? Of course, He does.

Our job is to pray for him and show what a life characterized by God's love and His goodness looks like. Do you know someone who doesn't believe in God? Are there people, perhaps in your family, who live as if there is no God? Try winning hearts rather than arguments. Show the unbeliever that the Lord is your refuge by the way you live your life.

God is, indeed, present in the company of the righteous. Therefore, our lives ought to be testimonies of His love and goodness toward the unbeliever. Remember, at one time, we didn't fully believe either.

For further reading: Ezekiel 11:19, Luke 23:24, 1 Timothy 1:16, 1 Peter 3:1-2

DAY 18

"LORD, who may dwell in your sanctuary?
Who may live on your holy hill?" (Psalm 15:1).

The Lord's sanctuary represented the very presence of God to the Old Testament believers. Nobody could be in the presence of God and live. When the high priest went into the Holy of Holies on the Day of Atonement, he had to go through all kinds of cleansing rituals. Even then, a rope was tied around him so that if he fell dead in the presence of God, he could be dragged out.

But David was a man after God's own heart. He had spent time talking to God, listening for His voice, singing and worshiping God, and he wanted to know who could come as a guest into the holy place of God.

The answer is not those who come with sacrifices or who perform certain Jewish rituals. Rather, those who may come into the presence of God are those who are blameless and righteous (Psalm 15:2). Those rituals were a temporary way of making one clean, pointing to the hope found in the Righteous One. God is holy. We are sinful. We cannot be in His presence apart from the blood of Jesus.

"This righteousness from God comes through faith in Jesus Christ to all who believe" (Romans 3:22). Those who have faith in Jesus are made righteous and blameless by His grace, granting us entrance into the presence of God for all eternity. In the Lord's presence is fullness of joy (Psalm 16:11).

We can't earn the right to be in God's presence, and we can never be good enough. We can only come to Him in Jesus' name and through His righteousness that covers us. When we are covered in Him, we are holy, blameless, and pure.

Jesus is our High Priest who by His own blood entered the most holy place, making a way for us to come into the presence of God.

"Such a high priest meets our need—one who is holy, blameless, pure, set apart from sinners, exalted above the heavens" (Hebrews 7:26).

Who may dwell in God's presence? Those covered by the righteousness of Jesus through faith.

For further reading: Psalm 16:11, Romans 3:22, Galatians 5:22, Hebrews 7:26

DAY 19

"LORD, you have assigned me my portion and cup;
you have made my lot secure" (Psalm 16:5).

Apart from the Lord, we have no good thing. Think about it: everything good in our lives is a gift from God.

"Every good and perfect gift is from above, coming down from the Father of the heavenly lights, who does not change like shifting shadows" (James 1:17).

The Lord assigns us our portion. For the Old Testament believers, this portion was their inheritance of land in fulfillment of His promise to Abraham. For us today, our inheritance is in heaven.

"Praise be to the God and Father of our Lord Jesus Christ! In his great mercy he has given us new birth into a living hope through the resurrection of Jesus Christ from the dead, and into an inheritance that can never perish, spoil, or fade—kept in heaven for you" (1 Peter 1:3-4).

Those who run after the things of this world will experience sorrow after sorrow. Those who seek the things of God will experience His peace and His presence, now and for all eternity.

Yes, we still face sorrows and struggles, but only in the context of God's heart toward us. We will not experience anything outside of His divine plan. The boundaries for us are pleasant. We are secure in our salvation. We have a delightful inheritance.

The Lord counsels us with His wisdom if we seek Him. Even in the dark of night, He will instruct us. If we keep Him always before us, we will not be shaken.

So, no matter what you are going through or what challenges you are facing today, you can trust the Lord to show you His path, where you will find joy and peace.

In Jesus, you have a cup that overflows with blessing, so rejoice!

For further reading: James 1:17, 1 Peter 1:3-4, 2 Peter 1:3

DAY 20

*"And I—in righteousness I will see your face; when I awake,
I will be satisfied with seeing your likeness" (Psalm 17:15).*

Are you satisfied in God?

We all are searching for something in life. We chase after the things we think will bring us peace and satisfaction, but so many are running after all the wrong things. David knew that only His pursuit of God would bring him lasting peace.

David looked to God for vindication when others accused him. He knew that only in the Lord could his heart truly be pure. David understood that his mouth could be an instrument of great sin and resolved not to let it be so.

He called on God, he sought God with all his heart, and as a result, David experienced the great love of God. He knew what it meant to be the apple of God's eye, to be hidden in the shadow of the Lord's wings.

You and I can know this love as well.

When we stop chasing after the things of the world and set our hearts on seeking God, we too will know what it is to be satisfied in His presence.

"'Blessed are you who hunger now, for you will be satisfied'" (Luke 6:21).

The Lord will still the hunger of those He cherishes. When our heart's desire is to seek God above all else, He truly satisfies our every need. We will be complete in Him.

What are you searching for? Do you long for comfort, peace, approval, acceptance, or love? Let go of your longings and give them to Jesus. In Him you will find all you need. One day you will awake to see Him face to face, and every desire of your heart will be complete.

For further reading: Isaiah 55:1-2, Matthew 5:6, Luke 1:53, 6:21

DAY 21

"He reached down from on high and took hold of me; he drew me out of deep waters" (Psalm 18:16).

I love superheroes. I'm by no means an expert, and I've never read a comic book in my life, but I do enjoy the superhero movies. I even know to stay in the theater and wait for the extra scenes after the credits. I sometimes get my universes mixed up, but I do love to see a good superhero save the day, defeat the enemy, and get the girl. A quick look at the box office will show you that America loves superheroes, too.

We identify with superheroes because they still struggle with being human. Yet in spite of opposition and adversity, they overcome, bringing hope and comfort to the world. The truth is we all need a Superhero. Here's why.

1. We can't save ourselves. We need a Savior.

"He brought me out into a spacious place; he rescued me because he delighted in me" (Psalm 18:19).

2. We can't defeat our enemy. We need someone to fight for us.

"He rescued me from my powerful enemy, from my foes, who were too strong for me" (Psalm 18:17).

3. We face injustice. We need One who is just.

"The LORD has dealt with me according to my righteousness; according to the cleanness of my hands he has rewarded me" (Psalm 18:20).

Yes, we love our superheroes, but they aren't perfect. That's one reason we identify with them: They are flawed just like us. But how much better to put our hope in a Superhero who actually chose to lay aside His power and glory to become human like us, to be tempted like us, and yet remained perfect in every way. We all need a Superhero, and His name is Jesus. He is the King of kings and Lord of lords. He is powerful enough to defeat every foe, and gentle enough to hold us in His arms. He is hope for the hopeless, help for the helpless, and a Hero for every time and place.

For further reading: John 3:17, 15:13, Ephesians 5:1

DAY 22

*"He trains my hands for battle; my arms
can bend a bow of bronze" (Psalm 18:34)*

God is a warrior who fights for us.

"I call to the LORD, who is worthy of praise, and I am saved from my enemies" (Psalm 18:3). In Psalm 18, David was being pursued by Saul, who wanted to kill him. David described God as his heavenly Warrior, descending amidst the shaking of the earth, breathing fire from His mouth, soaring on the wings of the wind. The Lord thundered from heaven to fight David's enemy.

"He shot his arrows and scattered the enemies, great bolts of lightning and routed them" (Psalm 18:14).

Can you picture this scene when the enemy comes against you, His child? When we cry out to the Lord, He comes to our aid, firing arrows of lightning bolts at the enemy. He not only takes on our foes, but He demonstrates His love through His divine protection and defense.

God defended David because of his righteousness (Psalm 18:20). As believers, our righteousness is in Christ. Because we have put our faith in Him as our Lord, He is our Divine Protector against the enemy. As we grow in our relationship with Him, He teaches us through His Word how to fight the enemy alongside Him.

"He trains my hands for battle; my arm can bend a bow of bronze. You give me your shield of victory, and your right hand sustains me; you stoop down to make me great" (Psalm 18:34-35).

Even as the Lord trained David for battle, God never left his side. David was aware that every victory came because the Lord sustained him and made him great. So, too, we will learn how to battle the enemy through worship, the Word, and prayer. God will strengthen and arm us for battle, but our Warrior King will never leave our side. He is a Warrior who is mighty in battle. And He's making little warriors out of us.

Further Reading: 2 Chronicles 20, Matthew 4:1-11, Ephesians 6:10-18, James 5:13

DAY 23

*"The heavens declare the glory of God;
the skies proclaim the work of his hands" (Psalm 19:1).*

All creation testifies to the glory and majesty of God. Even those who don't believe in God cannot scientifically provide any other plausible explanation for all of creation. Their attempts are seriously flawed at best, ridiculous at worst.

The sky itself speaks to us of the Creator: a sun that is the center of our universe; planets that revolve around the sun, bringing us seasons; an earth that rotates on its axis, bringing us night and day; an atmosphere that protects us from the sun, but allows just enough heat to provide food and warmth; a moon that controls the tides; gravity that keeps us grounded to earth; ocean currents that control the winds, that control the rains, that provide the crops.

We can look at the night sky and see stars, too many to count, and yet He knows them all by name.

The heavens during Old Testament times were objects to be worshiped. The ancients looked to the sun, moon, stars, thunder, and lightning as deities. They worshiped the creation rather than the Creator.

But the Word tells us that God's power is clearly seen in creation, so that man is without excuse.

"For since the creation of the world God's invisible qualities—his eternal power and divine nature—have been clearly seen, being understood from what has been made, so that men are without excuse" (Romans 1:20).

God's creation is a beautiful testament of His power, majesty, and glory. The most magnificent mountains and glorious beaches should bring us to our knees in wonder and awe. As you go about your business today, take some time to soak in the wonder of creation.

And give glory to the One who spoke it all into being with just the sound of His voice.

For further reading: Genesis 1, Psalm 147:4, Isaiah 55:12, Romans 1:20-25

DAY 24

"The law of the Lord is perfect, reviving the soul" (Psalm 19:7a).

The Word of God is powerful. God's Word not only spoke the world into existence, but it has the power to change our lives. David said the Words of God make us wise.

"The statutes of the Lord are trustworthy, making wise the simple" (Psalm 19:7b).

We need God's wisdom through His Word to guide us in our daily decisions.

His Word brings us joy.

"The precepts of the LORD are right, giving joy to the heart" (8a).

In a time when there are so many words everywhere that can cause us confusion and fear, God's Word brings joy because it is true and right.

God's Word is a sure thing.

"The ordinances of the LORD are sure and altogether righteous" (9b).

We can't always count on other people to be true to their word, but God's Word is always sure.

His Word warns us of trouble.

"By them is your servant warned; in keeping them there is great reward" (11).

We have God's Word to warn us of the consequences of sin. We don't always know what to do, but in God's Word we can find the answers to any question. We can look to God and His truth to guide us in our daily walk.

And when we lose our way, His Word will guide us back on the right path. If you are struggling with knowing truth in any situation, look to God's Word. His answers are always the right ones.

For further reading: Deuteronomy 8:3, Psalm 119, Isaiah 55:11, Colossians 3:16

DAY 25

"May the words of my mouth and the meditation of my heart be pleasing in your sight, O LORD, my Rock and my Redeemer"
(Psalm 19:14).

Nothing can get us in trouble faster than our words. James said if we could control the tongue we would be perfect!

"We all stumble in many ways. If anyone is never at fault in what he says, he is a perfect man, able to keep his whole body in check" (James 3:2).

What is it about our tongue that is so hard to control?

The words of our mouths come out of the meditations of our heart.

Jesus said it this way:

"For out of the overflow of the heart the mouth speaks" (Matthew 12:34b).

If we have a mouth problem, it's because we have a heart problem. So, what are we to do?

We can pray a daily prayer as David did, asking God to help make the words of our mouths *and* the meditation of our hearts be pleasing to Him.

We can't change our hearts or even fully know what is in our hearts.

"The heart is deceitful above all things and beyond cure. Who can understand it? I the Lord search the heart and examine the mind" (Jeremiah 17:9-10a).

Ask God to search your heart and mind and purify you from anything that is not of Him. Pray that the Holy Spirit would grant you self-control over your tongue. Then practice being quiet, waiting on God to urge you to speak.

Try memorizing Psalm 19:14 by meditating on it daily. The more of God's Word we hide in our hearts, the easier it will be to walk in His truth (Psalm 119:11).

For further reading: Psalm 119, Jeremiah 17:9-10, Matthew 12:34, James 3:2

DAY 26

"Some trust in chariots and some in horses,
but we trust in the name of the LORD our God" (Psalm 20:7).

Each day we are faced with many tasks—some easy, others more difficult. In every circumstance, we can choose to trust in ourselves, our money, our achievements, and our education, or we can choose to trust in God.

In order to walk in victory, David knew whom to trust. This psalm is a prayer for the Lord's help in time of distress, for the Lord's support in battle, and for the Lord to grant victory and success.

We all want God's help and support and success.

The key is to put our trust in Him in the first place. Often we step out in our own strength to do what only God can do. When we trust in ourselves, we will be brought down. But when our trust is in God, we will stand firm.

"They [who trust in chariots and horses] are brought to their knees and fall, but we [who trust in the name of the Lord] rise up and stand firm" (8, brackets added, see Psalm 20).

Before you begin any endeavor, whether it's a work project, a home budget, or fighting a spiritual battle, remember who is able to grant you success. He delights in giving you "the desire of your heart" and making "all your plans succeed" as you abide in Him and seek to do His will (4).

Give him your complete trust by bringing your needs to Him first. Acknowledge His authority in your life and your dependence upon Him for success. Then lay your project at His feet and ask for His help. There's no better place you can be than in a place of submission to God, waiting on the saving power of His right hand to bring you through.

Then you can "shout for joy when you are victorious (5)," giving Him all the glory for your success.

What (or whom) are you trusting in today?

For further reading: Proverbs 3:5, Isaiah 26:3, John 14:1, Romans 15:13

DAY 27

"You have granted him the desire of his heart
and have not withheld the request of his lips" (Psalm 21:2).

Have you ever had God grant you the desire of your heart—something you prayed for and believed God for, and He did it?

There is such joy when God brings victory in our lives and answers to the prayers we have prayed, maybe even for a long time.

If you are still praying and seeking God, don't give up. Look to His strength and continue to cry out to Him for the answers. God has given us so much already—eternal life through His Son, victory over death, hell, and the grave, eternal blessings, and joy in His presence.

Because He has already done so much for us, we should be encouraged as David was, that He hears our prayers and He is working on our behalf. As we trust in the Lord and His unfailing love, we will not be shaken.

Instead of focusing on the need, try focusing on the goodness of God.

If you are praying for a lost family member, try thanking God for what He is doing in that person's heart. Praise Him for His love for her. Sing and worship and give thanks to the Lord because He has made a way for your loved one to be saved.

Maybe you are believing God for healing or restoration of a relationship or a job. Whatever your need is, God hears your prayer. Come to Him with a thankful heart and rejoice that even in your circumstance, He is God and He is for you.

Will God grant you the desire of your heart? As you seek Him, His desires and your desires will become one. Remember that God is for you and His will is for your good. So praise Him for loving you enough to give you His best.

For further reading: Psalm 20:4, 40:8, 73:25, Romans 10:1

DAY 28

"My God, my God, why have you forsaken me?" (Psalm 22:1a).

Psalm 22 is a Messianic Psalm. David wrote these words prophetically of Jesus, hundreds of years before Jesus hung on the cross. The words remind us of the pain that Jesus suffered, not just physically, but emotionally as He took on our sin.

Sin separates us from a holy God. When Jesus bore the weight of our sin, He took upon Himself the wrath that was due us. As Jesus bore the punishment that we deserved, He felt abandoned by His Holy Father.

"At the ninth hour Jesus cried out in a loud voice, 'Eloi, Eloi, lama sabachthani?'—which means, 'My God, my God, why have you forsaken me?'" (Mark 15:34).

Can you imagine the wrath of God being poured out on His own perfect, sinless, holy Son? That is the price Jesus paid for you and me.

"But God demonstrates his own love for us in this: While we were still sinners, Christ died for us. Since we have now been justified by his blood, how much more shall we be saved from God's wrath through him! For if, when we were God's enemies, we were reconciled to him through the death of his Son, how much more, having been reconciled, shall we be saved through his life!" (Romans 5:8-10).

Since we have been spared the wrath of God and brought near to Him through Jesus, let us remember the great price He paid as we come into His presence to pray and worship Him.

Let us never lose sight of the suffering of Jesus on our behalf. May we never grow indifferent to the cross. Let it never become common to us. And may we never grow accustomed to the story so that it loses its impact on us.

I pray that every time we get used to the idea of Jesus dying for us, we will hear those words from the cross: "My God, my God, why have you forsaken me?" and we will remember that He was forsaken so we could be forgiven.

For further reading: Isaiah 53, Habakkuk 1:13, Mark 15:34, 2 Corinthians 5:21

DAY 29

"You are enthroned as the Holy One; you are the praise of Israel"
(Psalm 22:3).

God is enthroned on the praises of His people. From Jesus comes the theme of our praise: He has done it! He has gone to the cross on our behalf and achieved salvation for us. Praise God! Jesus did for us what we could never do for ourselves. Our praises storm heaven with honor, glory, majesty, worship, and thanksgiving for who He is and all He has done.

> "When he came near the place where the road goes down the Mount of Olives, the whole crowd of disciples began joyfully to praise God in loud voices for all the miracles they had seen:
>
> 'Blessed is the king who comes in the name of the Lord!'
>
> 'Peace in heaven and glory in the highest!'
>
> Some of the Pharisees in the crowd said to Jesus, 'Teacher, rebuke your disciples!'
>
> 'I tell you,' he replied, 'if they keep quiet, the stones will cry out'" (Luke 19:37-40).

Jesus is worthy of our praise! If we don't praise Him, even the rocks will cry out in our place. When we trust in Him, we are not disappointed. He has won salvation for us and made us co-heirs with Him. He has secured our redemption through His blood and by our faith in Him. What more could we ask?

The Lord is enthroned on our praises. In other words, when we praise Him, we see Him as He really is—high and exalted over all the earth and over our lives. We can't make Him higher than He is. Our praise just opens our eyes to His truth. What's holding you back from giving Him praise? He never withholds anything good from us. So, let's not withhold our praise from Him.

Let your praises storm heaven today!

For further reading: Luke 19:37-40, Hebrews 13:15, 1 Peter 2:9, Revelation 5:12

DAY 30

"The LORD is my shepherd, I shall not be in want" (Psalm 23:1).

Psalm 23 is probably one of the most well-known passages in the Bible. David was not only a poet and a king, he was also a shepherd. He understood what it meant for God to be his Shepherd-King.

The role of a shepherd is to care for the needs of the sheep. With God as our Shepherd, He takes care of us. He meets our needs so fully that we are in want of nothing. He makes us lie down in contentment and security, resting in green pastures of having all that we need. He leads us beside quiet, still waters that provide refreshment. He restores our souls. When we are weak, He strengthens us. When we are weary, He revives us. When we are broken, He makes us whole.

He guides us in paths of righteousness. Just like sheep, we are prone to stray from God. The world can be so tempting, and we still live in this flesh. But our Shepherd-King guides us in the right way if we seek Him. He will lead us down the path that is best for us.

Sheep are dumb. They will follow each other right off a cliff. But the Lord knows us.

"...for he knows how we are formed, he remembers that we are dust" (Psalm 103:14).

God knows our human limitations, and He loves and guides us still. The problem is that many of us don't want to be led. We are stubborn and want to do things our own way. God will let us, but we will bring trouble upon ourselves.

The Shepherd is good. His plans for us are good. His path for us is best. If you are tired of doing things your own way, you're in a good place. Yield to the Shepherd and let Him lead you down the right path. Rest in His care and let Him restore your soul. He will carry you as gently as a little lamb and love you right back into the fold.

For further reading: Isaiah 40:11, 53:6, Luke 12:32, John 10

DAY 31

*"Even though I walk through the valley of the shadow of death,
I will fear no evil, for you are with me" (Psalm 23:4).*

We often hear this Scripture quoted at funerals, and we find comfort in the fact that God is with us in times of grief. But any time we are going through a valley, this verse is appropriate.

I love what a friend recently shared with me about this verse. She heard someone say that the verse says we are walking "through" the valley, so don't get stuck there. When we are going through a difficult time, we just need to keep walking with God. He is the Good Shepherd who will stay with us and lead us through.

David tells us that the Shepherd's rod and staff brought comfort. The shepherd's rod is an instrument used for "counting, guiding, rescuing, and protecting sheep."[2] The shepherd's staff is used for support. The shepherd's counting of the sheep reminds me that He leaves the ninety-nine to go after the one. His guiding and rescuing is necessary for all the trouble we are likely to get ourselves into.

His rod protects us from the enemy just as a shepherd protects his sheep from the wolves.

"I am the good shepherd. The good shepherd lays down his life for the sheep. The hired hand is not the shepherd who owns the sheep. So when he sees the wolf coming, he abandons the sheep and runs away" (John 10:11-12a).

Jesus is the Good Shepherd who lays down His life for the sheep. He is with us to protect us from the enemy. No matter what we go through, we have a Shepherd for our souls. He will watch over us, guide us, and comfort us.

Are you walking through the valley today? Don't fear. Your Good Shepherd is with you to guide you, rescue you, and comfort you. Just keep walking.

For further reading: Ezekiel 34:11-16, Matthew 18:12-14, 25:32-46

DAY 32

"You anoint my head with oil; my cup overflows" (Psalm 23:5b).

Nothing compares with knowing Jesus, so whatever we give up will never measure up to the blessings of being in the kingdom of God. What are some of those blessings?

Provision

He invites us to His table and prepares a meal for us, even in the presence of our enemies. In other words, when the world is against us, God will show Himself strong on our behalf and provide for us as a demonstration of His love to a watching world.

Being invited to His table is a sign of blessing, provision, favor, fellowship, and connection. It signifies that we are His friends, and He desires to sit with us and break bread with us. It's intimate.

Anointing

Just as an honored guest in those days would be anointed with oil, Jesus calls us and anoints us with His Spirit so that we can do the work He has called us to do.

"But you have an anointing from the Holy One, and all of you know the truth" (1 John 2:20).

Overflow

God is so good to us that our cup of blessing overflows. There is abundance in the Lord. There is more than enough.

With Jesus as our Shepherd, goodness and mercy will always be with us, even as we pass from this life into the next. Today, you can celebrate the fact that you are a sheep carried in the arms of the Good Shepherd. Because of Him, you will always have more than enough.

For further reading: Matthew 6:25-34, Philippians 4:19, 1 Timothy 6:17, 1 John 2:20

DAY 33

"The earth is the LORD's, and everything in it,
the world, and all who live in it" (Psalm 24:1).

We sometimes tend to think that we own what we have earned by the work of our hands, but nothing could be further from the truth. As we work to provide for our families, we must never forget that everything we have belongs to God.

He provides for us out of His abundance, but ultimately we are just stewards of all He blesses us with. Knowing that truth should change the way we view our circumstances. When we don't think we have what we need, we can remember that God owns it all. He will meet our needs out of His abundance.

"And my God will meet all your needs according to his glorious riches in Christ Jesus" (Philippians 4:19).

When we are blessed with abundance, we should be willing to share with others in need.

"And do not forget to do good and to share with others, for with such sacrifices God is pleased" (Hebrews 13:16).

Because we don't really own anything, we should be willing to let go of it for His glory and someone else's good. When we have a decision to make regarding a purchase, we should remember who owns all that we have and ask for His guidance. We are no longer our own. All we are and all we have belong to God. Let us, then, seek Him for every decision we make.

When we come to God with clean hands and a pure heart through the blood of Jesus, God blesses us with His presence, His provision, His peace, and His holiness. We have all that we need in Him. So let us seek His face and not just His hand.

"But seek first his kingdom and his righteousness, and all these things will be given to you as well" (Matthew 6:33).

So don't worry about what you need. Trust the One who owns it all.

For further reading: Matthew 6:33, Philippians 4:19, Hebrews 13:16

DAY 34

"The LORD confides in those who fear him;
he makes his covenant known to them" (Psalm 25:14).

When we lift our souls to the Lord and put our trust in Him, He will not let us be put to shame. If we daily ask God to show us His ways and teach us His paths, He will guide us.

So many people want answers to life's questions, but they want the easy way out. They want the benefits of knowing God without putting in the time and effort to get to know Him.

This psalm instructs us to seek the Lord, to trust in Him, to put all our hope in Him, to surrender ourselves to Him, to humble ourselves before Him. When we fear the Lord and make Him our desire, He instructs us in His ways.

When we come to the Lord daily in humility and repentance, He leads us in the way we should go.

David knew that in order to know God's will, he had to surrender to God's ways. The Lord confides in those who fear Him. When we have a holy reverence and fear of God, He treats us as friends and confides in us.

If you are confused about the path to take in your life, surrender to God in humility and trust. Confess your failures and your pride. Ask God to teach you His ways and be willing to follow wherever He leads. God's way is always best, so don't be afraid to trust Him with your future.

As we submit to His authority in our lives, the Lord guards us. His integrity and uprightness will protect us.

Put your hope in God today and trust Him with the outcome.

For further reading: Jeremiah 33:3, John 10, Romans 10:17

DAY 35

*"I love the house where you live, O LORD,
the place where your glory dwells" (Psalm 26:8).*

There's nothing better than being in the presence of the Lord. Of course, God is always with us, but when we are made aware of His presence through prayer, worship, or just meditating on His goodness, we are blessed with peace and joy.

When David came into the presence of the Lord, he first asked God to examine his heart and mind. He wanted to come before the Lord holy and blameless. He wanted the love of God to go before Him. He wanted to walk in God's truth continually.

What a great pattern of prayer for us!

Do you love to be in the presence of God? Do you make it a habit to seek Him first every day? When we start our day with God, everything is better.

We can come before Him to be examined and washed clean, too. We can ask His love to go before us throughout our day. We can pray that we walk each day in God's truth, which is His Word, continually.

No wonder David loved the place where God's glory dwells! There he found forgiveness, love, and truth. In God's presence David found the strength to face each day. He found a place of vindication, redemption, and mercy.

If we want to live each day with our feet on solid ground, we need to start on our knees. Ask God to search you, cleanse you, fill you, and lead you before you start each day. You will walk in His praise all day long.

For further reading: Exodus 33:12-18, Jeremiah 29:13, Matthew 18:20, 1 Corinthians 3:16

DAY 36

"The LORD is my light and my salvation—whom shall I fear?
The LORD is the stronghold of my life—of whom shall I be afraid?"
(Psalm 27:1).

Do you struggle with fear? Honestly, there are so many reasons that we could be overwhelmed with fear, but fear is not of God.

"For God did not give us a spirit of timidity, but a spirit of power, of love and of self-discipline" (2 Timothy 1:7).

Just as this psalm tells us, if God is on our side, we have no reason to fear. He brings light into the darkness; He gives salvation to those who come to Him. When evil comes against us and the fear tries to take over, we can be confident in the Lord. He will keep us safe in His presence. He will cause the enemy to be defeated. We do not have to fear!

How do we go from the place of fear to a place of confidence? By being in God's presence. David said that when he sought the Lord, God answered Him and helped Him. The Lord gave him victory over the enemy because David had a heart for God.

Where's your heart? What do you treasure most in your life? What do you give most of your attention? Do you seek the things of God or do you seek to please yourself?

When we choose to seek God first, He keeps us safe in His dwelling. We don't have to wait until heaven to experience the goodness of God. David said he was confident that he would see the Lord's goodness in the "land of the living" (Psalm 27:13).

Whatever fear you are struggling with today, lay it down and just seek God's face. Worship Him for who He is and tell Him that you trust Him with your struggle. The Lord will receive you and lead you and fill you with confidence in Him. God hasn't given you a spirit of fear. He wants you to walk in power, love, and self-discipline. Surrender yourself to Him and His ways today.

For further reading: Joshua 1:9, Psalm 91, John 14:27, 2 Timothy 1:7

DAY 37

"One thing I ask of the LORD, this is what I seek: that I may dwell in the house of the LORD all the days of my life, to gaze upon the beauty of the LORD and to seek him in his temple" (Psalm 27:4).

I am not a multi-tasker. I know. I'm a woman. I should be able to balance multiple things at one time, but I just don't. I can only do one thing at a time. Just ask my husband.

As women, we often are required to juggle home, family, church, career, ministry, and a host of other things all at once. Sometimes we can become so overwhelmed with responsibility that we really just want to give up. I have found that when I prioritize my relationship with the Lord above every other responsibility in life, things run much more smoothly.

Several years ago, I made a commitment to the Lord to start every day seeking Him before anything else—before breakfast, the news, my family, Facebook, or anything. God wants to be first in our lives. When we make seeking Him our "one thing" like David did, we are much more capable of handling all the other responsibilities that come our way.

When Mary and Martha invited Jesus over for supper, Martha got busy preparing the meal, but Mary sat at Jesus' feet, listening to what He said. When Martha complained that Mary wasn't helping, Jesus responded:

"'Martha, Martha...you are worried and upset about many things, but only one thing is needed. Mary has chosen what is better, and it will not be taken away from her'" (Luke 10:41-42).

We have many things throughout our day that people want from us and things we want ourselves, but those things can cause us to be worried and upset. Jesus said only one thing is needed—time at His feet.

Like David and Mary, let's be intentional to seek out the one thing that really matters each day. The rest will fall into place.

For further reading: Matthew 6:33, 7:7-8, Luke 10:38-42, Philippians 3:12-14

DAY 38

"The LORD is my strength and my shield;
my heart trusts in him, and I am helped.
My heart leaps for joy and I will give thanks to him in song"
(Psalm 28:7).

Once again, David was facing the enemy. Do you sometimes feel that every time you turn around, there is another battle to fight?

David had so many enemies in his lifetime, but every time he was faced with a battle, he called on the Lord. David knew where His help came from. When facing Goliath, he didn't depend on his own strength to win the battle. He knew only God could give him victory.

"David said to the Philistine, 'You come against me with sword and spear and javelin, but I come against you in the name of the LORD Almighty, the God of the armies of Israel, whom you have defiled'" (1 Samuel 17:45).

David's power was not his own but was in the name of the Lord. We, too, will face many battles as we serve the Lord. We may even go through a season in which we feel we are in a constant battle. Don't be tempted to fight in your own power. Turn to the Lord for help.

"Submit yourselves, then, to God. Resist the devil, and he will flee from you" (James 4:7).

This submitting and resisting is sometimes an ongoing process, but as we submit ourselves to God, we are acknowledging our dependence upon Him. As we resist the devil, we are opposing him and his ways, not giving in to his temptation or taking the easy way out.

God will fight our battles if we trust in Him. He will repay those who have done evil towards us as we trust Him. Our place is to surrender to God. He is our strength. He will give us joy in the midst of the trial and put a song of praise in our hearts. Sometimes the best way to defeat the enemy is to walk in the joy of the Lord.

For further reading: 1 Samuel 17, 2 Chronicles 20, Ephesians 6, James 4:7

DAY 39

"Ascribe to the LORD the glory due his name;
worship the LORD in the splendor of his holiness" (Psalm 29:2).

This psalm is a hymn of praise to the Lord of all creation. As children of God, our hearts should always be drawn to praise. We were created to worship. Praise releases our emotions in a healthy way so that as we rejoice in God and all He has done, we experience a joy and peace that are good for the soul.

What has God done for you that you are thankful for today?

The Lord is strong and powerful. He is able to defeat every enemy. He has won salvation for us and made a way for us to know Him. He has provided all that we need for life and godliness.

The Lord is sovereign over all creation. He is majestic and beautiful! He is enthroned over every problem we face and every mountain we climb. He reigns over it all, and we cry, "Glory!"

The very voice of God spoken through His Word is powerful enough to break cedars and twist oaks. Meditate on His Word and praise Him for His awesome truth.

Give to the Lord the glory due his name. Worship him in the splendor of his holiness. He is King over all things, and there is nothing He holds back from us.

"The LORD gives strength to his people; the LORD blesses his people with peace" (Psalm 29:11).

Do you need strength and peace today?

God has all you need in His presence. Come to Him and give Him the worship He deserves. He will cover you with His presence and fill you with all that you need.

For further reading: Psalm 24:8, 136:1, Philippians 4:6, 1 Thessalonians 5:18

DAY 40

"O LORD my God, I called to you for help and you healed me"
(Psalm 30:2).

Have you ever been in the pit? My life before I came to know Jesus was like being in a deep, dark pit with no way out. I was lost, confused, and struggling to make sense of my life apart from God. I had no stability, no sense of peace or security, no wholeness or purpose.

I cried out to the Lord and He brought me out of the pit. He healed my brokenness and made me whole. Apart from Jesus we are all lost and in darkness, deserving the wrath of God because of the sin in our lives.

The sin in each of our lives is like a disease, a sickness that is surely bringing death to our souls.

But because of His great mercy, we have the opportunity to be made secure in Him. His anger toward our sin lasts a moment, but His favor toward our repentance lasts a lifetime.

The Lord makes us able to stand firm in Him. He turns our wailing into dancing and clothes us with joy. We deserve death—we get life. We deserve His wrath—we get His favor. We deserve punishment—we get His mercy.

That's why we can't be silent! That's why we sing and give Him thanks forever!

Are you thankful today that when you called out to God for help, He reached down and lifted you out of the pit and healed you?

If so, give thanks to Him in praise and worship today. Share your testimony with someone today. Let the world know what Jesus has done for you.

For further reading: 1 Chronicles 16:25, Ephesians 1:3-8, Hebrews 13:15, Revelation 5:13

DAY 41

"Into your hands I commit my spirit;
redeem me, O LORD, the God of truth" (Psalm 31:5).

Jesus quoted these words from the cross. He was able to entrust Himself to the Father because He knew He would not be abandoned to the grave. He knew the Father as the God of truth. Can you commit yourself into God's hands?

"I hate those who cling to worthless idols; I trust in the LORD" (Psalm 31:6).

The biggest idol we face is self. Do we trust in ourselves, or do we trust in God? In order to trust the Father as Jesus did, we have to know Him as the God of truth. God's Word is truth. Jesus is truth. Do we really believe that, or do we still look to the world to validate truth for us? Do we believe we need to look a certain way to be accepted by the world, or do we trust that we are fearfully and wonderfully made in the image of God?

"I praise you because I am fearfully and wonderfully made; your works are wonderful, I know that full well" (Psalm 139:14).

Do we believe we have to achieve perfection to be accepted by others, or do we trust that we are chosen and beloved in the Lord?

"For he chose us in him before the creation of the world to be holy and blameless in his sight" (Ephesians 1:4).

Do we believe we need relationships to validate our worth, or do we believe we are worthy because God says so?

"And even the very hairs of your head are all numbered. So don't be afraid; you are worth more than many sparrows" (Matthew 10:-30-31).

Do we really trust the Lord, or do we just trust in ourselves and what we can accomplish?

Commit your spirit into God's hands today, and let Him guide and direct your paths with His truth.

For further reading: Psalm 129, Matthew 10:29-31, Ephesians 1:3-8

DAY 42

"But I trust in you, O LORD; I say, 'You are my God.
My times are in your hands'" (Psalm 31:14-15a).

We all know deep down that our time here on earth is limited, but for the most part we live life as if we have all the time in the world. For instance, we may know we need to forgive someone, but we will hold onto that grudge. We may feel convicted to share the gospel with someone, yet we put it off until later.

Most of us have planners that we fill with events and activities, rarely seeking God for direction over our schedules.

David trusted God with his time. He committed his time to God and expected the Lord to deliver him from his enemies so that he could live another day.

We don't know what our future holds, but God does. All our events, circumstances, and experiences we can place in God's hands and trust Him to guide and direct us.

In the story of Esther, a young Jewish woman ended up in the palace at just the right time to save her people from an evil plot that would have eliminated the Jewish race. When deciding how to respond in this circumstance, her uncle said to her, "And who knows but that you have come to royal position for such a time as this?" (Esther 4:14).

What circumstance has God placed you in "for such a time as this"? We can miss the divine appointment if we are not entrusting our time into His hands.

Paul said "do this [love], understanding the present time. The hour has come for you to wake up from your slumber, because our salvation is nearer now than when we first believed" (Romans 13:11, brackets added).

We do not know the day or the hour when Christ will return, but we need to always be ready. Leave nothing unspoken that God has urged you to speak. Use your time wisely, knowing that every moment is a gift from God.

For further reading: Esther 4:12-16, Hosea 10:12, 2 Corinthians 6:2

DAY 43

*"Blessed is he whose transgressions are
forgiven, whose sins are covered" (Psalm 32:1).*

The Hebrew word for *blessed* means "happy."[3] We are happy when our sins are forgiven and covered by the blood of Jesus. That forgiveness goes into effect when we confess and renounce our sins. "If we confess our sins, he is faithful and just and will forgive us our sins and purify us from all unrighteousness" (1 John 1:9).

But when we try to cover them ourselves, we only bring pain and suffering to our lives. We can't hide our sins from God. And God is holy. His wrath is always poured out on sin because He understands the pain and devastation sin causes in our lives.

"When I kept silent, my bones wasted away through my groaning all day long. For day and night your hand was heavy upon me; my strength was sapped as in the heat of summer. Then I acknowledged my sin to you and did not cover up my iniquity. I said, 'I will confess my transgressions to the LORD'—and you forgave the guilt of my sin'" (Psalm 32:3-5).

How do we try to cover our sins? "Live as free men, but do not use your freedom as a cover-up for evil; live as servants of God" (1 Peter 2:16).

In other words, just because we are free from sin and living under grace doesn't mean we should choose to walk in sin and just let grace cover it. "By no means! We died to sin; how can we live in it any longer?" (Romans 6:2). That's an evil cover-up. And God sees it all anyway.

"Nothing in all creation is hidden from God's sight. Everything is uncovered and laid bare before the eyes of him to whom we must give account" (Hebrews 4:13). We have the freedom to not be bound by sin but to walk in the liberty of serving God. Are you struggling with some sin right now? Come clean from the burden of sin and let Jesus' blood do the covering. You will find freedom and happiness in Jesus.

For further reading: Romans 6:1-12, Hebrews 4:13, 1 Peter 2:16, 1 John 1:9

DAY 44

"For he spoke, and it came to be; he commanded, and it stood firm"
(Psalm 33:9).

We serve a God who literally spoke the world into existence. He breathed life into this world by His powerful Word.

"In the beginning was the Word, and the Word was with God, and the Word was God. He was with God in the beginning. Through him all things were made; without him nothing was made that has been made" (John 1:1-3).

"The Word became flesh and made his dwelling among us. We have seen his glory, the glory of the One and Only, who came from the Father, full of grace and truth" (John 1:14).

Jesus is the Word made flesh. He came to this world in fulfillment of prophecies spoken over thousands of years. He fulfilled every word to a T. What God has spoken has come to pass. What God has commanded has stood firm. Because God has been true to His Word over the ages, we can trust in every promise. God is not a man that he should lie (Numbers 23:19). His Word is Truth.

When you are struggling in any area of your life, find a promise in the Bible that you can cling to. Write it on a postcard, and put it somewhere that you will see it every day. Read it aloud and believe it in your heart.

Jesus is the Word. Every time you open your Bible, you are interacting with the Living God.

"For the word of God is living and active" (Hebrews 4:12a).

Let the living, breathing Word of God work in your life today as you believe it, speak it, pray it, and trust it.

"For the word of the LORD is right and true; he is faithful in all he does" (Psalm 33:4).

For further reading: Numbers 23:19; John 1:1-3, 14; Hebrews 4:12-13

DAY 45

"Blessed is the nation whose God is the LORD" (Psalm 33:12).

This Scripture was written of Israel, but God's principles apply to all nations. When a nation acknowledges God, He blesses that people. The opposite is also true. A nation who rejects God will experience the loss of those blessings. God's heart is for all people. He loves all those He made, and He has a plan and purpose for every nation.

"And they sang a new song: 'You are worthy to take the scroll and open its seals, because you were slain, and with your blood you purchased men for God from every tribe and language and people and nation'" (Revelation 5:9).

"Therefore go and make disciples of all nations, baptizing them in the name of the Father and of the Son and of the Holy Spirit, and teaching them to obey everything I have commanded you" (Matthew 28:19-20a).

This psalm tells us that God thwarts the plans of people, but his plans stand firm forever, through all generations (Psalm 33:11). We like to think that we make plans and elect leaders and devise governments, but the truth is that God is sovereign over all things.

Everything is filtered through His divine purpose to save His people. So, our job is to be part of a nation whose God is the Lord. We should pray for our nation and seek to make disciples as we have been commanded.

We should elect leaders who will seek the things of God so we can be a nation whose God is the Lord. But ultimately our trust should be not in leaders and governments but in the Lord, who is our help and our shield.

"From heaven the LORD looks down and sees all mankind; from his dwelling place he watches all who live on earth—he who forms the hearts of all, who considers everything they do" (Psalm 33:13-15).

He sees us all, but His eyes of favor are on those who fear him, that He may bless.

For further reading: Matthew 28:19-20, Revelation 5:9

DAY 46

"My soul will boast in the LORD; let the afflicted hear and rejoice"
(Psalm 34:2).

If anyone had reason to boast, David did. He was a warrior and had been anointed king. He could have boasted in his own power, strength, and wisdom. Instead, David boasted in the Lord. We all struggle to some extent with pride. Our sinful nature desires to be approved of by others and to be given credit when we do something well. We have a natural tendency to brag on ourselves, especially when it's something we worked hard for. But when we boast of our own abilities, we take the glory away from the One who gave us those abilities.

"May I never boast except in the cross of our Lord Jesus Christ" (Galatians 6:14). We really have no reason to boast apart from God. We certainly can't save ourselves.

"For it is by grace you have been saved, through faith—and this not from yourselves, it is the gift of God—not by works, so that no one can boast" (Ephesians 2:8-9).

At the same time, we need to have confidence to be able to serve God boldly. So how do we have humility and confidence at the same time? I call it holy boldness. "'But you will receive power when the Holy Spirit comes on you; and you will be my witnesses in Jerusalem, and in all Judea and Samaria, and to the ends of the earth'" (Acts 1:8).

The Holy Spirit empowers us with boldness and confidence, but it is in Jesus and His work in us—not in ourselves.

When Peter and John were arrested in Acts 4, they boldly spoke the truth to the rulers and elders who questioned them. "When they saw the courage of Peter and John and realized that they were unschooled, ordinary men, they were astonished and they took note that these men had been with Jesus" (Acts 4:13).

That's the kind of holy boldness we all need. Not a boastful attitude that says, "I'm better than you." But a humble confidence in the Lord and His saving power.

For further reading: Acts 1:8, 4:13, Galatians 6:14, Ephesians 2:8-9

DAY 47

"Taste and see that the LORD is good;
blessed is the man who takes refuge in him" (Psalm 34:8).

Have you ever been super hungry and craved something satisfying, but then you filled up on junk instead? There's that disappointment that comes when you settle for leftovers, and then your husband walks in with takeout.

We do that spiritually as well. We have a spiritual hunger that can only be satisfied in Jesus, but we spend our day trying to satisfy our hunger with everything else.

"Blessed are those who hunger and thirst for righteousness, for they will be filled" (Matthew 5:6).

The emptiness we often feel inside is a longing for the things of God. What we really need is soul food. We need to fill our hungry hearts with worship, the Word, and conversation with God. Oftentimes, however, we fill ourselves up on social media, television, food, or shopping.

When we choose to fill our longings with anything other than God, we are left still hungry because those things can never satisfy. Only Jesus, the Bread of Life, can satisfy our hungry hearts.

"Then Jesus declared, 'I am the bread of life. He who comes to me will never go hungry, and he who believes in me will never be thirsty'" (John 6:35).

Our souls—mind, will, and emotions—are constantly seeking to be satisfied. And we are quick to give them what they want. But our spirits—the part of us that connects with God—hunger for more of Him. I have found in my life that if I will feed my spirit first, my soul will be satisfied.

Today, give your spirit what it longs for—more of God. As you feed on the Word and dwell in God's amazing presence, your soul will be satisfied, because He is good!

Further Reading: Matthew 4:4, 5:6; Luke 1:53; John 6:35; Revelation7:16

DAY 48

"The lions may grow weak and hungry, but those who seek the LORD lack no good thing" (Psalm 34:10).

I wrote a book entitled *Seek Him First: How to Hear from God, Walk in His Will, and Change Your World*. Much to my surprise, it became an Amazon bestseller in eleven days. Most people want to know how to hear from God. Many want to know how to walk in God's will. And lots of people want to truly make a difference in the world. The way to have that kind of impact is simple: we seek God first, as our number one priority. The Lord has called us into relationship with Him. He knows us, and He wants us to know Him. We can't follow God if we don't make an effort to seek Him.

I have been married for twenty-six years. If I don't make an effort to spend time with Kenneth, to do things for him, and to show him my love, we wouldn't have much of a marriage. What God desires for us is a real relationship—not just religious rituals.

The word *seek* means to "frequent a place." I have a particular place that I go to every morning to spend time with God. *Seek* also means "to consult or inquire of, to ask for, to practice, study, follow, seek with application." [4]

In my daily time with the Lord, I read a devotional, much like this one; I keep a journal of my thoughts and prayers to God in response to His Word as I study; I spend time talking to God, confessing my sins, thanking Him for my many blessings, and asking Him to meet needs around me. I also take time to just listen and respond to God as He speaks to me.

I love my time with the Lord each day, and I can honestly say that I lack no good thing in my life. He meets me right where I am, and He truly satisfies me in His presence. Do you have a daily time and place to seek the Lord? He is waiting for you and longs for you to come away to the secret place with Him.

"Seek the LORD while he may be found; call on him while he is near" (Isaiah 55:6).

For further reading: Isaiah 55:6, Jeremiah 29:13, Hosea 10:12, Matthew 6:33, Hebrews 11:6

DAY 49

"The LORD is close to the brokenhearted and
saves those who are crushed in spirit" (Psalm 34:18).

I have a dear, sweet friend who lost her husband this past year. She has been so devastated and heartbroken, that I almost can't bear it. Yet this verse was a daily reminder as I prayed for her, that the Lord was holding her close to His heart. Our God is a warrior, but He is a tender warrior. He's not so big and mighty that He can't come to us with gentleness and soothe our broken places. He's not either loving or wrathful; He's both. He's not either soft or strong; He's both. He's the Lion of the Tribe of Judah, and He's the Lamb that was slain for the salvation of the world.

While we praise Him as King of kings and Lord of lords, the Bright and Morning Star, the Mighty God—we also worship Him as the sweet presence in our time of deepest hurt, the Balm of Gilead who soothes our pain, the Father to the fatherless, and the Comforter to those who weep. Jesus read Isaiah 61 in the synagogue and applied this prophecy to Himself:

"The spirit of the Sovereign LORD is on me, because the LORD has anointed me to preach good news to the poor. He has sent me to bind up the brokenhearted, to proclaim freedom for the captives and release from darkness for the prisoners, to proclaim the year of the LORD's favor and the day of vengeance of our God, to comfort all who mourn, and provide for those who grieve in Zion— to bestow on them a crown of beauty instead of ashes, the oil of gladness instead of mourning, and a garment of praise instead of a spirit of despair" (Isaiah 61:1-3a).

Jesus came to bring vengeance against sin but also to bind up the brokenhearted. Aren't you glad we serve a Tender Warrior who can bend the bow of justice and heal a broken heart at the same time? Jesus understands your brokenness today. He is more than able to heal your hurts and bring you comfort. Give your brokenness to Jesus, and let Him bring beauty out of the ashes.

For further reading: Psalm 68:5, Isaiah 61:1-3, Jeremiah 8:22, 2 Corinthians 1:3-5

DAY 50

"Contend, O LORD, with those who contend with me;
fight against those who fight against me" (Psalm 35:1).

Have you ever had someone accuse you wrongfully or be against you for no fault of your own? That's a very difficult place to be in. In our flesh or human nature, our desire is to retaliate, to defend ourselves, or (a very popular response) to post something on social media. I often see people post responses that I'm pretty sure they didn't really think about. And they surely didn't pray about.

When we try to defend ourselves against wrongdoing or retaliate in any way, we are basically admitting that we don't trust God to vindicate us. We want to get even ourselves and set the record straight. I'm not saying there's never a situation we need to clarify. We may even need to apologize if we hurt someone, even unintentionally. But David knew that if his heart was right with God, the Lord would defend him. Not only would God defend David, but David also depended upon the Lord to set the record straight. He called on the Lord to vindicate him.

"Awake, and rise to my defense! Contend for me, my God and Lord. Vindicate me in your righteousness, O LORD, my God; do not let them gloat over me" (Psalm 35:23-24).

David trusted God to bring vindication to his cause and put to shame those who had mistreated him. We can trust God to do the same for us.

Sometimes we have been so deeply wronged by others that we think we need to take action. Just remember that your God is more than able to bring shame on those who have mistreated us. He will do this in order to draw them to himself.

So the next time you find yourself at the end of someone else's mistreatment, before you fire off that post, go to the Lord in prayer. Ask Him to vindicate you and set the record straight. Then praise Him for the victory and go on about your business.

Further Reading: Psalm 24:5, Isaiah 26:3, 53:7

DAY 51

*"Your love, O LORD, reaches to the heavens, your
faithfulness to the skies. Your righteousness is like the mighty
mountains, your justice like the great deep" (Psalm 36:5-6).*

The love of God is limitless and unconditional. To the ancients, the heavens represented the dwelling of God, the universe, the atmosphere, and everything beyond what they could see. To say that God's love reaches to the heavens is to describe it as unending. It's God's love that draws us to Him. Perhaps one of the most tender expressions in Scripture of God's love for us is found in Zephaniah.

"The LORD your God is with you, he is mighty to save. He will take great delight in you, he will quiet you with his love, he will rejoice over you with singing" (Zephaniah 3:17).

The greatest expression of the love of God is through His Son.

"But God demonstrates his own love for us in this: While we were still sinners, Christ died for us" (Romans 5:8).

The faithfulness of God reaches to the skies. The skies would be the farthest limit of what the ancients could actually see. God's righteousness is like the mighty mountains—high, lofty, and unattainable—except through faith in Christ. God is holy, perfect, and majestic. In Him there is no flaw whatsoever. His righteousness is something so high that no man can achieve. But through the grace of God, we can enter into His righteousness by faith (2 Corinthians 5:21).

And His justice is like the great deep—unfathomable to the ancients. "Yet the LORD longs to be gracious to you; he rises to show you compassion. For the LORD is a God of justice. Blessed are all who wait for Him" (Isaiah 30:18).

Praise the Lord today for His love, righteousness, faithfulness, and justice.

For further reading: Isaiah 30:18, Jeremiah 31:3, Lamentations 3:22-23, Zephaniah 3:17, Romans 5:8, 2 Corinthians 5:21

DAY 52

"Delight yourself in the LORD and he will
give you the desires of your heart" (Psalm 37:4).

This Scripture is one of my favorites, and I definitely believe it to be true. Psalm 37 is about seeing the wicked prosper without growing upset or envious. David says we are to remember that they will soon wither away. Nothing they have achieved or obtained will last. But our instruction as believers is to trust the Lord and do good, to delight ourselves in Him, to commit our way to Him, and to trust Him with our lives.

In other words, when we see people around us who don't acknowledge God in their lives, but they seem to have it made, we can sometimes become disillusioned with the Christian life. The Lord is telling us in His Word not to be fooled by appearances or distracted by others. While others carry out wicked schemes, we are to keep our eyes on God and follow Him.

The psalm goes on to tell us that the meek will inherit the earth and enjoy great peace (Psalm 37:11). I don't know about you, but I am at the point in my life where I highly value peace. The idea that if we will just be faithful to what God has called us to without looking around at what others have, we will inherit it all for eternity is enough for me.

So, what does it mean to "delight yourself in the Lord"? It means to find our pleasure and satisfaction in seeking the things of God rather than the things of the world. Chasing after the world's pleasure is easy—following God is not always easy. But if we choose to delight in God, He will give us the desires of our hearts. What this means is that God places His desires in our hearts. The truth is that what God desires for us is better than anything we can even think or imagine. So when we delight in Him, we rest in a place of fulfillment and peace. We have all that we need and all that we want.

If you have seen unbelievers around who seem to have it all, remember that when they lie down at night, they are still empty inside. And at the end of the day, they will lose it all. So instead of fretting or being envious of them, ask God to give you a heart of compassion for them. Then share His love so they too can know His peace.

For further reading: Psalm 145:19, Isaiah 30:15, John 15:10, Hebrews 11:6

DAY 53

"I was young and now I am old, yet I have never seen the righteous forsaken or their children begging bread" (Psalm 37:25).

God takes care of His own. He is Jehovah Jireh, our Provider. We may not always have what we want, but we will always have what we need.

"Better the little that the righteous have than the wealth of many wicked" (Psalm 37:16).

There's more to life than money and stuff. God does sometimes bless His people with wealth, but true wealth is found in those things that money can't buy.

"The wicked borrow and do not repay, but the righteous give generously" (Psalm 37:21).

God will not forsake His own. He will provide all that we need—not just to pay our bills but what we need for life and godliness.

"His divine power has given us everything we need for life and godliness through our knowledge of him who called us by his own glory and goodness" (2 Peter 1:3).

Whatever you may feel you lack, trust God to provide. Give out of a generous heart, and trust God to meet your needs.

I would rather have love, joy, and peace than a big house, fancy car, and lots of clothes or jewelry. I think the older we get the more we realize what we truly need and what makes us happy. Many people spend their whole lives searching for more and more stuff. But we came into this world naked, and that's how we're going.

David realized that he had never seen those who walk in God's righteousness being forsaken by Him. Neither have I. Because true prosperity is to grow in the Lord and bear fruit for Him.

For further reading: Psalm 128, John 15:16, 2 Peter 1:3, 3 John 2

DAY 54

"All my longings lie open before you, O LORD;
my sighing is not hidden from you" (Psalm 38:9).

Have you ever had to suffer very painful and/or public consequences of sin?

In this psalm, David is suffering as a result of his sin.

"My guilt has overwhelmed me like a burden too heavy to bear" (Psalm 38:4).

All sin has consequences, even if we have confessed and received forgiveness. After David committed adultery and essentially murder by having Bathsheba's husband put on the front lines of battle, he was confronted by the prophet Nathan.

David realized the gravity of his sin and repented. We have a beautiful written account of that confession in Psalm 51. Even though the Lord forgave David, he still spent the rest of his life dealing with the consequences of that sin.

Sin brings pain and destruction into our lives. That's why God hates it so. He loves us, and He doesn't want us to live with such painful consequences.

At one time, David's longing was for Bathsheba. He gave in to that sinful longing and suffered as a result. In this psalm David is again suffering the pain of sin. His longing and sighing are probably for relief.

I've been there.

To me, this psalm is an encouragement and a reminder of the dangers of sin. We may think sometimes that a "little" sin is okay, but sin is like a cancer that spreads.

"Don't you know that a little yeast works through the whole batch of dough?" (1 Corinthians 5:6).

Let's strive to walk in holiness and avoid the pain and suffering that come as a result of sin.

For further reading: Psalm 51, 1 Corinthians 5:6, 1 John 1:9

DAY 55

"I said, 'I will watch my ways and keep my tongue from sin; I will put a muzzle on my mouth as long as the wicked are in my presence'" **(Psalm 39:1).**

It's sometimes tough to be around unbelievers who gossip, curse, or tell coarse jokes, and not get caught up in it. Or listen to them talk about politics or religion and not want to share our opinion in a not-so-nice way. Or to always be positive and full of hope around them because you don't want to ruin your witness.

David's remedy for being around the wicked was to just muzzle his mouth. But it didn't work. The longer he tried to sit there and be quiet, the more his anguish increased until he could stay quiet no longer. "But when I was silent and still, not even saying anything good, my anguish increased. My heart grew hot within me, and as I meditated, the fire burned" (Psalm 39:2-3).

Jeremiah had a similar experience with the Word of the Lord. When he spoke God's truth, he was mocked and ridiculed, but when he tried to hold it in, he couldn't. "...his word is in my heart like a fire, a fire shut up in my bones" (Jeremiah 20:9b).

When David finally spoke, he prayed. He asked the Lord to show him how fleeting life is so that he would be reminded to put his hope in God.

When we are faced with the opportunity to work with or spend time around unbelievers, our words are so important. There may be times when we have to ask God to just set a guard over our lips and keep our mouths shut.

"Set a guard over my mouth, O LORD; keep watch over the door of my lips" (Psalm 141:3).

Then there will be times that God's Word will burn in our hearts and we will have to share it, regardless of how it is received. Ask God to give you boldness when you need to share truth and silence when you need to be quiet.

For further reading: Psalm 141:3, Jeremiah 20:9, Matthew 12:36, James 3:1-12

DAY 56

"I waited patiently for the LORD; he turned to me and heard my cry. He lifted me out of the slimy pit, out of the mud and the mire; he set my feet on a rock and gave me a firm place to stand. He put a new song in my mouth, a hymn of praise to our God" (Psalm 40:1-3a).

There are different kinds of pits. There's the pit we get thrown into, like Joseph. And then there's the pit we dig for ourselves.

I didn't grow up in church or in a Christian family. I was insecure and fearful because of instability in my family, but I also suffered because of my own choice to sin. I never enjoyed the peace of knowing I was safe or whole or cleansed. I wanted to get out of that pit, but I didn't know how. And it wasn't something I could do on my own.

But when I heard the truth about Jesus, and I cried out to Him, He heard my cry. He lifted me out of chaos and dysfunction and set my feet on a rock. I found stability, security, and confidence in Him.

He took away my shame and filled me with hope.

He delivered me from sin and filled me with His Spirit.

He changed my sadness into joy and put a song of praise in my mouth.

God hears our cries when we come to Him and seek forgiveness, healing, and restoration. He will not only lift us out of the pit, but He will give us "a firm place to stand." My security and peace are found in Him.

I will never cease to praise Him for all He has done for me. I will sing, worship, pray, preach, shout, serve, surrender, sacrifice, love, give, and tell the story over and over for what God has done for me.

What's your Jesus story? Who can you share it with today?

For further reading: John 4:1-42, Acts 1:8, Colossians 4:5-6, 1 Peter 3:15

DAY 57

"I desire to do your will, O my God; your law is within my heart"
(Psalm 40:8).

Do you truly desire to do the will of God?

Many people say they want to know God's will for their lives. If we want to do God's will, all we have to do is tell Him. Go to the Lord in prayer and tell Him that you desire to do His will.

Here's the thing. His will can be found in His Word. God's will never contradicts His Word. So spend time in the Word and ask God to show you His will for your life.

Seeking God first every day as our number one priority is crucial to knowing God's will. If we seek Him and show that we honor and prioritize Him above all else, He will make His will known to us. He's not trying to keep it a secret.

When we are pursuing God's will, we should follow peace. If we don't have peace about a particular direction, we need to stop heading that way. The presence of peace will accompany those choices that are in His perfect will.

Sometimes we think we have peace because we are following our own desires and silencing the conflict within. Remember, His will aligns with His Word. True peace will never come at the expense of obedience.

Many times we know what God wants us to do, but we don't want to do it. We need to get our will in line with His. This starts with surrender to God's authority in our lives. He is God. We are not. He knows what the future holds and what is best for us, so there is no fear in surrender.

Come to God with an open heart and seek His face. Through prayer, His Word, peace, and obedience, we will be able to follow God's will for our lives.

"But may all who seek you rejoice and be glad in you; may those who seek your salvation always say, 'The LORD be exalted!'" (Psalm 40:16).

For further reading: Matthew 6:10, Romans 12:1-2, 1 Thessalonians 5:18, 1 John 5:14

DAY 58

"Blessed is he who has regard for the weak;
the LORD delivers him in times of trouble" (Psalm 41:1).

A king's duty was to defend the weak and powerless. David knew that if he had regard for the weak when they were in trouble, God would take care of him when he was in trouble. God also calls us to care for the weak and powerless— orphans, widows, the hungry, the imprisoned.

"For I was hungry and you gave me something to eat, I was thirsty and you gave me something to drink, I was a stranger and you invited me in, I needed clothes and you clothed me, I was sick and you looked after me, I was in prison and you came to visit me" (Matthew 25:35-36).

God calls us to have mercy and compassion on those who have needs around us. Jesus said when we do it for "the least of these" it's as if we are doing it for Him.

Who do you know who could use a meal, a visit, or clothing? How can you help meet the needs of the weak in your community?

We are surrounded by widows and orphans who need love, encouragement, and help. Maybe God is calling you to foster or adopt a child. Maybe He wants you to visit someone and pray with them. It doesn't always take a lot to make a difference.

Jesus said even a cup of cold water in His name would bring a reward (Matthew 10:42).

Start with those needs closest to you—your family and your church. Then look for those in your community who need a helping hand. And don't forget that our greatest need is for Jesus. So be sure to share His love and His truth with all you reach out to in His name.

What can you do to show regard for the weak today?

For further reading: Matthew 10:42, 25:31-46, Acts 6:1-7, 1 Timothy 5:8, James 1:27

DAY 59

"As the deer pants for streams of water, so my soul pants for you, O God. My soul thirsts for God, for the living God. When can I go and meet with God?" (Psalm 42:1-2).

Longing for God, thirsting for God, desperate for the presence of God—that's where God wants our hearts to be. The psalmist is remembering how he used to go up to the temple with the multitude to the house of God to worship, but now he no longer can.

He is longing for fellowship with God to be restored.

We can be in God's presence any time. The only thing that ever separates us from God is when we choose to turn from Him because of sin. But that fellowship can easily be restored. All we have to do is surrender to God and confess our sin to Him. He will forgive us and restore us to a right relationship with Him.

Is there anything between you and God right now? Nothing can separate you from His love, but sin can keep you from intimacy with Him.

"For I am convinced that neither death nor life, neither angels nor demons, neither the present nor the future, nor any powers, neither height nor depth, nor anything else in all creation, will be able to separate us from the love of God that is in Christ Jesus our Lord" (Romans 8:38-39).

If you feel there is something between you and God, you can be sure that it's not God. Nothing can separate you from His love, but your sin will break fellowship with Him.

Surrender to the Living God right now and ask Him to restore you. Then you can again rejoice in His presence and drink from His cup. He wants to pour out life-giving water for your thirsty soul.

And He alone can satisfy.

For further reading: Psalm 23:2, John 4:10, 7:38, Romans 8:38-39, 1 John 1:8-9

DAY 60

"Why are you downcast, O my soul? Why so
disturbed within me? Put your hope in God, for I will
yet praise him, my Savior and my God" (Psalm 42:5).

Downcast—a word that describes a depressed soul. It's a deep sadness that won't seem to go away. Have you ever been there?

The psalmist was depressed because he was out of fellowship with God. He was unable to go to the temple where God's presence dwelled because his people were in exile.

We sometimes are out of fellowship in the church for different reasons. We may have gotten sick and couldn't go to church. Maybe we missed a couple of Sundays and then got lazy. Or maybe something happened that made us not want to go back. Whatever the reason, we need the fellowship of other believers to encourage us in our walk with the Lord, so it is important that we find our way back to church, even if it means finding another church.

"And let us consider how we may spur one another on toward love and good deeds. Let us not give up meeting together, as some are in the habit of doing, but let us encourage one another—and all the more as you see the Day approaching" (Hebrews 10:24-25).

Just as a charcoal removed from the fire will quickly die out without the heat of the other bricks, so too we will quickly lose our fire for the Lord when we get out of fellowship with other believers. Not being in fellowship can definitely lead us to depression, but the cure is right here in the psalm. Put your hope in God and praise Him. Let your faith encourage more faith.

If you are feeling down or missing out on fellowship with other believers, you can decide to hope in God and praise Him no matter how you feel.

So look to your Savior and God, and jump back into fellowship with your church family. They've been missing you!

For further reading: Romans 15:5, 2 Corinthians 7:5-7, Hebrews 10:24-25, 1 John 1:5-7

DAY 61

*"It was not by their sword that they won the land, nor
did their arm bring them victory; it was your right hand, your
arm, and the light of your face, for you loved them" (Psalm 44:3).*

We sometimes feel forsaken by God, crushed, rejected, humbled, and broken. How are we to respond to a God whom we know to be all-powerful and good, yet whose goodness towards us we can't always see?

We can follow the example of the psalmist, who looked to God in his time of trouble. He began by remembering the goodness of God in the past. He described all that God had done for him, acknowledging that none of it came as a result of his own power but only from the hand of a loving God. Then the psalmist admitted that he still trusted in God and not in himself to bring him out of his current situation. He was submitting to the One who was able to help.

Next, he described his plight—they had fallen to the enemy, and, contrary to the teaching of his day, "all this happened to us, though we had not forgotten you or been false to your covenant" (Psalm 44:17). Oftentimes, we, too, suffer unjustly. We believe that if we have been seeking and serving God, then He should protect us from suffering.

But the truth is that suffering comes to all of us in this life because we live in a fallen world. What God promises is that in the midst of our suffering, He will be with us. Like the psalmist, all we can do is look to God and ask Him to "rise up and help us; [and to] redeem us because of [His] unfailing love" (Psalm 44:26, brackets added).

If you are going through a trial through no fault of your own, follow the example of this psalm. Remember the goodness of God to you in the past, acknowledge that He is your only source of help, and ask God to help you. He will because He loves you. Remind God of His promises, and then trust Him with your present.

For further reading: Romans 5:1-8, 8:18-39, 1 Corinthians 15:56-58, 1 John 5:4

DAY 62

*"The king is enthralled by your beauty; honor
him, for he is your lord" (Psalm 45:11).*

What an awesome privilege to be the bride of Christ! And that is what we are. He is the Bridegroom, and we will one day sit down with Him at the wedding supper of the Lamb.

Most women struggle with feelings of insecurity, a lack of self-worth, often based on how we see ourselves in terms of the world's eyes. Our culture is so obsessed with beauty. Few of us feel that we measure up to the standard set by magazines, television, and social media. We use filters, cover-ups, make up, fake tans—anything to make us feel better about how we look to the rest of the world. And all the while, our King is enthralled by our beauty!

This psalm is a wedding song for a king in the line of David, but it also foreshadows Christ. Jesus said all the Scriptures concern Him (Luke 24:27), so we can look at this psalm as our own wedding song. The King is Jesus, and we are His bride. He is enthralled by our beauty. He looks at us and sees us through eyes of grace. His desire is for us, so much so, that He was willing to die for us.

There is no greater love than that which gives his life for another. We all want a hero who rides in on a white horse and sweeps us off our feet, who looks at us with love in his eyes and longs for our hearts. That's Jesus.

He is everything our hearts have ever longed for and more. He loves us with an everlasting love. He sees us as perfect in His eyes. We can stop trying to measure up in the world's eyes, because we are already beautiful in the King's eyes.

"Charm is deceptive, and beauty is fleeting; but a woman who fears the LORD is to be praised" (Proverbs 31:30). What makes us beautiful is our heart for God. This world and all its magazine covers and social media posts are passing away. Our love for God endures. And so does His love for us.

For further reading: Proverbs 31:30, Jeremiah 31:3, John 15:13, Revelation 21:1-2

DAY 63

"There is a river whose streams make glad the city of God, the holy place where the Most High dwells" (Psalm 46:4).

Fear can grip us like nothing else can. It can keep us awake, shake us to our core, paralyze us, and overwhelm us. This psalm tells us that we don't have to fear because God is our refuge and strength. He is our help in times of trouble.

How did the psalmist find peace in the midst of turmoil? He recalled the river that flowed through Jerusalem, the city of God.

Only, there is no river that flows through the Holy City. Other major cities had a river—Thebes, Damascus, Ninevah, and Babylon.[5] But Jerusalem had no river. The river the psalmist refers to is the presence of God, "the holy place where the Most High dwells."

Because Jerusalem had the life-giving, refreshing, renewing presence of God flowing through her, the psalmist was able to declare "God is within her, she will not fall" (Psalm 46:5).

When fear grips your heart, remember that the Holy Spirit of Jesus is within you. He is all-powerful and magnificent. He is mighty and ever-present. Nothing can get past Him to get to you.

If He allows it, remember that He is exalted over it. Sometimes we need to just get still and quiet before Him and remember who He is.

"Be still, and know that I am God; I will be exalted among the nations, I will be exalted in the earth" (Psalm 46:10).

God is exalted far above anything that can come close to us. And He is in us.

"So do not be afraid, little flock, for your Father has been pleased to give you the kingdom" (Luke 12:32).

Let the River of God's love and peace flow through your spirit today.

For further reading: Joshua 1:8-9, Isaiah 43:1-3, Luke 12:32, John 14:15-27

DAY 64

"Sing praises to God, sing praises; sing praises to our King, sing praises" (Psalm 47:6).

Nothing can lift our spirits quite like a song. Have you ever been having a really bad day, and then a song came on the radio that spoke to your heart and lifted your emotions?

There is something about music that has the ability to touch us in a deep place in our souls. A friend of mine once said he believed music had the power to bypass our brains and go straight to our souls. That truth can be a good thing or a bad thing. What are you listening to?

If you are listening to music with questionable lyrics, you may think it's not really affecting you because you just like the beat, or you're not really listening to the words. But the truth is that music is touching your soul at a level you can't even comprehend. On the flip side, if you are listening to godly music that lifts and praises the Lord, you are allowing the Holy Spirit to touch your soul in a way that nothing else can.

There have been times that I was really sad or down and a song just filled me with joy. There have been times when I was fearful, but a song gave me peace. There have also been times that I felt alone or far from God, but when I began to lift my voice to the Lord, I once again felt His presence. We can argue all day about styles of worship and music in the church, but when it comes down to it, what really matters is that a song brings praise to God. Many times in the Bible, we are instructed to sing to the Lord, especially in celebration of who He is.

To a nation whose God lived in the heavens or in the temple, but did not dwell at that time in the hearts of men, praise was seen as a way to bring God close to them. How much more then can we, indwelt with the Spirit, draw near to God through a song?

For further reading: Ephesians 5:19, Colossians 3:16, James 5:13, Revelation 5:9

DAY 65

"As we have heard, so have we seen in the city of the LORD Almighty, in the city of our God: God makes her secure forever" (Psalm 48:8).

We all have a need for security. If we grew up without a secure home, a solid foundation, or parents who affirmed their love, we may suffer with insecurity. Oftentimes, insecurity will spill over into our relationships with others and cause a lack of trust.

Jerusalem, or the city of God, is often used in the Bible as a metaphor for the presence of God, because He dwelled among the Israelites in the temple. He did this for no other nation on earth. The psalmist celebrates the security found within the walls of Zion. Jerusalem was not secure because of her walls or her army. Jerusalem was secure because of her God (Psalm 48:3).

Guess what? God makes you secure forever as well. If you have surrendered your life to God and asked Jesus to be your Lord, He lives within you. He has secured your relationship with Him for all eternity. Nothing you can ever say or do will cause Him to love you less or let you go. The Lord is our citadel. He himself is our fortress, not just for protection of our bodies, but from the insecurity, doubt, and mistrust that can plague our minds.

If you struggle with insecurity as I once did, look for Scriptures like these to meditate on and think about the security that you have in the Lord. This one helped me when I first came to Christ:

"About Benjamin he said: 'Let the beloved of the LORD rest secure in him, for he shields him all day long, and the one the LORD loves rests between his shoulders" (Deuteronomy 33:12).

Benjamin was the youngest son of Jacob and the smallest tribe of Israel. Yet to him, the promise was given that he would rest secure in the love of the Lord. He is the one the Lord loves. And he rests between God's shoulders, just like a kid seated on her daddy's shoulders for a ride. Rest secure in His unfailing love today.

For further reading: Deuteronomy 33:12, Psalm 16:5, 112:8, Proverbs 14:26, Hebrews 6:19

DAY 66

*"No man can redeem the life of another or give to God a ransom for him—the ransom for a life is costly, no payment is ever enough"
(Psalm 49:7-8).*

We can sometimes take for granted the price Jesus paid for us. We wear a cross around our necks or sport a Jesus fish on our car. We go about our day as if knowing God is the most casual thing in the world, forgetting that Jesus gave His life for us to know Him. The ransom for a life is costly. Jesus paid a great price to ransom us from sin and the grave. No man could redeem us. No other price could ever be enough.

"Surely he took up our infirmities and carried our sorrows, yet we considered him stricken by God, smitten by him, and afflicted. But he was pierced for our transgressions, he was crushed for our iniquities; the punishment that bought us peace was upon him, and by his wounds we are healed" (Isaiah 53:4-5).

Jesus suffered greatly to pay the price for us. And He did it willingly, of His own accord. "The reason the Father loves me is that I lay down my life—only to take it up again. No one takes it from me, but I lay it down of my own accord" (John 10:1).

Because God paid a great price for us to be in a saving relationship with Him, we ought to remember that we are not our own (1 Corinthians 6:19-20).

We have been purchased by the Lord. When we come to Him, we give up our right of ownership. We now belong to Him. Every decision we make should be in light of His ownership of us, seeking His will for our lives.

Today, be reminded of the great price Jesus paid for you. His price assigns you great value, so walk today like the blood-bought, Spirit-filled, priceless child of God that you are!

Further reading: Isaiah 53:4-5, Mark 10:45, John 10:11, 1 Corinthians 6:19-20

DAY 67

"He who sacrifices thank offerings honors me, and he prepares the way so that I may show him the salvation of God" (Psalm 50:23).

In the Old Testament, the people of God lived under the sacrificial system of worship. They had to bring offerings to God to atone for their sin, in which the blood of an animal was spilled, because without the shedding of blood there is no remission of sins (Hebrews 9:22).

Over time, the way to God became more about ritual than relationship. They couldn't come into His presence without a sacrifice, yet the sacrifice became more important than His presence. God just wanted their hearts.

"The LORD says: 'These people come near to me with their mouth and honor me with their lips, but their hearts are far from me. Their worship of me is made up only of rules taught by men'" (Isaiah 29:13).

We, too, can sometimes get caught up in the ritual of Christianity. We go to church, pay our tithes, sing in the choir, maybe even read a daily devotional. But our hearts are far from Him. We know all the right words to say, but aren't actively seeking Him every day.

Of all the offerings instituted in their sacrificial system, God wanted their thank offerings, because those required something of their hearts. Bulls and goats can be brought without much thought, but He wanted them to call on Him.

"Sacrifice thank offerings to God, fulfill your vows to the Most High, and call upon me in the day of trouble; I will deliver you and you will honor me" (Psalm 50:14-15).

We honor God when we acknowledge our thanks and dependence upon Him for life; when we seek Him for who He is and not just what He gives; when we call on Him in times of trouble instead of depending upon ourselves and our own abilities. Today, acknowledge your dependence upon the Lord and call on Him for help. Let your worship be from the heart.

For further reading: Isaiah 29:13, Jeremiah 29:13, Acts 2:37, Hebrews 9:22

DAY 68

"Cleanse me with hyssop, and I will be clean;
wash me, and I will be whiter than snow" (Psalm 51:7).

Isn't it interesting that someone the Bible calls "a man after God's own heart" (Acts 13:22) is one who broke about half the commandments?

One of the primary reasons for this can be seen in Psalm 51. About a year after David's sin with Bathsheba, the prophet Nathan came to him and confronted him (2 Samuel 11:1-12:25). David's response can be seen here in this psalm as he cries out to the Lord in repentance and sorrow over his sin. "Have mercy on me, O God, according to your unfailing love" (Psalm 51:1a).

Upon conviction of his sin, David immediately cried out to God to be merciful. He didn't try to run, hide, or deny his sin. He acknowledged it before God and called on His mercy. David had sinned against Bathsheba, Uriah, Joab, and himself, but he knew that ultimately his sin was against the Lord.

Our sin has consequences and affects others around us, but ultimately, it grieves the Spirit of God. To confess means that we agree with God about our sin. God calls our sin evil, and we have to get in agreement with Him that what we have done is evil in His sight. "Against you, you only, have I sinned and done what is evil in your sight, so that you are proved right when you speak and justified when you judge" (Psalm 51:4).

David acknowledged his sinful nature but didn't make excuses for it. He knew that God had taught Him better. "Surely you desire truth in the inner parts; you teach me wisdom in the inmost place" (Psalm 51:6).

We, too, will sometimes fall into sin. We can follow David's example of repentance by confessing our sin against God, acknowledging our sinful nature, agreeing with God about our sin, and seeking to turn away from it and live by the truth and wisdom His Word teaches us (Psalm 51:8).

God longs to show mercy to us and restore to us joy and gladness. Let's give Him the opportunity.

For further reading: 2 Samuel 11:1-12:25, Matthew 23:25, Acts 13:22, 1 John 3

DAY 69

"Then I will teach transgressors your ways
and sinners will turn back to you" (Psalm 51:13).

God has a call on each of our lives, but often when we mess up, we think He's changed His mind about us. Granted, we do still suffer the consequences of sin. God cannot be mocked; a man reaps what he sows (Galatians 6:7).

But God operates in grace. If we come to Him with a truly repentant heart, He will restore us completely. We may have to deal with the consequences of our choices, but God doesn't change His mind about us. He knew we were sinners when He called us.

In Psalm 51, David asked the Lord to restore to him the joy of salvation, to grant him a willing spirit, and to allow him to continue to teach others the ways of God.

That's what's so great about the divine plan of God. He can take our mistakes and use them to minister to others. We can take what we have learned from our sins and help someone else not make the same choices. We can choose to do the right thing, even when it hurts and be a witness to others of what God can do.

What God desires in us is "a broken and contrite heart" (Psalm 51:17). When we come to Him, truly broken over what we have done, He is able to restore us and still use us for His glory. Nothing is wasted in God's kingdom. Even those things that bring us shame can be used to show others a better way.

What are you running from that God has called you to do, but shame has kept you stuck? God's forgiveness is complete. If He could use you before, He can use you now. If you need time to deal with consequences and grow in your relationship with Him, then take that time to seek Him.

But don't give up on letting Him use you. We are all broken and marred vessels, but through us His light can still shine.

For further reading: 1 Corinthians 1:26-31, Galatians 6:7, 1 Thessalonians 5:24, 1 Timothy 6:11-12

DAY 70

"But I am like an olive tree flourishing in the house of God"
(Psalm 52:8a).

We live in a polarized culture where left is left and right is right, and there is very little in between. We can quickly become discouraged as we see traditional values become discarded and a new generation arise with little regard for the things of the Lord. Can you bear to scroll through a social media feed on a day when something polarizing has happened? It seems no one has regard for his neighbor. Many only see things in terms of their own opinion, and they are quick to share it.

If someone has an opposing view, they are immediately branded as ignorant or uninformed, while truth is hard to come by. We may think we are living in a time unlike any other, but in many ways, nothing has changed since David penned these words. David, too, had to deal with evil people who boasted of their evil ways and plotted destruction. He had to listen to those who "love every harmful word" (Psalm 52:4).

But in the midst of such darkness, David testified of his position in the Lord. He said "I am like an olive tree flourishing in the house of God" (Psalm 52:8a). The olive tree, known as the "tree of eternity," is a staple to Middle Eastern living. They live for hundreds of years and are not easily uprooted. Olive trees provide shade, food, and oil, which can be used for heat, cooking, and many other things.[6]

David knew that although the wicked in the land were deceitful and plotted David's downfall, he was secure because his hope was in the Lord. The wicked, God would "uproot from the land of the living" (Psalm 52:5). But David would stand firm in the presence of God.

We, too, can be firmly planted in God's presence. As we seek Him through prayer, worship, and the Word, God will make us firm and steadfast, so that we are able to stand. We can put our hope in the Lord and praise Him for what He has done. In the end, God will deal with His enemies. Meanwhile, let's be found flourishing in the house of God.

For further reading: Proverbs 14:11, Isaiah 7:9, Romans 14:4, 1 Corinthians 15:58

DAY 71

"There they were, overwhelmed with dread,
where there was nothing to dread" (Psalm 53:5).

This psalm may sound a little familiar. It's almost an exact repeat of Psalm 14. But verse five is different, which is what made it stand out to me. The reference is to the enemy whom God overwhelmed with dread when actually they were not even being threatened—at least not by a human enemy.

How often are we overcome with dread when, in reality, there is nothing to dread? I've heard it said that dread is a cousin to fear, and there may be some truth to that. *Dread* means to "to be apprehensive or fearful" or "to feel extreme reluctance to meet or face."[7] So when we dread something, we fear the possibility of something unpleasant in the future.

The problem with dread is that it steals the present from us. For instance, let's say it's the last day of your vacation, and tomorrow you have to go back to work. Rather than enjoying your day, you spend your time dreading work the next day.

Most of the time when we are "overwhelmed with dread" there is really nothing to dread. We are worrying about or anticipating something that is not going to be as bad as we think. But we wasted precious time allowing our minds to dwell on that negative thought, rather than enjoying the present time we do have.

Remember in this psalm, it was the evildoers who were overwhelmed with dread. These were the fools who didn't trust in God. But we are the people of God who rejoice and are glad in Him. We have every reason to celebrate the present moment and be thankful for all God has done.

So the next time you feel yourself starting to dread some unpleasant activity, remember not to be the "fool" who is overwhelmed with dread when there was nothing to dread. Instead, be of those who seek God and look for what is good in every situation. God will deal with evildoers, but we can enjoy the peace and presence of being found in Him.

For further reading: Matthew 6:25-34, Philippians 4:6, 1 Peter 5:7

DAY 72

"Surely God is my help; the LORD is the one who sustains me"
(Psalm 54:4).

In times of sickness, grief, pain, and suffering, we often feel that we cannot go on. We may feel on the verge of collapse, weak, helpless, and unable to bear up under the strain. During these times, we can call on God to be "the one who sustains" us. He is the only one who can help us in times of extreme suffering. When it's a friend who is suffering, sometimes we don't know what to say. We want to help, we want to offer comfort and support, but we know our words won't mean much.

In these times, we can offer our presence rather than our words. Sometimes our friends just need to know we are there. They need a hand to hold, a shoulder to cry on, an ear to just listen. We want to fix everything, but we have to understand that's not our job. If we could make everything right, they wouldn't need God.

When a friend is suffering, the best thing we can do is pray for her. Cover her constantly in prayer. Put a note that says "Pray for _____" on your desk or on your refrigerator so you remember to pray for her often. Don't try to come up with spiritual sounding things to say—they will sound trite in the face of your friend's suffering. Instead, ask the Lord to be her source of comfort, to sustain her, and to give her the strength she needs moment by moment.

If your friend asks you for advice, don't be quick to respond. Spend some time in prayer and ask the Lord to give you a word of encouragement for her.

"The sovereign LORD has given me an instructed tongue, to know the word that sustains the weary. He wakens me morning by morning, wakens my ear to listen like one being taught" (Isaiah 50:4).

If you are accustomed to spending time with God every day and you know His voice, then share the word He gives for your friend. But remember that ultimately the only One who can sustain the hurting is Him.

For further reading: Psalm 18:35, Isaiah 46:4, 50:4, Hebrews 1:3

DAY 73

"But as for me, I trust in you" (Psalm 55:23b).

Church hurts are the worst kind. There's a level of trust within the body of Christ that, when broken, leaves a hole in us that's hard to heal.

"If an enemy were insulting me, I could endure it; if a foe were raising himself against me, I could hide from him. But it is you, a man like myself, my companion, my close friend, with whom I once enjoyed sweet fellowship as we walked with the throng at the house of God" (Psalm 55:12-14).

Even David knew the pain of that kind of betrayal. He said his heart was in anguish (Psalm 55:4) and he wished he could flee from the whole mess (Psalm 55:6-8).

I've been there. But here's the truth: God doesn't want us to run away from it. He wants us to look to Him in it. He is more than able to handle church hurts and abuses. The church isn't perfect. We will still fellowship with brothers and sisters who make mistakes, say the wrong things, do the wrong things, and some even may not be saved.

We will make the situation worse, however, if we gossip, complain, and try to find people to take our side on an issue. While it is tempting to want our opinion validated by others, strife will soon follow. We are then playing right into the hands of the enemy whose goal is to divide and conquer. Instead, we need to follow the example of David (16-17).

Take your concerns to the Lord in prayer, crying out to Him. If the offense is something serious, go to your pastor and ask for help. But don't go the phone or the parking lot to make your case heard. "Without wood a fire goes out; without gossip a quarrel dies down" (Proverbs 26:20).

Some things will resolve themselves if we pray and leave them alone. Some things require pastoral intervention. And sometimes we need to forgive and let go. Give other people space to grow spiritually. Have patience with those who are weaker in their faith. And trust God to be big enough.

For further reading: Proverbs 19:11, 26:20, Romans 15:1-2

DAY 74

"When I am afraid, I will trust in you" (Psalm 56:3).

What are you afraid of? Some are afraid of death or losing loved ones, cancer, snakes, spiders, heights, storms, or darkness. Some fear disapproval, failure, rejection, and loneliness. Others fear loss of income, job, wealth, or stability. What do you fear?

We are going to confront our fears today, okay? Honestly, I'm afraid of everything listed above (Well, not really ALL of them, but most of them).

David had a reason to be afraid. The Philistines had seized him and were planning to kill him. His very life was threatened. But even in his fear, he trusted God. God doesn't want us to fear. He's given us 365 "fear nots" in Scripture—one for every day of the year. But He knows we are human. When we are afraid, we can trust in Him.

The best expression of trust in the midst of fear is to stand on God's Word.

"In God, whose word I praise, in the LORD, whose word I praise—in God I trust; I will not be afraid. What can man do to me?" (Psalm 56:10-11).

These verses remind me of something Jesus said:

"'I tell you the truth, my friends, do not be afraid of those who kill the body and after that can do no more. But I will show you whom you should fear: Fear him who after the killing of the body, has power to throw you into hell. Yes, I tell you, fear him'" (Luke 12:4-5).

Those who threaten the people of God are the ones who should fear. We, on the other hand, are safe in the security of our salvation. Therefore, we actually have no reason to fear.

If you struggle with fear, stand on the truth of God's Word as David did. Find verses about fear and copy them down, study them, memorize them, and post them in places where you will see them daily as a reminder that God has said, "Fear not!"

For further reading: Isaiah 41:10, 43:1-3, 2 Timothy 1:7, 1 John 4:18

DAY 75

"I cry out to God Most High, to God, who fulfills his purpose for me"
(Psalm 57:2).

God has a divine purpose for each of our lives, and that purpose will not be thwarted. We can choose not to live for the Lord and reject His plans for us, but if we are seeking God, no devil in hell and no man on earth can keep the Lord from fulfilling His purpose for us.

"'I know that you can do all things; no plan of yours can be thwarted" (Job 42:2).

Do you know what your purpose is? Our primary purpose is to live with God forever.

"Now it is God who has made us for this very purpose [eternal life] and has given us the Spirit as a deposit, guaranteeing what is to come" (2 Corinthians 5:5, brackets added).

While on this earth, our purpose is to bring Him glory through our lives. All we say and all we do should be about the Lord and His glory. When we get focused on ourselves and our purposes, we miss opportunities to be used by God to fulfill His purposes.

"...for it is God who works in you to will and to act according to his good purpose" (Philippians 2:13).

He will work in you and help you to fulfill His call on your life. If we are seeking the Lord, He will fulfill His purpose for us. If we choose to reject Him, He can still use us without our consent, but we will never live the life He created us to enjoy.

Seek Him, surrender to Him, serve Him, and fulfill the purpose for which you were made.

For further reading: Job 42:2, Romans 9:17, 2 Corinthians 5:5, Philippians 2:12-13

DAY 76

"Then men will say, 'Surely the righteous are still rewarded; surely there is a God who judges the earth'" (Psalm 58:11).

We serve a God who is a righteous Judge. When we see evil in the world, our hearts cry out for justice. When children are abused and sold into slavery, when the elderly are mistreated, when women are raped and killed, we long for every wrong to be made right and for those who are evil to be punished.

God put that innate sense of justice within us. When we read the words of David in this psalm, at first it may seem harsh—especially when we read that "the righteous will be glad when they are avenged, when they bathe their feet in the blood of the wicked" (Psalm 58:10). David's desire for the death of his enemies doesn't seem to jive with the command to love our neighbor as ourselves.

We have to remember two things.

First, the psalms are descriptive and not always prescriptive. In other words, we see David describe his thoughts and feelings honestly to the Lord, but that doesn't mean God is prescribing how our behavior should be. When we have feelings and thoughts such as David's, a good policy is to be honest with God and express them to Him in prayer as David did. Often when we express our emotions to God, He will soothe us and fill us with His Spirit so that we can react in the right way.

Second, David trusted God to bring justice and pay back those who had wronged him. When he cried out for the blood of his enemy, it's because that enemy had shed the blood of his people—usually the poor and innocent. Just as we are horrified when we hear of the brutal mistreatment of others, so David was calling on God's justice to avenge the wrongs that had been done.

We all long for justice to be done and for the poor and innocent to be avenged. One day every wrong will be made right and all men will see that "surely there is a God who judges the earth" (Psalm 58:11b).

For further reading: Isaiah 42:1-4, Matthew 12:15-21, Romans 3:26, 2 Thessalonians 1:6

DAY 77

"But I will sing of your strength, in the morning I will sing of your love; for you are my fortress, my refuge in times of trouble"
(Psalm 59:16).

God is our refuge in times of trouble. Trouble can look like a lot of things: relationship problems, a sickness, financial strain, loss of a job, a wayward child, a misunderstanding. In our flesh, our tendency is to complain. Honestly, it's hard not to. But God calls us to turn those problems into praises. Instead of complaining to a friend, we can pour out our hearts to God and know that He hears us. Not only does He hear, He delivers. He protects us from the enemy, and He will give us victory.

I love that in the midst of bloodthirsty men who wanted to kill David, he sang praises. I am reminded of a New Testament story of praising in the face of a trial. In Acts 16, we read of Paul and Silas's imprisonment following Paul's casting a demon out of a girl. The crowd attacked them and they were ordered to be stripped and beaten. After what the Bible describes as being "severely flogged" they were thrown in prison.

I'm not sure we can truly appreciate the physical pain and suffering of being flogged. While these men were fastened in stocks, suffering from their torture, they began praying and singing hymns to God. Can you imagine? The "hymns" they would have sung are what are known as the *Hallel*, Psalms 113-118. But among what they could have sung that night were words like these:

"I love the LORD, for he heard my voice; he heard my cry for mercy. Because he turned his ear to me, I will call on him as long as I live" (Psalm 116:1-2).

When God heard the sounds of their praises, all hell broke loose. An earthquake shook the foundations of the prison and all the doors flew open. Everybody's chains came loose! We may be in deep pain and anguish, not knowing what to do; but if we will turn our complaining into praising, God will hear our cry and set us free. Don't let the enemy convince you that all hope is gone. Sing a hymn of praise and let those walls come down.

For further reading: 2 Chronicles 20, Psalm 116:1-2, Acts 16:16-40

DAY 78

*"But for those who fear you, you have raised a banner
to be unfurled against the bow" (Psalm 60:4).*

In Old Testament times, when a nation was defeated in battle, it was understood to be a sign of God's anger and rejection. It never signified the breaking of His covenant but was interpreted as a break in His blessings.

Israel repeatedly went through cycles of seeking God, then turning away from Him, crying out to Him for help, and being delivered by God.

When we as a people turn from God and reject His ways, the nation may suffer a loss of the blessing of God. In the last days, many will fall away from God in every nation. As He removes His hand of blessing, we are reminded to cry out to Him for restoration. Revival begins with the people of God.

Even in times of apostasy, there is usually a remnant that stays true to God. As they cry out to God on behalf of the people, God raises a banner for them. Banners were used to call people into battle, to rally the troops, and to lead them forth. As small groups gather for prayer, God will rally more troops into the battle until restoration comes.

Do you grieve over your city or nation as many fall away from God and desperate times come? Cry out to God on behalf of your people. Watch Him raise a banner against the foe and call forth intercessors to pray with you. All it takes to start a revival is a few faithful who fear the Lord.

"If my people, who are called by my name, will humble themselves and pray and seek my face and turn from their wicked ways, then will I hear from heaven and will forgive their sin and will heal their land" (2 Chronicles 7:14).

Even though this was originally a promise made to Israel, God's chosen people, the principle remains true for us. God seeks after the people who seek after Him. God will give us aid and bring us victory as we faithfully seek Him in prayer. Go to battle for your city.

For further reading: 2 Chronicles 7:14, Isaiah 11:12, Romans 11:1-6, 2 Timothy 3:1-5

DAY 79

"From the ends of the earth I call to you, I call as my heart grows faint; lead me to the rock that is higher than I" (Psalm 61:2).

The King James Version of this verse says, "when my heart is *overwhelmed:* lead me to the rock that is higher than I." If there's anything we understand today, it's what it means to be overwhelmed. When we have so many things coming against us at one time that our minds and emotions can't handle it, we are overwhelmed. The word *overwhelm* means "to cover over completely; to overpower in thought or feeling."[8] I can certainly identify with that definition, can't you?

Whether it's work or bills or pain or responsibilities, we can feel as if we are drowning beneath it all. Thank God, there is a Rock that is higher than we are. We can cry out to God and ask Him to lift our heads above the water. David said, "Lead me to the rock that is higher than I" because David knew he could do nothing on his own to fix his problem. He needed the Lord, his refuge, his strong tower. So do we.

When life has us overwhelmed, we need to go to the Rock. We need to climb up and stand up and place our feet firmly on the Rock, knowing that we are secure in Him. And if we will continue to build from that foundation, we will be less likely to get overwhelmed in the future. We can give God our finances, our workload, and our responsibilities. We can start praying before we spend or take on more duties. We can keep our feet firmly planted as we learn how to say "No."

I don't know what you may be going through today, but know this: God loves you and He will see you through it. He will allow times of testing to grow us and purify us. As we seek Him for strength and comfort, He will lift us up and set us on the Rock (Psalm 40:1-2).

Moment by moment, day by day, His love encourages us to keep striving for the Rock.

For further reading: Psalm 46:10, Isaiah 40:31, Matthew 19:26, 2 Corinthians 4:8-9

DAY 80

"My soul finds rest in God alone; my salvation comes from him. He alone is my rock and my salvation; he is my fortress, I will never be shaken" (Psalm 62:1-2).

There is a rest for the people of God that can only be found in God's presence. It's a soul rest that relieves us from striving and pursuing so that we can just be. No matter what is going on around us, we can find peace in the rest of God.

"Come to me, all you who are weary and burdened, and I will give you rest. Take my yoke upon you and learn from me, for I am gentle and humble in heart, and you will find rest for your souls. For my yoke is easy and my burden is light" (Matthew 11:28-30).

So many of you are tired and weary. You have tried to carry burdens that were not yours to carry. You've put so much pressure on yourself to perform and to meet others' expectations. You've taken on more responsibility than you can bear. Your soul—mind, will, and emotions—can only handle so much. You weren't created to take on the weight of the world. It's time to stop striving and rest in God's presence.

He is calling you to come away with Him to the secret place and let Him teach you how to serve under His yoke and not the one that the world puts on you or that you have put on yourself. Jesus said His yoke is easy. He calls us to do one thing: Follow Him.

Maybe you need to recommit yourself to consistent quiet time with the Lord every day. Maybe you are so tired you need a few days away to spend with the Lord. Find the time and make it happen. Don't try to fill the space with noise. Put away the tech and have a spiritual retreat with just God and His Word.

He will give you rest for your soul—your mind, your will, and your emotions. Feed your spirit with what it desires: Jesus.

For further reading: Psalm 23, Matthew 11:28-30, Luke 10:38-42

DAY 81

"O God, you are my God, earnestly I seek you" (Psalm 63:1a).

The word translated *earnestly* can also mean "early" (KJV). I know, I know. Most people don't want to hear about seeking God early. We all love our sleep! But let me just share a few thoughts about seeking God first thing in the morning.

I have never considered myself to be a morning person, so when I first committed myself to spending time with God every day, I tried different times of the day. I tried having my quiet time in the afternoons when I first came home from work, but I would be distracted by laundry and kids' homework and supper. I tried doing it at night before I went to sleep, but by then I was exhausted and wouldn't be able to concentrate.

The only time I could find when I would not be distracted and I could focus my attention (after coffee, of course) was in the morning. At first, I hated having to get up so early. But then something happened. God began to reveal Himself to me through His Word and answer my prayers and change my heart. Pretty soon, I couldn't wait to get up to spend time with Him.

"Because your love is better than life, my lips will glorify you. I will praise you as long as I live, and in your name I will lift up my hands" (Psalm 63:3-4).

I found a love that was worth getting up for. The more time I spend with the Lord, the more time with Him I want. Honestly, I can't get enough of Him!

"My soul will be satisfied as with the richest of foods; with singing lips my mouth will praise you" (Psalm 63:5).

Jesus satisfies a place in us that nothing else can. You may not be a morning person, but there is something special about mornings. It's the first part of our day. We are giving Him our best—not our leftovers. It sets the tone for the rest of our day. And we are seeking Him first, as our priority above everything else.

Seek Him first, however that works best for you. Soon, you will hunger for more.

For further reading: Psalm 5:3, Lamentations 3:23, Matthew 6:33, Mark 1:35

DAY 82

"All mankind will fear; they will proclaim the works of God and ponder what he has done. Let the righteous rejoice in the LORD and take refuge in him; let all the upright in heart praise him!" (Psalm 64: 9-10).

At times it seems that evil will win. We can look around and quickly get discouraged at the state of the world. When we see violence, evil, and injustice, what should be our response? When we witness lies, fake news, and the erosion of our culture, what can the righteous do? I'm sure there were times that David felt the same way. He, too, witnessed evil and injustice all around.

"They encourage each other in evil plans, they talk about hiding their snares; they say, 'Who will see them?' They plot injustice and say, 'We have devised a perfect plan!' Surely the mind and heart of man are cunning" (Psalm 64:5-6).

Yep, the mind and heart of man can be so evil that we sometimes want to bury our heads in the sand and pretend the evil doesn't exist. But David didn't. He knew ignoring it wouldn't make it go away. He asked God to protect him and hide him from their conspiracies. He asked the Lord to bring down the wicked so that all mankind would fear Him and proclaim what He had done. And David called on other believers to join him in taking refuge in the Lord and praising Him.

The Bible tells us that in the last days, wickedness will increase. We can't pretend it's not there or argue it away. Evil people are living in darkness. They need the hope of Christ. As believers, we need to turn to the Lord for help and cry out on behalf of our nation.

He may be calling us to speak up or get involved. He may be calling us as intercessors to pray and rally others to pray. And He is definitely calling us to praise Him, even in the midst of divisive and confusing times. Let us look to the God of our salvation and find refuge in Him.

For further reading: 2 Samuel 22:29-31, Romans 5:1-5, 1 Thessalonians 5:15-18, 2 Peter 3:10-13

DAY 83

"Blessed are those you choose and bring near to live in your courts! We are filled with the good things of your house, of your holy temple" (Psalm 65).

We are so blessed because we are chosen.

"You did not choose me, but I chose you and appointed you to go and bear fruit—fruit that will last. Then my Father will give you whatever you ask in my name" (John 15:16).

We were chosen by God and appointed to bear fruit for Him—the fruit of the Spirit: love, joy, peace, patience, kindness, goodness, faithfulness, gentleness, and self-control. We can only do so as we abide in the Vine.

"I am the vine; you are the branches. If a man remains in me and I in him, he will bear much fruit; apart from me you can do nothing" (John 15:5).

That's why God calls us to come near to Him and "live in his courts." Living in His courts means dwelling in His presence, spending time with Him, listening for His voice, and following the promptings of His Spirit.

As we draw near to God, we are "filled with the good things" of His presence. Do you need more of the goodness and blessing and favor of God on your life? Do you want more of the anointing and grace of God?

Well, that's what you were chosen for!

All that is good can be found in relationship with God, but we must pursue that relationship and grow in Him. As we seek His presence daily, we will be filled with the blessings of His peace and His presence.

He is our hope, "who stilled the roaring of the seas, the roaring of their waves, and the turmoil of the nations" (Psalm 65:7).

You are chosen, and you are blessed.

For further reading: John 15:1-17, Ephesians 1:4, 2 Thessalonians 2:13, 1 Peter 2:9

DAY 84

*"Come and listen, all you who fear God; let me
tell you what he has done for me" (Psalm 66:16).*

With whom have you shared your testimony lately?

When Jesus met the woman at the well in John 4, she had lived a life of longing for love and acceptance. She had been in several relationships with men and was currently with a man who was not her husband. But Jesus met her right where she was and met her need for love.

He offered her Living Water that would quench every thirst so she would never thirst again.

Her response?

She told everyone she met.

"Many of the Samaritans from that town believed in him because of the woman's testimony" (John 4:39).

She shared her testimony with others. She didn't keep the good news of what Jesus had done to herself. But so often, that's what we do. Sure, we may tell others when we first get saved, but do we continue to praise God and tell the world what He has done for us?

Do we celebrate each day that we get to live in the kingdom, realizing how far God has brought us? Do we remember what He saved us from? Do we daily think about His goodness and what our lives would be like without Him?

The psalmist is willing to tell to anyone who will listen what God has done for him. What about you? What has God done for you?

Go and tell someone today.

For further reading: Mark 16:15, John 4:39, Romans 1:16, 1 Peter 3:15

DAY 85

*"May God be gracious to us and bless us
and make his face shine upon us" (Psalm 67:1).*

When Moses met the Lord at the burning bush, God revealed Himself in flames of fire. God called to Moses and instructed him to take off his shoes. The very ground where Moses stood was holy. And Moses hid his face because he was afraid to look at God.

Later, when Moses asked God to show him His glory, God graciously covered Moses with His hand so that Moses could experience His glory and not die (Exodus 33:22-23). Abraham fell to his face in God's presence (Genesis 17:3), Isaiah was completely undone (Isaiah 6:5), and John fell as though dead before Him (Revelation 1:17).

God is so, so holy. Yet, the psalmist asked for God to make His face shine upon him. For the light of God's face to shine was a common expression asking God for His favor and deliverance. It was part of the priestly blessing in Numbers 6:24-25 that God instructed the priests to use in blessing the people.

For the face of God to shine on us means that God accepts and blesses His people with divine favor. Oh, how we need the favor and blessing of God! For those still in darkness, the veil remains, keeping them from seeing the glory of God and understanding the truth of His Word. Only in Christ can the veil be removed, by faith.

Our job is to pray for unbelievers that the veil be removed and God would give them eyes to see, ears to hear, and hearts to receive the gospel. Then they, too, can enjoy the favor of the Lord and receive His blessing and deliverance.

Pray for those whose hearts are darkened by sin that the Lord would be gracious and bless them and make His face shine upon them that they might believe.

For further reading: Genesis 17:3, Exodus 33:22-23, Numbers 6:24-25, Isaiah 6:5, 2 Corinthians 3:18, Revelation 1:17

DAY 86

"A father to the fatherless, a defender of widows, is God in his holy dwelling" (Psalm 68:5).

My father left home when I was twelve years old. I visited him but never really developed much of a relationship with him until much later into my adult years. When I gave my life to Jesus in my early 20s, I began to experience what it means to have God as my Father.

This psalm is "a processional liturgy celebrating the glorious and triumphal rule of Israel's God."⁹ David recounted Israel's history from Mount Sinai as Moses led the people out of Egypt and into the Promised Land, to Mount Zion, the holy city of Jerusalem, the city of David.

He described the power and majesty of God as He destroyed the enemies of Israel—the earth shook and God poured down rain (Psalm 68:8). Armies fled and their camps were plundered (Psalm 68:12). Israel celebrated the victories of God as He showed Himself strong on their behalf.

And yet even as David described the power and majesty of God in defeating the enemies of Israel, he praised the One who is a Father to the fatherless, a defender of widows, the Tender Warrior who both loves and leads.

And that is the God you serve today. He is with you as your Provider, Protector, and Defender. He is the Judge who will one day right every wrong. And He is also your Father, Friend, Counselor, and Comforter. Verse 19 tells us that God daily bears our burdens. Nothing is too big for Him, and nothing is too small for Him. If it concerns us, it concerns Him. In verse 27, David described the "little tribe of Benjamin leading them" in the procession of praise.

How fitting that even the smallest tribe can lead the "great throng" of people, even royalty! Doesn't that thought bring a smile to your face? We can praise the God who "thunders with mighty voice" and yet "gives strength to His people."

Sing and celebrate the Tender Warrior today.

For further reading: Isaiah 9:6, Matthew 6:9, Romans 8:15, 1 John 3:1-3

DAY 87

"Save me, O God, for the waters have come up to my neck"
(Psalm 69:1).

I imagine we all have felt like David at times—drowning in the "miry depths" and unable to find our feet beneath us. Deep waters. Engulfed. There are times when we come under such persecution from the enemy that we even feel God can't hear us. We grow weary, crying out for help. We look for God, but we see no answer in sight.

David described such a time in his life, but He also spoke prophetically of the persecution of Jesus on the cross. In verse 21 David said, "They put gall in my food and gave me vinegar to drink."

In Matthew 27:34, Jesus was offered wine mixed with gall, which was supposed to act as a sort of pain reliever, but Jesus refused to drink it. Then in Matthew 27:48, Jesus was given a sponge soaked in wine vinegar to drink.

Jesus was in deep waters. Engulfed. But for our sake, He refused to take comfort from the pain. He suffered so we wouldn't have to face eternal punishment for our sins.

When we are at our lowest point, just like David, we can look to Jesus. David turned to the God he knew, assured of His favor, love, and salvation (Psalm 69:13). He called on God to answer him out of his goodness and mercy (Psalm 69:16). And we can do the same. Even when it seems as if we are sinking with no way out, we can look to God in our pain and distress and trust Him. We can trust God to be just, to be righteous, and to be unchanging. He will bring justice to our situation and mercy for our need.

Turn to the God who is able and praise Him in song, glorify Him with thanksgiving. Look for the good in the midst of your trial. This is what pleases the Lord (Psalm 69:30-31). The Lord will save you and rebuild you, and if your trust is in Him, He will one day lead you home where "those who love his name will dwell" (Psalm 69:36).

For further reading: Isaiah 35:4, 63:1, John 12:47, 1 Thessalonians 5:18, Hebrews 7:25

DAY 88

"But may all who seek you rejoice and be glad in you" (Psalm 70:4a).

What are you seeking?

The world has much to offer—relationships, material possessions, substances, more money, popularity, approval—the list goes on and on. From the time we are old enough to recognize our own emptiness and desire for fulfillment, we are surrounded with idols crying out for our hearts.

David's enemies were seeking something—his life (Psalm 70:2)! They wanted to kill him. We're not sure to whom David was referring in this psalm, but his enemy could have been seeking his life for revenge, power, or wealth.

David's prayer was that they would be "turned back in disgrace" (Psalm 70:2). When we seek after the things of the world, we will end up in shame, confusion, and disgrace. None of those desires will lead to fulfillment. People will hurt us, material possessions will grow old and obsolete, substance abuse will destroy us, money and popularity will flee, and the approval of man is fickle.

Only seeking after God will bring peace and fulfillment to our lives. All the rest is a cleverly-designed illusion to keep you from the Lord. Don't fall for the trap of the enemy.

David knew that those who seek the Lord would rejoice and be glad. Those who rest in His salvation have every reason to say "Let God be exalted" because they have understood the truth: Only an intimate relationship with Jesus Christ can satisfy the deepest needs of the human soul.

What are you seeking?

I encourage you to seek the Lord today. He is ready, willing, and more than able to meet your needs and deliver you.

For further reading: Isaiah 55:6, Jeremiah 29:13, Hosea 10:12, Hebrews 11:6

DAY 89

"Rescue me and deliver me in your righteousness" (Psalm 71:2a).

How long have you been following Jesus? In this psalm, David says God has been his hope since his youth (Psalm 71:5). Sometimes when we have been walking with the Lord for a long time, we begin to develop a works-based mentality. In others words, we are saved by grace, but gradually we begin to think that our right living earns us favor before God. I've been there.

The problem with this line of thinking is that 1. It's not true. 2. We will never be good enough. 3. We become judgmental. 4. We become self-righteous.

But David didn't. He didn't look to his own righteousness to save him. David knew that only the righteousness of God could rescue him (Psalm 71:2), and he was determined to live by God's righteousness alone.

"I will proclaim your righteousness, yours alone" (Psalm 71:16b).

One reason David understood the ways of God is because he had looked to the Lord to teach him since his youth (Psalm 71:17). David knew the world would lead him astray; he needed the instruction of the Lord. So do we. We need to stay in the Word and keep our eyes on Jesus, the only example of righteousness.

What about you? Have you begun to depend on your own righteousness to bring about the life you desire? Do you sometimes find yourself looking down on others who aren't as spiritual as you are? Are you proud of yourself for your righteous lifestyle? If so, know that your own righteousness is like filthy rags in the eyes of God (Isaiah 64:6).

Turn to God in repentance and thank Him for giving you His righteousness. Turn your focus away from yourself and to the only truly righteous One.

Like David, you can give praise to God for a righteousness that reaches to the skies. He alone has done great things (Psalm 71:19).

For further reading: Isaiah 64:6, Matthew 23, Luke 18:9-14, Ephesians 2:8-9, Titus 3:5

DAY 90

"Praise be to the God of Israel, who alone does marvelous deeds"
(Psalm 72:18).

Have you ever made a promise you couldn't keep? Has anyone ever broken a promise to you? A person's word is important, and when people break their word to us, we can often be deeply hurt.

In this psalm, we see the promises of God kept through thousands of years. About 4,000 years ago, God called a man named Abram and promised to make him the father of many nations and to bless all nations through him (Genesis 18:18).

Somewhere around 3,000 years ago, God called forth a man named David and promised him that he would reign over Israel and that he would never fail to have a descendant on the throne (2 Samuel 7:16).

About 2,000 years ago, God sent His Son Jesus to be the fulfillment of both those promises. A descendant of both Abraham and David (Matthew 1:17), Jesus Christ now reigns on the throne of God where He will live forever, and through faith in Him, all nations of the earth can be blessed.

God is true to His promises, even if they take thousands of years to fulfill. God exists outside of time. A day is like a thousand years to Him (2 Peter 3:8). He is not a man that He should lie (Numbers 23:19). He is the same yesterday, today, and forever (Hebrews 13:8). He does not change like shifting shadows (James 1:17).

Hallelujah!

His promises to us are many. Spend some time searching out the promises of God to you in His Word. Man may let you down, but your God never will.

"Praise be to the God of Israel, who alone does marvelous deeds (Psalm 72:18)."

For further reading: Genesis 18:18, Numbers 23:19, 2 Samuel 7:16, Matthew 1:17. Hebrews 13:8, James 1:17, 2 Peter 3:8

DAY 91

"But as for me, my feet had almost slipped" (Psalm 73:2a).

How easy it is to look around at the world and feel as if we have kept our hearts pure in vain (Psalm 73:13). I mean, face it: The wicked in this world sure do seem to prosper and get away with sin. Often we see those who spurn God and live evil lives prosper. They often walk about in pride and look down on those of us who try to follow Jesus.

If we're not careful, like the psalmist, our feet will begin to slip down the shiny incline of resentment. We can easily begin to resent the fact that we are sacrificing the pleasures and sins of the world because we want to be pleasing to God—especially when we suffer for it.

I think somewhere deep inside, we begin to believe the lie that if we do everything right, God at least owes us a decent life, right? We start to think that if all we will get for our efforts is pain and suffering, then why bother?

The truth is that we have to enter the presence of God as the psalmist did in order to have our hearts awakened to truth. "When I tried to understand all this, it was oppressive to me till I entered the sanctuary of God; then I understood their final destiny" (Psalm 73:16-17).

Only in the presence of God can we experience the peace and joy that come from knowing Him, a gift far greater than anything this world has to offer. And beyond this world, we live for the life that is to come.

Those who reject God may seem to get away with it now, but one day every knee will bow and every tongue confess that Jesus is Lord (Philippians 2:9-11). I would rather bow to Him now and spend eternity with Jesus, than reject Him now and face eternity without Him.

If you are struggling with doing the right thing when everything seems wrong, spend some time in the presence of God. Worship Him for who He is. He will show you your destiny is with Him, and that is worth any sacrifice now.

For further reading: Ephesians 4:31, Philippians 2:9-11, Hebrews 12:15, 1 Peter 5:10

DAY 92

"My flesh and heart may fail, but God is the strength of my heart and my portion forever" (Psalm 73:26).

We chase after so many things in life we think will make us happy. But we are left wanting, empty, still unfulfilled with the things of the world.

Think of all the things you have sought to bring you comfort—relationships, food, shopping, approval. Even when we do attain them, they never bring the peace and satisfaction we are looking for. We always seem to be left empty somehow, still seeking something to make us feel complete.

Once the psalmist realized what he had in God, he was moved to exclaim, "Whom have I in heaven but you? And earth has nothing I desire besides you" (Psalm 73:26).

Oh, the blessing, peace, and joy that come from knowing Jesus! Once we understand the reality of life in Christ, we can rest in the calm assurance that earth truly has nothing that compares. No relationship, no food, no material possession, no job, achievement, award, drug, or vacation can compare to what we have in Jesus.

To the psalmist, the heart represented more than just an organ pumping blood throughout the body; the heart represented the thoughts, attitudes, emotions, desires, and motivations of the human spirit. It also represented courage. Even though our own hearts and our own fleshly desires may fail us, God is our strength.

If we are following Jesus, we have all that we need in Him. He forgives, restores, sets free, comforts, relieves, revives, refreshes, sustains, completes, and fulfills. All that we need can be found in Him. He is our portion, our part, our possession.

We can give up the chase for everything but God.

For further reading: Nehemiah 8:10, Isaiah 41:10, Ephesians 6:10, Philippians 4:13

DAY 93

"But you, O God, are my king from of old;
you bring salvation upon the earth" (Psalm 74:12).

Have you ever felt rejected by God?

The Israelites had been exiled and the temple destroyed. Israel was taunted by her enemies and surely felt that God had rejected them. But this one promise brought them hope: From the time of God's covenant with them, He promised salvation. Jesus Christ is the fulfillment of that promise. When Jesus was born, Joseph and Mary were instructed to give Him the name Yeshua—the Lord saves.

Sometimes we too feel rejected by God. Maybe we have prayed for something for a long time with no answer. Perhaps we are struggling with sin, and sin keeps winning. Maybe we believed a promise for our future, but it didn't come to pass the way we expected.

Just as the psalmist did, we may need to remember who our God is—He is our King from of old. He has brought salvation on the earth. Because we are redeemed, we no longer have to fear being rejected. The word *salvation* means deliverance, welfare, and victory.[10]

We are not only delivered from sin, death, and the grave, but welfare implies that God provides healing, comfort, security, and protection. In other words, He is taking care of us. He has taken on responsibility for our welfare. You cannot be rejected by God.

So what if the healing doesn't come? What if the answers don't look as they should?

Then like the psalmist—who with his natural eyes saw only the devastation and destruction of his people, but with his spiritual eyes looked to the promise of God—we, too, must turn our eyes to the King who brings salvation upon the earth. Yeshua saves. And therein lies our victory.

For further reading: Psalm 27:10, Isaiah 49:15, Luke 1:31, John 15:18, 1 Peter 2:4-5

DAY 94

"It is God who judges; he brings down one, he exalts another"
(Psalm 75:7).

So often we feel threatened by the forces of evil and the instability of our world. While it is true that the enemy is the prince of this world (John 12:31) and the god of this age (2 Corinthians 4:4), it is equally true that he has been utterly defeated on the cross.

What may have looked like a victory for Satan as Jesus humbly allowed Himself to be nailed to a cross, became the ultimate good for all mankind. Through the crucifixion, death, and resurrection of Jesus Christ, all humanity has been given the opportunity for eternal life.

It is God who judges, and Satan has been convicted and sentenced.

Because he has been judged and condemned, Satan's time is short. So as we see everyday examples of what may appear to be victory for Satan, let us remember that out of it can flow the greatest good.

Joseph, who was hated by his brothers, sold into slavery, and accused of sexual assault by his boss's wife, was able to one day look at his brothers and say, "You intended to harm me, but God intended it for good to accomplish what is now being done, the saving of many lives" (Genesis 50:20).

When we see the darkness descending and hate seems to be winning, remember that God brings down one, and He exalts another. As we humble ourselves before Him and entrust ourselves to Him, He will bring good out of those situations that seemed only evil.

"Humble yourselves before the Lord, and he will lift you up" (James 4:10).

As long as we bring ourselves before the Lord with humility and in holy fear of Him, we need not fear the enemy. God will use his wrong for our good.

For further reading: Genesis 50:20, John 12:31, 2 Corinthians 4:4, James 4:10

DAY 95

"His tent is in Salem, his dwelling place in Zion" (Psalm 76:2).

One of the beautiful aspects of Hebrew poetry is parallelism. This literary feature uses repetition of a statement to emphasize its importance. Often a phrase will be repeated but using similar language, such as in the above verse.

"His tent is in Salem" means the same thing as "his dwelling place in Zion." Both statements stress the fact that the God of all creation has chosen to dwell among His people.

Salem comes from the Hebrew *shalom* and literally means "peace."[11] It was an early name for Jerusalem.

Zion refers to Mount Zion, a mountain found in Jerusalem. *Zion* comes from a root meaning "parched place,"[12] and is another name for Jerusalem.

In Revelation we learn that one day God will create a new heaven and earth; and the Holy City, Jerusalem, will come down to earth.

"Then I saw a new heaven and a new earth, for the first heaven and the first earth had passed away, and there was no longer any sea. I saw the Holy City, the New Jerusalem, coming down out of heaven from God, prepared as a bride beautifully dressed for her husband. And I heard a loud voice from the throne saying, 'Now the dwelling of God is with men, and he will live with them. They will be his people, and God himself will be with them and be their God'" (Revelation 21:1-3).

The word *dwelling* literally means "tabernacle" and is the same word used here in John. "The word became flesh and made his dwelling among us" (John 1:14).

So, the God who chose to dwell among His people in Israel sent His Son to dwell among us so that we could dwell forever with Him. Jesus came to turn the parched places of our hearts into a place of peace.

And one day we will dwell with Him forever face to face.

For further reading: John 1:14, 1 Corinthians 13:12, Revelation 21:1-3, 22:4

DAY 96

"Your path led through the sea, your way through the mighty waters, though your footprints were not seen" (Psalm 77:19).

Sometimes we cry out to God and don't feel any comfort. Such was the case of Asaph in this psalm. He couldn't sleep at night; he felt rejected by the Lord. He was in complete distress. But he decided to recall all the times God had been faithful to Israel in the past.

He remembered the God of miracles who had redeemed the people and shown His mighty power. He remembered how God had led the Israelites out of slavery, through the Red Sea, and into the Promised Land.

When we face times of great distress and cannot be comforted, we too, can meditate on God's Word and recall His deliverance in the past. We can remember what Jesus has done for us on the cross. We can also call on God to carry us through.

"When you pass through the waters, I will be with you; and when you pass through the rivers, they will not sweep over you. When you walk through the fire, you will not be burned; the flames will not set you ablaze" (Isaiah 43:2).

I'm sure when the Israelites were on the run from Pharaoh with waves of the sea all around them, they were scared, confused, and distressed. I'm willing to bet that at that moment, they didn't feel very comforted and assured of God's presence.

But Asaph, looking back, knew that God carried them, even if His footprints couldn't be seen. I bet He's carried you a time or two as well.

What are you despairing of today? Let your heart remember those times He carried you, and be encouraged that He is carrying you still.

"He tends his flock like a shepherd: He gathers the lambs in his arms and carries them close to his heart; he gently leads those that have young" (Isaiah 40:11).

For further reading: Isaiah 40:11, 43:2, John 16:33, 1 Peter 5:7

DAY 97

*"He decreed statutes for Jacob and established the law in Israel
which he commanded our forefathers to teach their children"*
(Psalm 78:5).

The only way for our children to walk in the ways of God is if we teach them. Teaching is 50% words and 50% actions. How will they know God's truths if we don't tell them and show them? It's not the church's responsibility or the school's responsibility or our neighbor's responsibility. It's our responsibility.

You may not have kids of your own, or your children may now be adults, but chances are there are some kids in your life who are watching you. How are you teaching the next generation the ways of God?

I wasn't raised in a Christian home, so when I began to follow Jesus, I wanted to teach my kids to do the same. When our kids were young, we had nightly devotions with them. When they got older and wanted to do devotions on their own, we started having dinner devotions together as a family. We served in our local church, and our kids were always part of that. Our home life definitely wasn't perfect, but we tried to be real. If we messed up, we owned up. We took seriously God's command to teach our children His ways.

"These commandments I give you today are to be upon your hearts. Impress them on your children. Talk about them when you sit at home and when you walk along the road, when you lie down and when you get up" (Deuteronomy 6:6-7).

If we love our children, then we will want them to have a personal relationship with Jesus Christ. They can't fly into heaven on our coattails or experience His peace by osmosis. Each of the young people God has put in our lives must experience God for herself.

How can you share your love for Jesus in a genuine, authentic way with the children in your life today?

For further reading: Deuteronomy 6:6-7, Proverbs 22:6, Isaiah 54:13, Ephesians 6:4

DAY 98

"Help us, O God our Savior, for the glory of your name; deliver us and forgive our sins for your name's sake" (Psalm 79:9).

As a nation, America has strayed so far from the moral foundation of our forefathers. Just as Israel's history included a cycle of seeking God, turning back to sin, crying out to God for help, and experiencing His deliverance, so America has followed a similar pattern.

Revival fire has swept through America several times since our inception, and we are so in need of revival today. According to the Barna Group, an independent company that does research into faith and culture, 48% of Americans are considered post-Christian, meaning they consider themselves Christians but do not attend church, read the Bible, or pray on a regular basis.[13]

The only way for America to experience the revival fire we so desperately need is for people to cry out to God for forgiveness. We have to once again be desperate for God and seek His help, not for our glory, but for the glory of His name.

"If my people, who are called by my name, will humble themselves and pray and seek my face and turn from their wicked ways, then will I hear from heaven and will forgive their sin and will heal their land" (2 Chronicles 7:14).

I think we've heard this Scripture so much, we don't even really pay attention to it anymore. But Asaph was reminding us in this psalm that apart from God, we are just objects of wrath, and we can easily fall to the nations around us. What will it take for America to turn back to God? Will it take another disaster, another terrorist attack, another civil war?

What will it take for you and me to take this Scripture seriously and put it into practice?

Let us humble ourselves, pray, seek His face, and turn from sin, today.

For further reading: 2 Chronicles 7:14, Psalm 85:6, Acts 3:19-21, James 4:8

DAY 99

*"Restore us, O God; make your face shine
upon us, that we may be saved" (Psalm 80:3).*

The word *restore* means "to turn back."[14] This prayer of Asaph's came after Israel had been "ravaged by a foreign power."[15] Oftentimes, we have to be ravaged by the enemy and face dire consequences for our sins before we turn back to God. But it doesn't have to be that way. Jesus has made a way for us to come to the Father at any time and repent. Through our confession of sin, we are restored to fellowship with God.

"If we confess our sins, he is faithful and just and will forgive us our sins and purify us from all unrighteousness" (1 John 1:9).

God has done everything in His power to make a way for us to know Him. That's the reason Jesus came (John 17:3). The only thing He won't do is take away our free will. We have the freedom to choose whether we will walk in right standing with Him or not. Nothing changes His love for us (Romans 8:38-39). But sin creates a wall between us and God and keeps us from enjoying fellowship with Him. And it will make us miserable.

Once we surrender our lives to Jesus, and He fills us with His Spirit, there will always be a struggle between the Spirit and our flesh. If we give into sin, the Spirit will convict us. He will be grieved within us over that sin and urge us to repent.

If we don't listen to Him and turn away from our sin, eventually our conscience will become seared. We will no longer experience His conviction, and we will fall away from fellowship with Him.

All we have to do is repent and be restored.

Jesus made the way for us. Come clean with Him and enjoy the glory of His presence shining on you today.

For further reading: Isaiah 59:2, John 17:3, Galatians 2:20, 1 Timothy 4:1-2, 1 John 1:8-9

DAY 100

"I am the LORD your God, who brought you up out of Egypt. Open wide your mouth and I will fill it" (Psalm 81:10).

Could God speak any more beautiful words to us?

The Israelites had been slaves in Egypt, forced to do manual labor, no longer possessing the land God had called them to through Abraham. In this psalm, the Lord reminded them that He is the One who brought them out of Egypt. He was the One who provided for them, protected them, and whose presence led them. And He wanted to fill them.

But how often the Israelites forgot the God who saved, delivered, provided, and protected them. They were quick to think their own hand had saved them. They were quick to complain about what they had, forgetting it was all a gift from their Father.

We too often forget that God is the One who has saved us and set us free from our sins. He is the One who provides for us, protects us, and leads us with His presence. God longs to be good to His children. He wants to bless us with good things. But we tend to get hard-headed and think we are the ones who worked hard to have what we have. We start to think all we have is ours. We forget that God gives us the ability to work, to understand, to create, to build wealth.

"If you then, though you are evil, know how to give good gifts to your children, how much more will your Father in heaven give good gifts to those who ask him!" (Matthew 7:11).

All because He loves us.

What are you longing for today? More peace, hope, forgiveness, or joy?

Acknowledge the Giver of all good gifts in your life. Thank Him for being your Savior, Deliverer, and Provider. Ask Him to teach you how to steward those gifts for His glory.

Then open wide your mouth and watch Him fill it.

For further reading: Matthew 7:11, John 4:10, Ephesians 2:8-9, James 1:17

DAY 101

*"Defend the cause of the weak and fatherless;
maintain the rights of the poor and oppressed" (Psalm 82:3).*

God is just, and He will one day bring justice on the earth. Every wrong will be made right. He is the God who "presides in the great assembly" or the Hall of Justice (1 Kings 7:7) in heaven.

Until then, we are called to be the hands and feet of Jesus in this world. As ambassadors of the gospel, we too should care for widows, orphans, the poor, and the oppressed.

"'The King will reply, "I tell you the truth, whatever you did for one of the least of these brothers of mine, you did for me"' (Matthew 25:40).

Who are the "least of these" in your community? Do you know widows who are lonely or need help around their house? Are there foster kids in your community waiting for families to take them in? Are there children who go to bed hungry at night or elderly folks who sacrifice heat or air to pay for medications?

There are many causes we can rally around and efforts we can support—homeless shelters, abused women, victims of sex trafficking—but often we get so caught up in our own families and careers that we fail to take the time or make the commitment to care for the "least of these."

We don't have to do everything or be everything to everybody. We just need to be aware of needs around us and then ask God how we can help.

Jesus said even a cup of cold water in His name brings a reward.

We can't right every wrong, but we can bring love and kindness in the name of Jesus so the world sees the truth of who He is.

Who needs to see Jesus in you today?

For further reading: 1 Kings 7:7, Proverbs 14:21, Matthew 6:2, 10:42, 25:40

DAY 102

"Let them know that you, whose name is the LORD—
that you alone are the Most High over all the earth" (Psalm 83:18).

Wouldn't it be great if all the enemies of God were destroyed so that His name alone received glory in the earth? Wouldn't it be awesome if all of the sin, evil, and wickedness in this world were suddenly vanquished, and the pain and suffering caused by sin were wiped out once and for all?

That's the heart of the psalmist in this prayer. His desire was to see the enemies of God destroyed so that the powers of evil couldn't lead people astray. He wanted God and His peace and His righteousness to reign over Israel.

If we're honest, that's the cry of our hearts as well. Sin leads to suffering. Evil brings pain. When wicked people come to power in a nation, everybody suffers for it—the godly and ungodly alike.

The truth is that Jesus is on His throne and He reigns over all; but until He returns, the evil one still roams the earth, looking for someone to devour. Our responsibility is to resist him and to stand firm in prayer and in faith.

"Be self-controlled and alert. Your enemy the devil prowls around like a roaring lion looking for someone to devour. Resist him, standing firm in the faith, because you know that your brothers throughout the world are undergoing the same kind of sufferings" (1 Peter 5:8).

The more we submit ourselves to God, the more we are resisting the devil. We must stay alert to his tactics so that we do not fall prey to his schemes and lies. Like the psalmist, we too want to see God's name be lifted high over all the earth, especially when our world shows little fear of God. The good news is that one day we will.

I'm looking forward to that day!

For further reading: Philippians 2:9-11, James 4:7, 1 Peter 5:8

DAY 103

"Even the sparrow has found a home, and the swallow a nest for herself, where she may have her young—a place near your altar, O LORD Almighty, my King and my God" (Psalm 84:3).

Is that not beautiful? I can just picture Korah (the psalm writer) looking up and seeing the tiny birds building a nest under the eaves of the temple columns. In his day, God's presence dwelt only there in the Holy of Holies. And even the birds wanted to be there.

Are we building our homes in the presence of God and raising our young there? We need more of the power and presence of God in our homes.

"Blessed are those who dwell in your house; they are ever praising you" (Psalm 84:4).

That's where I want to be: dwelling in the presence of God, ever praising Him. And the only way that will happen is if I start my day in the throne room with God—not just reading a devotion or praying a prayer, but seeking the face of God and surrendering my heart to Him in worship.

It's time to go to the throne room of God and seek His face. The wonderful news is that we have been invited in. What was mysterious and holy and off-limits to everyone but the high priest in Korah's day has now been opened to us through the blood of Jesus. We have access through our Savior into the holy and mysterious but no longer off-limits presence of God.

"Therefore, brothers, since we have confidence to enter the Most Holy Place by the blood of Jesus, by a new and living way opened for us through the curtain, that is his body, and since we have a great high priest over the house of God, let us draw near to God with sincere heart in full assurance of faith" (Hebrews 10:19-22a).

Do you desire to have more of the power and presence in your life as I do?

Let's ask Him by faith for more!

For further reading: Exodus 33:12-17, Matthew 7:24-27, Hebrews 10:19-22

DAY 104

*"As they pass through the Valley of Baca,
they make it a place of springs" (Psalm 84:6a).*

In this world we will face both joy and sorrow, pain and comfort, ups and downs; that is the natural cycle of things. But if we learn to live in the presence of God, we can rise above the thoughts and emotions that overwhelm us. The psalmist wrote this during the time when God's presence dwelt only in the temple. He had been barred from access to the temple and yearned to be able to go and enjoy the sweet fellowship that he had known there with the Lord.

"Blessed are those whose strength is in you, who have set their hearts on pilgrimage. As they pass through the Valley of Baca, they make it a place of springs; the autumn rains also cover it with pools. They go from strength to strength, till each appears before God in Zion" (Psalm 84:5-7).

You see, the psalmist knew that blessings would come for those who set their hearts on seeking God. "Who have set their hearts on pilgrimage" is literally translated "in whose hearts are the highways...."[16] The highways to what? The place of worship. If we will just set our heart on the highways to worship, God will bring us the comfort and peace that we long for.

The Valley of Baca is an interesting name. No place is known to have had that name, but the word *baca* means "weeping" or "balsam tree,"[17] which is a type of tree that grows in dry, arid places. So as these pilgrims set their hearts on worship, even as they passed through times of sorrow or despair, their worship turned it into a place of springs. The Hebrew for *pools* can also mean "blessing."[18] Blessings come to those who hope in the Lord, even through their tears. Though the valley of weeping may come, if we will set our hearts on worshiping our God, He will turn our place of weeping into a valley of praise. We will go "from strength to strength" as we journey through this life—not our strength, but God's.

Do you need strength today in your valley of weeping? Set your heart on the highway to worship and let the Lord be your strength.

For further reading: 1 Chronicles 16:29, John 4:24, Romans 12:1-2, Hebrews 10:1

DAY 105

"Better is one day in your courts than a thousand elsewhere"
(Psalm 84:10a).

When it comes right down to it, there's no place I'd rather be than in His presence. We know that God is everywhere, and there's nowhere we can go to flee from His presence.

But are we always dwelling there? I know I'm not—not in my mind, my heart, my attention. I know that I can accomplish nothing apart from Him, so I need more of Jesus in my life.

"I am the vine; you are the branches. If a man remains in me and I in him, he will bear much fruit; apart from me you can do nothing" (John 15:5).

So, how do we dwell in God's presence and abide in Him so that we can bear fruit on a daily basis? For me, I have to spend time in His presence in worship.

Worship is what will draw my heart to the throne of God faster than anything else. Worship will keep a song in my heart throughout the day so that I depend more on God and less on myself. Worship recalibrates my attention to the majesty and power and truth and grace of my God.

"How lovely is your dwelling place, O LORD Almighty! My soul yearns, even faints, for the courts of the LORD; my heart and flesh cry out for the living God" (Psalm 84:1-2).

Does your soul yearn so much to be in God's presence that you feel as if you will faint without Him? Sometimes I go and do so much in my own strength, that I know I will utterly faint if I don't let go and let Him have it all.

Is it time for you to let go in His presence and let Him have your struggles, your questions, your strength?

Seek God's presence today in worship and let go of anything that keeps you from experiencing His best and bearing more fruit for Him.

For further reading: Psalm 95:1-2, 139:7-10, John 15:1-17, Colossians 3:2

DAY 106

"Righteousness goes before him and prepares the way for his steps"
(Psalm 85:13).

Our God is in the business of restoration. He shows favor, forgives and covers sins, and revives those who seek Him. All because of His unfailing love.

Our sin deserves His wrath—He shows us His salvation.

Because of His great love, we want to listen to Him and not return to our folly. We don't serve in order to be saved; we serve because we are saved.

When our lives were characterized by selfishness, deception, sin, and strife, all we had to do was humble ourselves before Him and turn away from our sin. And He freely forgave us and restored us into the image of His glory.

What a mighty God we serve! No one can compare to Him. He is a holy, righteous God, and yet He made a way for us to walk in His righteousness.

"'Though your sins are like scarlet, they shall be as white as snow; though they are red as crimson, they shall be like wool'" (Isaiah 1:18).

Praise God that what He did for you and me, He will do for those we love. Does your heart ache for a friend or loved one who is lost in sin? Remember that our God is in the business of restoration. It doesn't matter how far they have fallen or how far away from God they may seem; He is able to save.

"Surely the arm of the LORD is not too short to save, nor his ear to dull to hear" (Isaiah 59:1).

God desires for all people to be saved. Pray and believe God to work in their hearts, remove the veil of unbelief from their eyes, and convict them of sin. You are praying according to His will, so rejoice that He is preparing the way for His steps.

For further reading: Isaiah 1:18, 59:1, Zephaniah 3:17, Matthew 1:21, Luke 19:10, John 3:17

DAY 107

"Teach me your way, O LORD, that I will walk in your truth;
give me an undivided heart, that I may fear your name"
(Psalm 86:11).

You know why David had such a heart for God? He was devoted to Him. "Guard my life, for I am devoted to you. You are my God; save your servant who trusts in you" (Psalm 86:2). The word translated *devoted* is the Hebrew word *hasid* which means "godly, saints, the people of God with a focus on their faithfulness; faithful people, faithful servants, consecrated people."[19] The King James Version renders it "holy."

In Old Testament times, the articles in the temple used for worship were set apart as holy unto the Lord—they were consecrated for His service and couldn't be used for anything else (Exodus 25-28). That's the idea behind the word *hasid*. David was *hasid*—he was devoted, dedicated, set apart unto the Lord. He asked God to give him an undivided heart. Perhaps this psalm was written after David's fall into sin, and he was all the more aware of his weaknesses. Maybe David was crying out to God to help him not fall into sin again but stay devoted to Him.

Do we have that desire in our hearts to be set apart for God, faithful, devoted, so dedicated to the Lord that our hearts long only for Him? That's a tall order, isn't it? Because we have families, friends, church family, co-workers, and so many other relationships that can pull our attention away from God. How can we stay so devoted that we have an undivided heart for Him? Like David, we can pray and ask for help. God knows our weaknesses. "But he said to me, 'My grace is sufficient for you, for my power is made perfect in weakness'" (2 Corinthians 12:9).

He has grace to meet us right where we are. The question is, "What do we desire?" Do we desire, like David, that the Lord would teach us His way and lead us in His truth? Do we truly desire to have an undivided heart?

If so, ask God today to help you be devoted to Him.

For further reading: Matthew 6:24, Acts 2:42, 2 Corinthians 12:9, Colossians 4:2

DAY 108

"As they make music they will sing, 'All my fountains are in you'"
(Psalm 87:7).

This psalm is a celebration of Jerusalem, the City of God. Jerusalem was the place God chose to dwell among His people and show His love. She was loved more than any other place on earth because she was the place of God's chosen people. Today, you are the place God chooses to dwell. If you have surrendered your life to Jesus, He has come to live within you.

"Don't you know that you yourselves are God's temple and that God's Spirit lives in you?" (1 Corinthians 3:16). So God celebrates you as the place He now chooses to dwell. He gave His very life for you, and He rejoices over you.

"The LORD your God is with you, he is mighty to save. He will take great delight in you, he will quiet you with his love, he will rejoice over you with singing" (Zephaniah 3:17).

God doesn't just tolerate you. He doesn't put up with you because He has to. He didn't save you just because you were part of a multitude of people throughout all history that needed saving. He looked down and saw you as an individual and decided He wanted to die for you.

The psalmist celebrated and sang because he belonged to the people of God, and he knew all his fountains—all that refreshes the heart and makes glad—could be found in God. We too can celebrate that all our fountains are in Him.

The Israelites are still God's chosen people, but we have been invited to receive salvation and become part of the family of God. We are chosen too. "You did not choose me, but I chose you and appointed you to go and bear fruit—fruit that will last" (John 15:16a).

"God chose us in him before the creation of the world to be holy and blameless in his sight" (Ephesians 1:4). Chosen one, celebrate the fountains of the Lord today—the Living Water poured out for you.

For further reading: Zephaniah 3:17, John 15:16, 1 Corinthians 3:16, Ephesians 1:4

DAY 109

*"But I cry to you for help, O LORD; in the
morning my prayer comes before you" (Psalm 88:13).*

As I have walked with my friend through the sudden death of her husband, everything about her life has been turned upside down. She is a woman of great faith and believed God would heal her husband of his sudden illness, but He didn't.

Although some days she can barely breathe because the pain is so raw and sharp, she has trusted the grace of Jesus moment by moment to get her through. I have watched her carry the weight of grief with peace and joy, even in the midst of questions that go unanswered.

Only a life-giving relationship with Jesus Christ can sustain us through such times. In this psalm, Korah expressed the deepest grief, pain, and trouble of his life, yet he started his song by crying out to "the God who saves me" (Psalm 88:1).

Sometimes life doesn't go the way we thought it would, and we are left trying to pick up the broken pieces. Try as we might, we can't make the pieces go back together to form the picture we thought our life was becoming.

Only by trusting our source of help and salvation can we learn to fit the pieces together into a new image, a different illustration of what God intends for our life to be. You may feel as if God has abandoned you. You may question why things had to turn out the way they did. You might wonder if God still has a plan for your life.

The answer is yes, God still has a plan and purpose for your life. He hasn't abandoned you. In fact, the Word tells us He's closer now than ever before (Psalm 34:18). He's working all things together for your good (Romans 8:28).

One day, you will look back and see that all the broken pieces have created a beautiful mosaic, telling a story of a faithful God who uses our deepest pain to color our lives with His hope and grace.

For further reading: Psalm 34:18, Romans 5:1-5, 8:28, 15:13

DAY 110

"Blessed are those who have learned to acclaim you,
who walk in the light of your presence, O LORD" (Psalm 89:15).

"Who have learned to acclaim you" in the KJV is rendered "that know the joyful sound." The Hebrew word translated *acclaim* in the NIV literally means "trumpet blast, battle cry, shouts of joy, give a shout."[20]

To acclaim the Lord means that we know the joyful sound of victory, the shout of joy that comes when the battle is won. It's a cry of celebration of all that God has done.

The word *acclaim* means to "praise enthusiastically and publicly."[21] When we know the joyful sound of victory, we can't help but praise Him with enthusiasm for all to see. We aren't shy about it. We aren't reserved. We hold nothing back. We have to let the world know what our God has done.

We all worship in different ways according to our personalities or traditions. Some people may be more reverent in their worship and others more enthusiastic. But all I know is that I have been to a lot of ballgames in my lifetime. I'm married to a former coach, and I've raised two children.

Have you ever seen a mama at a ballgame? I don't care how quiet and reserved she usually is, when her child is on the field or the court, she becomes a megaphone. Her hands can't stay still. Her mouth can't be silent. She is going to let the world know that's her baby with the ball.

When we truly understand all that God has done for us—I mean really get that we deserve hell and we are getting paradise—it should cause everything within us to erupt with praise. We ought to be out of our seats, singing and celebrating the God of victory so the world will know that's *our* God. It's okay if you don't like to be demonstrative in your worship, but at some point I hope you will let go of all your reservations and rejoice with joy and celebration.

Blessed are those who know the joyful sound. They know it. They feel it. And they have to let it out.

For further reading: Psalm 47:1, 66:1, 100:1, Isaiah 12:6, 54:1

DAY 111

*"Teach us to number our days aright,
that we may gain a heart of wisdom" (Psalm 90:12).*

What does it mean to "number our days aright"?

The word *number* means "to count, reckon, number, assign, tell, appoint, prepare."[22] So to number our days rightly means we think about how many days we will live on the earth.

The psalmist Moses was asking God to help him realize how short his days on earth were compared to eternity. When we realize how quickly life passes by, we gain perspective on our circumstances. Things that hurt us deeply can then seem trivial. Priorities can shift when seen in light of eternity.

Moses also expressed the realization that life is difficult, and only knowing God's love can make us glad for the days we are here.

Another idea behind this verse is that we appoint or prepare our day rightly. In other words, we start our day with the Lord.

"Satisfy us in the morning with your unfailing love, that we may sing for joy and be glad all our days" (Psalm 90:14). True wisdom is in knowing that when we make God our number one priority every day, He satisfies us and fills us with joy, even in the midst of difficult circumstances.

What a great prayer for us to pray each day, that God would teach us how to number our days—to understand the brevity of life so that we don't live in bitterness, unforgiveness, or complacency in serving God and to assign value and priority to our appointments as we plan our day.

If we order our day to seek God first, we are surely gaining a heart of wisdom. As we surrender to Him and allow Him to teach us and lead us, He will make the number of our days blessed indeed.

For further reading: Ecclesiastes 12:1, Luke 11:3, 2 Corinthians 4:16, 2 Peter 3:8

DAY 112

"May the favor of the Lord our God rest upon us; establish the work of our hands for us—yes, establish the work of our hands" (Psalm 90:17).

No matter what your station in life—whether a student, employer, employee, homemaker, or retiree—you need God's favor and blessing on your life to succeed.

God's *favor* is His "pleasantness, grace, and beauty."[23]Wouldn't you love to have that on your life every day? What does that favor look like?

I have prayed this prayer over me and my family for a couple of years now, and I can tell you that God will show us favor and bless the work of our hands if we ask Him to. He has opened doors for our family we would never have thought possible.

He has provided and protected and established us in our work and in our ministries. I'm not saying everything has been perfect. All real work and ministry come with trials. But we have been blessed beyond measure.

When God's pleasantness and grace are on us, He will meet our needs in incredible ways and lead us down paths that only He knew about.

When God establishes the work of our hands, we are efficient and productive. But we have to be willing to submit to Him first to enjoy these blessings. When we pray this prayer, we are asking God to take over the work and ministry He has called us to and have His way.

I want His favor to rest on us. I want Him to establish the work of my hands in whatever way He sees fit—not according to my plans and purposes, but His.

So wherever you are in your life today, I am praying that He will show you His favor and establish the work of your hands.

For further reading: Luke 1:30, 2:14, 4:19, Matthew 6, James 1:12

DAY 113

"He who dwells in the shelter of the Most High will rest in the shadow of the Almighty" (Psalm 91:1).

Psalm 91 is a prayer that celebrates the covering protection of the Lord and has been whispered by many believers in times of danger or uncertainty. The promise in these holy words is that the person who chooses by faith to abide in the shelter or secret place of the Lord comes under His divine protection and care.

The Hebrew word translated *shelter* means "hiding place, secret place, shelter, covering, veil."[24] The word for *dwell* means "to sit down, remain, stay."[25] I love that, because what we understand is that God's promise is not for those who live for themselves, expecting God to protect them. He's under no obligation to do so.

But for those who choose to not only live for Jesus but inhabit His presence and stay with Him, abiding in Him, abiding in His Word, walking in His truth—nothing can harm them.

Does that mean nothing bad can ever happen in their lives on earth? Certainly not! Almost all the disciples were martyred, followed by many Christians after them. But it means that nothing can touch them outside of God's divine plan for their lives. It's an eternal promise, not a temporal one.

Psalm 91 says that when we make God our refuge, He will save us from the enemy. His faithfulness is our shield. We do not have to fear. No harm can come near us, for He will command His angels to guard us.

His promise is for those who love Him, who acknowledge Him—not just with their lips but with their lives. Even in trouble, sickness, or death, a devoted follower of Jesus is safe in the shadow of His wings.

So whenever you feel afraid or threatened, just speak the words of this psalm and remember by faith that as long as you dwell in the secret place with Jesus, nothing can harm you.

For further reading: Jeremiah 29:11, Matthew 23:37, 1 John 5:18

DAY 114

"Planted in the house of the LORD, they will
flourish in the courts of our God" (Psalm 92:13).

I love church! I have served in four different churches in my lifetime, each one of them special in its own way. I may be old-fashioned, but I adore Sunday school, singing songs, and worshiping with other believers. I enjoy the fellowship of the saints—young and old, black and white, rich and poor—joining hands to worship one true God.

There's something so special about being "planted in the house of the LORD." There is a stability and security that come from having roots. The traditions of the Lord's Supper and water baptism bind us together with a simplicity and profoundness all their own. Where else can you go to eat bread and drink juice together while all meditating on the sacrifice of the body and blood of Jesus? Where else can you find a commonality that binds different flavors into one beautiful dish?

The church is a body of believers—different gifts, abilities, backgrounds, weaknesses—broken in so many ways, yet strikingly beautiful to our God. When we gather to celebrate new birth and the washing and renewing symbolized in baptism, we share in one banner proclaiming "Jesus is Lord." For all her failures and foibles and false witnesses, there is still a sacredness and serenity of serving in a local church body. I find that only within the context of church do I truly flourish and grow.

Church is a beautiful, broken, blessed representation of the Bride of Christ. No church is perfect, and we won't find all our needs met in a building. But if we will keep our eyes on Jesus and come with a heart to serve Him, we can find a place to proclaim his love and faithfulness along with other sojourners who need Him deeply, too.

"For you make me glad by your deeds, O LORD; I sing for joy at the works of your hands" (Psalm 92:4). If we make church about us, we will never be satisfied. Make church about Jesus and flourish in the house of the Lord.

For further reading: Psalm 52:8, Matthew 16:18, John 2:17, Ephesians 5:23, Colossians 1:18-24

DAY 115

"Mightier than the thunder of the great waters, mightier than the breakers of the sea—the LORD on high is mighty" (Psalm 93:4).

We serve a mighty God. There is nothing He can't do. He created the universe with the words of His mouth. He was and He is and He is to come. There is no one above Him, no one beside Him, and nothing that can be compared to Him.

The poetic nature of the psalms is never more vivid or majestic than when describing the glory and power of God. He reigns supreme over everything. He is robed in majesty (Psalm 93:1).

The Hebrew word translated *majesty* in this verse literally means "surging sea, rising smoke."[26] I think the psalmist tried to find the most glorious words he could think of to describe the majesty of God, but words fail.

He is "mightier than the thunder of the great waters, mightier than the breakers of the sea." Have you ever stood on the beach when it was empty and void of vacationers and just listened to the powerful sound of the waves breaking on the shore? He's mightier than that.

He is from all eternity. He exists outside of time and space in a way we can never wrap our finite minds around. We can't explain Him. We can't understand Him. We can't fit Him in a human box of our own imaginations.

He is God. He is three in One. He is the Alpha and Omega, the Beginning and the End. All of life is in His hands, and if we belong to Him, we will one day reign with Him.

The Lord our God is strong and mighty! There's nothing our God cannot do.

For further reading: 1 Chronicles 16:27, Psalm 93, 2 Peter 1:16, Jude 25

DAY 116

"Does he who implanted the ear not hear?
Does he who formed the eye not see?" (Psalm 94:9).

As I was leaving school one day, I had only gone a couple of blocks when a car ran a stop sign and hit me. I had not gone very far, was not speeding, and did not break any traffic laws. My car was totaled, but we were all unhurt.

Later, though, we found out that the incident report said I was speeding, which caused the other insurance company to make me 20% liable for the accident. As you can imagine, I was upset. We called a lawyer friend to help us, but in the end we didn't want to sue, so I was left being partially responsible. The car that we had almost paid off had to be replaced, and we started all over making payments. But we sucked it up. I'm sure we've all figured it out by now: Life isn't fair.

As long as we live in this fallen world, we will have to deal with injustice. We can seek legal counsel when necessary, but the truth is that even the court system isn't perfect. "Do not put your trust in princes, in mortal men, who cannot save." (Psalm 146:3).

Life isn't fair, but God is. We can trust Him to work all things together for our good and to one day make every wrong right. Until then, we may have to deal with problems we didn't cause or face unfairness at the hands of bosses, insurance companies, or neighbors. How does God expect us to respond in such situations?

"Commit your way to the LORD; trust in him and he will do this: He will make your righteousness shine like the dawn, the justice of your cause like the noonday sun" (Psalm 37:5-6).

I love this verse because it promises us that we will see justice one day. And God will cause all people to see the truth. Until that day, we commit our way to Him and live at peace with those around us. Who knows that God may use our example to be a witness to someone else?

For further reading: Psalm 37:5-6, 146:3, John 10:10, Colossians 3:1-17

DAY 117

"Come, let us bow down in worship, let us kneel before the LORD our Maker" (Psalm 95:6a).

God calls us every day to come into His presence with worship. Most days I am too busy and reserve my praises for Sunday morning. But verse seven begins with *"Today*, if you hear his voice." Not just Sunday morning or Wednesday night, but today we are called to bow our knees in worship. Worship is more about the attitude of our hearts than the words on our lips, but what if we began each day as the psalmist described:

"Come, let us sing for joy to the LORD; let us shout aloud to the Rock of our salvation. Let us come before him with thanksgiving and extol him with music and song" (Psalm 95:1-2)?

It's so easy with music at the tip of our fingers on our smartphones to pull up a song of praise and sing along. When we start our day by singing, we set the atmosphere for the rest of our day. We set the attitude of our own hearts to be one of praise and thanksgiving, even if we awoke on the wrong side of the bed.

We also start our day by declaring into the spirit realm that our God is "the great God, the great King above all gods" (Psalm 95:3). Whether we feel like it or not, we are setting our heart on our God and starting our day in His presence.

It doesn't matter if we sing like an opera star or can't carry a tune in a bucket. God's favorite song is the one in our hearts and on our lips. Worship is warfare. Worship will set our hearts in line with who God is. Worship will turn our hearts away from our problems and set them straight on our God who is the Greater One.

So, as we begin each day with the Lord, spending time with Him in prayer and Bible reading, let us also bow down in worship and sing a song of praise. Our worship will align our hearts with Jesus, and that's the best way to start our day.

For further reading: 1 Chronicles 16:29, Psalm 100:2, John 4:24, Romans 12:1, Hebrews 10:1

DAY 118

"Sing to the LORD a new song; sing to the LORD, all the earth"
(Psalm 96:1).

Yesterday we talked about singing during our personal time with the Lord. Today we are talking about corporate worship. When we gather together as the Body of Christ, singing is an act that joins our hearts together as one.

My husband and I went to Guatemala in 2005 on a missions trip. One of my favorite moments was worshiping with the believers in two languages. As we sang a very popular worship song—the Guatemalans in Spanish and our team in English—the sound of praises in different languages melted together as one anthem to our God. It was a spectacular moment.

Corporate worship is an opportunity for believers to express their love and adoration for Jesus as one voice. When we stand side by side with our brothers and sisters and declare that our God reigns, our faith is solidified.

When we lift our voices throughout the pews and express words that thousands of Christians have sung for decades, our hearts are connected across the world and across the years.

When believers come together and sing with all their might the truth of the beautiful gospel of Jesus Christ, our worship is a witness to any unbelievers who hear us.

Likewise, if we stand in the sanctuary and half-heartedly move our lips but never allow our hearts to connect to the One we are there to worship, we show unbelievers that Jesus isn't worthy of our praise.

Congregational singing is one of the greatest evidences of a healthy church. Saved people are singing people.[27]

When you attend your place of worship this week, don't allow anything to keep you from expressing your heart to God in worship. Open your heart and open your mouth and sing!

For further reading: Exodus 15:1, Ephesians 5:19, Colossians 3:16, James 5:13

DAY 119

"The LORD reigns, let the earth be glad" (Psalm 97:1a).

In a world where evil sometimes seems to be winning and darkness can be overwhelming, aren't you glad to know that the Lord reigns?

This psalm describes God with righteousness and justice as his foundation. He sends forth His lightning and lights up the world. Even mighty mountains melt like wax in His presence. The very heavens display His glory for all the world to see.

God is right. God is just. God is good. And our God reigns.

We need never fear that evil will win or darkness take over, because our God reigns.

We don't have to worry that the earth is spinning out of control or disaster will destroy us forever, because our God reigns.

We can trust that we are on the winning side, because our God reigns.

"You, dear children, are from God and have overcome them, because the one who is in you is greater than the one who is in the world" (1 John 4:4).

All the earth can be glad because our God reigns. He reigns over sin, sickness, lies, and darkness. God reigns over death, hell, and the grave. He reigns over strife, abuse, and confusion. Jesus reigns over those who serve Him and those who don't.

No matter what you are facing today, know that your God reigns over that, too.

"Rejoice in the LORD, you who are righteous, and praise his holy name" (Psalm 97:12).

For further reading: Isaiah 24:23, 52:7, Luke 1:33, Revelation 11:15, 19:6

DAY 120

"The LORD has made his salvation known and revealed his righteousness to the nations" (Psalm 98:2).

Have you ever said, "I just wish I could find God's will for my life"? Sometimes we feel as if God is playing some cosmic game of hide-and-seek. Nothing could be further from the truth. Yes, He is a God of mystery, and we will never fully understand Him, but God wants to make Himself known and reveal His will to us.

God went to great lengths to make a way for us to know Him. The God of the universe sent His Son into the world to live among us—the Word made flesh—to teach and to serve and to die so we could know Him. Apart from a personal relationship with Jesus Christ, we could never know God. But Jesus came so we *could* know God.

"Now this is eternal life: that they may know you, the only true God, and Jesus Christ, whom you have sent" (John 17:3).

The Apostle Paul was a well-educated religious leader before he came to know Jesus. But he said he considered his education, status, and power as nothing compared to knowing Jesus. "But whatever was to my profit I now consider loss for the sake of Christ. What is more, I consider everything a loss compared to the surpassing greatness of knowing Christ Jesus my Lord, for whose sake I have lost all things" (Philippians 3:7-8a).

The question is not whether God is hiding His will from us. (He's not.) The question is whether we are willing to do His will, which will always align with His Word. God isn't hiding from us. He wants us to know Him. He wants to reveal more of Himself to us, and He does that through His Word and His Spirit. Do you want to know God's will for your life? Just submit to His authority and ask Him. He will show you (Romans 16:25-27).

For further reading: Matthew 6:10, John 7:17, 17:3, Romans 16:25-27, Philippians 3:7-8a

DAY 121

"Exalt the LORD our God and worship at his holy mountain, for the LORD our God is holy" (Psalm 99:9).

God is holy.

Abraham fell face down in the presence of Almighty God (Genesis 17:3, 17).

Isaiah was completely undone before the Lord (Isaiah 6:5).

John fell at his feet as though dead (Revelation 1:17).

Yet the Almighty has made a way through His Son for us to come boldly to His throne of grace and find mercy there (Hebrews 4:16). Holy meets human through Jesus. Holy walked the streets of Israel for over three decades, ate and drank, made friends and made enemies. He laughed, He cried, He healed, He delivered. He fed and shared and rebuked and led.

Holy walked the earth with skin on, took up a towel to dry crusty feet, then took up a cross and walked up a hill. Holy laid down His life for unholy. Around the throne of God, angels continually praise Him:

"'Holy, holy, holy is the LORD God Almighty; the whole earth is full of his glory'" (Isaiah 6:3).

"'Holy, holy, holy is the Lord God Almighty, who was, and is, and is to come'" (Revelation 4:8b).

One day we will join the angels around the throne and cry, "Holy!" For now, we walk with Him by faith and seek just a glimpse of holy in us (Hebrews 10:14).

We are being made holy as we learn to walk by the Spirit and not by the flesh, but one day we will know true holiness as we fall at His feet in worship and cry, "Holy are You, Lord!"

For further reading: Genesis 17, Isaiah 6:3-5, Romans 8:1-17, Galatians 5:16-26, Hebrews 4:16, 10:14, Revelation 1:17, 4:8b

DAY 122

"Enter his gates with thanksgiving and his courts with praise; give thanks to him and praise his name" (Psalm 100:4).

I can remember when our kids were young, what a hassle it sometimes was to get to church. The enemy doesn't want us to enjoy the Lord's Day in His house with other believers, and he will do everything he can to get our hearts and minds off the Lord. Often, my husband and I would begin arguing or our children wouldn't get ready on time. I would start stressing about being late, and then everybody would be in a bad mood.

Or, have you ever gotten in your car to go to church and whoever last drove your car had the radio on a secular station? You may not even realize it at first, but something in the atmosphere is not quite right. Or, have you ever gotten out of your car at church and someone there began complaining or gossiping about something going on in your church?

These are all tactics of the enemy to cause us to not come to God's house with our hearts ready to worship. We can be at church for three hours on a Sunday morning and never even experience the presence of God, never worship, and never receive from God's Word because our hearts weren't right.

"The LORD says: 'These people come near to me with their mouth and honor me with their lips, but their hearts are far from me" (Isaiah 29:13a).

The best way to prepare our hearts for worship is to spend quiet time with the Lord before we go to church. Don't skip your quiet time on Sundays; seek the Lord and ask Him to prepare your heart to come before him with thanksgiving and praise.

Ask the Lord to cleanse you of anything that is not of Him, to focus your heart and mind on His presence, to fill you with joy and peace, and to prepare your heart to sing and worship and honor Him and to receive His Word with hunger.

The enemy wants to steal your praise. Don't let him. Worship before you enter God's courts; and your heart will be ready to worship when you get there.

For further reading: Isaiah 29:13, Luke 10:40, Colossians 3:2, James 4:7, 1 Peter 5:8

DAY 123

"I will walk in my house with blameless heart.
I will set before my eyes no vile thing" (Psalm 101:2b-3a).

One reason many kids who are raised in church walk away when they are old enough to decide for themselves is because they have witnessed an inconsistency between what they experienced at church and what they experienced at home. Our relationship with Jesus should permeate every part of our lives. The psalmist David (don't laugh that it's David) said he would walk about his house with a blameless heart and set no vile thing before his eyes. Of course, we all know about Bathsheba. This psalm is believed to have been written for the coronation of his son Solomon, which would have been well after David's confession and repentance of his sin.

Make no mistake: nothing can teach us quite like experience. David knew the grave cost of his sin. That's why he was determined to not even let his eyes look upon something that would cause him to sin. He wanted his walk to be pure and blameless, whether at home or at work. Only Jesus has kept completely pure and without sin, but having the desire to be pure is half the battle. By declaring our intentions to the Lord in prayer and stating them out loud, we at least are professing what we want to be. And through the help of the Holy Spirit, we can overcome.

The other half of the battle is taking the actual steps to be pure. Our first step should be to spend time with God first every day. Then we may need to take measures to reduce the temptation to sin. We can choose what music, books, television shows, and websites we allow in our homes. We can choose our topics of conversation, the tone of our voices, the words we use. We can choose how we love others, starting with those in our own households. And we can choose to seek forgiveness when we blow it, rather than hiding, justifying, or playing the blame game. Others benefit when they see us being real.

Let's make up our minds today to walk with blameless heart; then let's take the steps to do our part to live a holy life.

For further reading: 1 Thessalonians 4:7, 1 Timothy 2:2, Hebrews 10:14, 1 Peter 1:15-16

DAY 124

"But you remain the same, and your years will never end"
(Psalm 102:27).

One thing we can count on is that God remains the same. He will never change, and He will never cease. Life is inconstant, unstable, and always shifting. We can sometimes feel that we have no firm foundation beneath us, especially in the face of loss or turmoil.

Psalm 102 describes a time of great distress and sorrow. The psalmist laments that his life is wasting away as he doesn't even remember to eat, so great is his grief. Sleep has escaped him as he lies awake at night, and his drinks are mingled with his tears. In this cry to God, the psalmist declares that it is time for the Lord to arise and show favor to His people, because they have suffered so greatly (Psalm 102:13).

Just as he appeals to God on the basis of His love, we too can cry out to God in our pain because He loves us. He weeps with us over the things that hurt. His heart breaks with our hearts. He hasn't forgotten or forsaken. He hears our cries.

The psalmist recalls the power of God in creating the heavens and the earth, knowing that same God has power over his circumstances as well. And that is the God who doesn't change.

God doesn't love us one day and hate us the next. He doesn't call us to Himself and then reject us later. The God who loves us, loves us in spite of the sin He hates. The God who calls us, keeps us, in spite of our finite wisdom and weakness. Life may shift beneath us; circumstances may vary and change—but our God does not.

"Jesus Christ is the same yesterday and today and forever" (Hebrews 13:8).

Does your life feel shaky and unstable? Call on the God who never changes and let His love establish you in peace.

For further reading: 1 Samuel 15:29, Malachi 3:6, Hebrews 7:21, 13:8, James 1:17

DAY 125

"Praise the LORD, O my soul, and forget not all his benefits— who forgives all your sins and heals all your diseases, who redeems your life from the pit and crowns you with love and compassion, who satisfies your desires with good things, so that your youth is renewed like the eagle's" (Psalm 103:2-5).

This is a go-to psalm for me when I have a bad day, when I am down, or when I'm upset about something. We serve a God who forgives all our sins. All our sins. Think about that. We all have things we've thought or said or done that we would rather just forget, things for which we are ashamed. If we have repented, He has forgiven and forgotten (Psalm 103:12).

This psalm tells us that God is "gracious and compassionate." He does not treat us as our sins deserve. If we come to Him in humility and repentance, He restores us completely by His grace. That's something to celebrate!

He heals all our diseases. I know many would argue that God hasn't healed all our diseases. If that were the case, everyone on earth would be in perfect health. But because we live in a fallen world where sin and sickness abound, we sometimes don't see God heal every disease. How do we make our experience align with God's truth? We have to look beyond the natural to the spirit realm. God does heal all our diseases eventually. He will either give us healing now or in eternity, but He is true to His Word. He heals our sin-sickness, and that changes our eternity.

He redeems our life from the pit. When we were lost in sin, we were in a deep, dark pit of destruction, but God lifted us up and crowned us with His love and compassion.

And He satisfies our desires with good things. I'm so thankful that God delivered me from sinful desires and filled me with a hunger for more of Him. I am so completely satisfied in Jesus.

If you are having a rough day, get your Bible out and read this psalm and praise the Lord for all His benefits today.

For further reading: Isaiah 53:5, Matthew 26:28, Acts 10:43, Colossians 1:14

DAY 126

"How many are your works, O LORD! In wisdom you made them all"
(Psalm 104:24a).

Morning Music

An aviary worship team welcomes the morning,
The low bellow of bovine adds the bass.
Dark clouds hang along the horizon,
Warm sun trying to keep up the pace.
Winged flight makes several passes,
Tuning their hearts to the key of day.
Silently I wait for the morning to dawn—
The first notes of what God has to say.

I love mornings and the outdoors, so I enjoy my morning quiet times on my back porch as many mornings of the year as I possibly can. Even when the temperature begins to drop, I will put on a sweatshirt, bundle in a blanket, and bring my coffee to the back porch to talk to God and study His Word.

I feel God's presence more deeply when I am surrounded by open skies, trees, and the sounds of nature. Honestly, I will turn off the worship music on my phone and just listen to the birds and sounds of the morning.

God is all in His creation. Whether we are hiking a mountain trail or strolling a pier over the ocean, the glory of God can be seen in the works of His hand.

"O LORD my God, you are very great; you are clothed with splendor and majesty" (Psalm 104:1b).

Even if you don't particularly enjoy the outdoors, try going for a walk and paying attention to the things God created all around you. Or lie on a blanket and look at the night sky. Praise Him for His works in creating a beautiful place for us to enjoy.

Let creation draw you to the beautiful heart of our Creator.

For further reading: Job 12:7-10, John 1:3, Romans 1:20, 8:19

DAY 127

*"Glory in his holy name; let the hearts of
those who seek the LORD rejoice" (Psalm 105:3).*

Jesus didn't come for us to have religion. After all, the Pharisees already had religion and were pretty content with it. That's why they didn't recognize Jesus as the Son of God—they didn't really know God. But Jesus came so that we could be set free from sin and truly know Him.

Jesus said that real, lasting life is found in knowing God. But many of us settle for a religious experience instead. Paul was a man well-acquainted with religion. Paul was zealous for what he believed was the pursuit of God because he had been blinded to truth. He was actually pursuing religious status, legalistic self-righteousness, and, in fact, working against the Lord.

What about us? Are we working really hard, pursuing religious status in the church, trying to obtain a legalistic self-righteousness, secretly proud of how well we are serving God, and yet not even spending time with Him, truly connecting with Him in worship, or hungering and thirsting for His Word?

Oh, beloved, God wants so much more for you. Once Paul encountered the Lord in all of His glory on the road to Damascus, he was forever ruined. He could never go back and be the same. He was changed from the inside out. He no longer cared about the religious life he had previously pursued. He only wanted to know God more.

God wants us to come to Him through His Son, seek His face, hunger and thirst for Him in worship, surrender to His Spirit, and live the life we were made for. We can stop striving to be perfect, to do better, to perform more, or to act religious. That's not what the Father is looking for. He just wants us.

Be encouraged today to let the Lord set you free from religious striving and lead you to His table. Come and sit at His feet, drink from His hand, feed on His Word, and rest in His presence. That is the life Jesus died to give you. He knows you, beloved. He wants you to know and love Him. He will take care of the rest.

For further reading: Proverbs 8:17, Jeremiah 29:13, John 10:14-15, Philippians 3:7-10

DAY 128

*"But they soon forgot what he had done and
did not wait for his counsel" (Psalm 106:13).*

We humans are fickle and forgetful. We can read an account of our nation's history and be astounded that our forefathers committed such grievous sins. But we often repeat the same mistakes we condemn in them. The same was true of the Israelites.

Time and time again, God rescued them when they cried out to Him for help against their adversaries. Yet sooner or later, they would fall right back into the sins of idolatry and rebellion. The psalmist recalls their storied history—how God led His people out of Egypt, rebuking the Red Sea before them, only to have them put God to the test in the wilderness.

They complained, grumbled, and turned to idol worship, forgetting the power and majesty of the God who led them out and performed miracles on their behalf. How soon they forgot what God had done!

How soon do we forget what He has done for us? Do we forget that it was grace that saved us when we start trying to perform? Do we not remember that we too were lost in sin when we begin to judge unbelievers in their sin? Have we so soon forgotten that if our God can save us, He can do anything?

After we see the hand of God work in our behalf, do we then take matters into our own hands and not wait for His counsel? Oh, yeah, we forget. Way too often, we forget. We need to learn from our history. We need to recall every day what God has done on our behalf, lest we lose sight of His glory amidst our ordinary. We need to put ourselves in remembrance of all that He has said when we begin to struggle with our doubts and fears.

We need to remember. Because if we remember, we will seek His counsel and wait upon the Lord. We will be less likely to repeat our folly if we remember the pain of past mistakes. Lord, help us remember Your work and Your Word, and teach us to wait on You.

For further reading: Proverbs 3:1-35, Ecclesiastes 12:1, Luke 22:19, John 14:26, 2 Timothy 2:8

DAY 129

"...for he satisfies the thirsty and fills the hungry with good things"
(Psalm 107:9).

What's your go-to comfort food? You know, that food you reach for at the end of a long, stressful day? For me, it's pizza—crispy crust, savory sauce, and any kind of veggies. But then I usually eat until I'm overstuffed, and along with that comes *discomfort*. What I thought would comfort me had the opposite effect. We often turn to things for comfort when we are hungry, tired, mentally stressed, or emotionally drained. But God longs to comfort us.

"I, even I, am he who comforts you" (Isaiah 51:12). So how does the Lord bring comfort? Let me offer a few suggestions.

Prayer: When we pray, we release all of those burdens that have weighed us down all day. It may just be a prayer for help with our responsibilities or with a relationship. 1 Peter 5:7 tells us that we can cast all our anxiety on Him because He cares for us. Releasing those burdens will bring comfort in knowing that God is in control.

Worship: There's nothing quite like worship to get our minds off ourselves and on our mighty God. Worship lets us express our hearts to God and focus on how good He is no matter what our situation. David expressed quite a range of emotions in the psalms.

The Word: Reading and confessing God's Word has the power to renew our minds and relieve some of the mental stress of our day. Even if it's just reminding ourselves of His promises and His faithfulness, the Word is a great source of comfort.

So the next time you come home at the end of a long day, before you reach for the pizza and the remote, spend some time with the Lord and let Him bring you the real comfort that your heart desires.

Jesus said that He is the Bread of Life. Take and eat!

For further reading: Matthew 5:6, 2 Corinthians 1:3-7, 1 Thessalonians 2:10-12, 1 Peter 5:7

DAY 130

"My heart is steadfast, O God; I will sing and make music with all my soul. Awake, harp and lyre! I will awaken the dawn" (Psalm 108:1-2).

To me, there's nothing like the quiet of early morning, just before the sunrise. I love to be awake before everyone else, to enjoy the stillness of morning, and to watch the sun quietly slip above the horizon. When the sun begins to stretch her arms as if awakening from a deep sleep, the birds chatter about breakfast, and Jesus comes to meet with me in the quiet place—all is right with the world.

When I read these verses in Psalm 108, I identify with the psalmist. God's love and faithfulness are so great, they reach to the skies, farther than my eyes can see. I truly feel that the worship and devotion in my heart can cause the sun to rise, that my praise can awaken the dawn!

Something deep within the human soul longs to bring forth music and singing in response to all God is and all God does. We echo the music of all creation when we say,

"Be exalted, O God, above the heavens, and let your glory be over all the earth" (Psalm 108:5).

I used to wonder how God could be exalted or lifted up, because He is already high and holy—far above all principalities and powers. How can we lift Him any higher than He already is?

One day I realized that we don't lift Him higher than He already is, we lift Him higher in us. We let Jesus be on the throne—far above everything that we worship and we desire. When we exalt the Lord, we are giving Him first place in us—right where He deserves to be.

As you begin your day, give Jesus His rightful place on the throne of your heart, far above all other desires. Awaken the dawn with your words of praise today!

For further reading: 2 Samuel 23:3-5, Psalm 143:8, Isaiah 50:4, 2 Corinthians 4:16, 1 Thessalonians 5:5-6

DAY 131

"Let them know that it is your hand, that you, O LORD, have done it"
(Psalm 109:27).

I'm sure if you have lived any length of time on this earth, you have been betrayed or hurt by a friend. It's almost inevitable, that at some point in life we are wounded by those with which we allow ourselves to be vulnerable.

Few wounds cut as deeply. And if we are in church for any time at all, we will probably be hurt by someone in the church.

The bottom line is that we are all wounded people. Out of our own disappointments, insecurities, and pride, we will inevitably hurt and be hurt. The cure for such betrayal is to keep our eyes on Jesus.

When the psalmist was wounded by a close friend, he looked to God for help. He prayed for those who hurt him (Psalm 109:4b). The psalmist trusted that God would repay as the Judge of all men. Because God is just, we can love our enemies and do good to them, just as Jesus taught.

We can look to Jesus who was betrayed and denied by His own disciples as an example of loving our enemies. God can use our response to such hurts as a testimony of His goodness and grace.

When we offer a gentle reply to harsh words, when we refuse to spread gossip, when we don't retaliate, we show a watching world that there is something different about us—and that difference is Jesus.

If you are suffering the sting of rejection, betrayal, or pain caused by a friend, remember that by your example, you can demonstrate the love of God, and "let them know that it is [His] hand" that has done it.

For further reading: Proverbs 15:1, 26:20, Isaiah 53:3, Matthew 5:43-48, Romans 12:17

DAY 132

"The LORD says to my Lord: 'Sit at my right hand until
I make your enemies a footstool for your feet'" (Psalm 110:1).

As I sit here this morning writing this devotion, my feet are resting on a beautiful footstool, belonging to my mother-in-law. My feet rest there, but not my full weight. My full weight is on the chair on which I sit. God's full weight or glory resides in heaven. We may see glimpses of His glory on earth, but this earth is just His footstool. It could never contain all of His glory. So, too, when we are in Christ, we are seated in heavenly places with Him.

"And God raised us up with Christ and seated us with him in the heavenly realms in Christ Jesus" (Ephesians 2:6). We walk and talk and live in this physical realm of earth, but this world is not our home. Therefore, we must keep our hearts and minds set on the glory of God.

"Since, then, you have been raised with Christ, set your hearts on things above, where Christ is seated at the right hand of God. Set your minds on things above, not on earthly things. For you died, and your life is now hidden with Christ in God. When Christ, who is your life, appears, then you also will appear with him in glory" (Colossians 3:1-4).

The things of this world are passing away, but praise God, we will one day be with Him in glory! This world is full of pain, sorrow, and difficulty, but we who are in Christ overcome the world (John 16:33).

So today, no matter what you are going through or what you have been through, if you belong to Jesus, it's just a footstool problem. Set your feet upon it, and set your eyes above, on the glory of God.

For further reading: Isaiah 66:1, John 16:33, Ephesians 2:6, Colossians 3:1-2, Hebrews 11:10

DAY 133

"Great are the works of the LORD; they are pondered by all who delight in them" (Psalm 111:2).

Do you delight in the works of the Lord? Do you take pleasure in your relationship with Jesus? When is the last time you pondered on the works of the Lord—really marveled over His ways?

Part of my daily quiet time is spent in writing out in my journal everything I am thankful for. On some days, I think about prayers God has answered and all the good things He has done for me, my family, and my church.

I ponder the works of God on my behalf—His salvation, healing, deliverance, protection, provision, guidance, and wisdom.

At times I meditate on His love, grace, mercy, peace, joy, faithfulness, blessings, favor, and goodness.

Other times, I simply ponder who He is to me—Father, Friend, Savior, Helper, Deliverer, Faithful Judge, Refuge, Strong Tower, Healer, Creator.

When I think of the power of His Word, His love in sending His Son to die for me, His mercy to forgive me over and over, and the grace that He still chooses to use me in spite of my sin, I am overwhelmed at the goodness of the Lord.

We all need to take some time every day to ponder the works of the Lord. If we are not delighting in Him, it's probably because we don't truly think about who He is and all He has done.

"He provided redemption for his people; he ordained his covenant forever— holy and awesome is his name" (Psalm 111:9).

Today, take some time to delight in the Lord by pondering His works on your behalf.

For further reading: 1 Chronicles 16:8-10, Luke 2:19, Colossians 2:7, 3:15, 1 Thessalonians 5:18

DAY 134

"Blessed is the man who fears the LORD, who finds great delight in his commands" (Psalm 112:1b).

As a young woman, I can remember thinking that the Bible was just a bunch of rules that keep us from having fun. I wasn't raised in church, and I didn't understand the character of God. Once I came to know Jesus, my understanding of His Word changed.

My first pastor once explained God's commands this way: He said imagine that you are a soldier who has found himself in a minefield. You are filled with fear because you have no idea where the mines are hidden. One wrong step, and you're gone.

But along comes a man who tells you that he was there when the mines were hidden in the ground. He has a blueprint and knows exactly where every mine is located. If you will trust him, he will guide safely through the field by telling you which steps to take.

Each time the Lord gives us a command, He is leading us safely through the minefield of this world. When He says, "No! Don't step there," it's because He knows that choice will be deadly. God's commands are not to keep us from having fun; on the contrary, they free us to truly enjoy life.

When we choose to live in rebellion to God's ways, we open ourselves up to destruction and disaster; but when we surrender to His authority, He leads us down the path that is life and peace.

"He will teach us his ways, so that we may walk in his paths" (Micah 4:2b).

I want to encourage you today to find great delight in the commands of the Lord. They are for your good. They are God's way of loving you and leading you through the dangers of life safely home.

"This is love for God: to obey his commands. And his commands are not burdensome, for everyone born of God overcomes the world" (1 John 5:3-4a).

For further reading: Isaiah 30:21, Hosea 14:9, Micah 4:2b, 1 John 5:3-49

DAY 135

*"From the rising of the sun to the place where it sets,
the name of the LORD is to be praised" (Psalm 113:3).*

I was very intentional about choosing our children's names. Names are significant in Scripture, and we wanted to give our children names that would be prophetic in a sense of who they would become. Our first child, Josiah, was named for the boy who became king of Judah at the age of eight, then went on to bring revival. The Bible says he never turned aside to the right or the left but always did what was right in the eyes of the Lord (2 Kings 22:2). The name Josiah means "fire of the Lord."

Our second baby, Bethany Grace, was named for the place Jesus went to hang out with His friends, Mary, Martha, and Lazarus. It's where the woman with the alabaster jar poured her love and worship on Jesus, and it's also the place where Jesus ascended into heaven.

My point is that we know names are meaningful, yet we sometimes fail to grasp the power in the name of Jesus. This psalm tells us that the name of the Lord is to be praised everywhere. His name is holy and represents all that He is. When we speak the name Jesus, we are calling on all the power of God evidenced in His name.

When we are overwhelmed and can't even find the words to pray, we can whisper, "Jesus," and all the forces of heaven come to our aid. When we pray in His name, we are declaring that what we ask Him to do, He has the power and authority to carry out. All that God is can be found in the name of Jesus, because Yeshua means "The Lord saves," and that's who He is. There's nothing He can't do and nothing good He will withhold.

At the name of Jesus, demons flee, angels are summoned, chains are broken, hearts are mended, sins are forgiven, and peace is found.

If you find yourself in a difficult place today and you don't know where to turn, just call on the name of Jesus. There's power in the name.

For further reading: Matthew 1:21, John 14:13, Acts 2:21, 4:12, Philippians 2:9-10

DAY 136

"Tremble, O earth, at the presence of the LORD" (Psalm 114:7a).

We don't tremble much at the presence of the Lord, do we?

In a soft culture of cheap grace and weak faith, our overfamiliarity with God can cause us to lose some of the shock and awe of the glory of the Almighty. We're much more likely to walk in smug confidence than trembling grace.

I'm reminded of the story of the two men who went up to the temple to pray—one a Pharisee and the other a tax collector. The Pharisee is proud of his association with God and thankful he's not like "other men" who sin. He's so proud of his self-righteousness.

But the tax collector won't even look up to heaven but cries out to God to have mercy on him, because he knows he's a sinner in the presence of Almighty God.

Sometimes we get so familiar with the God who calls us friend that we forget just how holy and powerful He truly is. As we prepare today in South Carolina for potentially one of the worst storms we've seen in decades, I am reminded of how big God is and how very little I am.

A category 5 hurricane capable of catastrophic and devastating damage is no match for the God who can destroy heaven and earth with a single breath.

Let's not take His presence for granted. Yes, He invites us into the holy of holies with Him and draws us into intimacy and friendship. But never doubt, He is still God. And that should cause us to tremble.

The Pharisee knew much about God but not enough to bow in His presence.

Let us know Him today as He truly is, and may it fill us with reverence and awe.

For further reading: Matthew 10:28, 2 Thessalonians 1:6-10, Hebrews 12:28-29, Revelation 1:14-17

DAY 137

"Not to us, O LORD, not to us but to your name be the glory, because of your love and faithfulness" (Psalm 115:1).

It's easy to start basking in our own glory.

We are naturally self-centered people. It's just who we are. It's in our nature to focus on ourselves and our needs and our desires. We have to recalibrate our attention daily.

All that we are and all that we do should be for God's glory—for His name to be lifted up and not our own. When we share the gospel with someone, it's for His glory. When we feed the hungry or clothe the poor, it's for His glory. When we teach a class or sing on the praise team, it's for His glory. When we memorize Scripture or rise early to seek Him, it's for His glory.

In a culture that glorifies self at every turn, we really have to fight the sinful nature that wants to make everything about us. I have found that it is a daily battle to keep my focus on the Lord and not myself. Even those things we do with the best of intentions can shift to a self-glorifying satisfaction if we aren't careful.

What have you done for the Lord lately that may have been for His glory, but you now enjoy some of the praise? If the praise of people is more important to us than the praise of the Lord, we probably need to do a heart check.

Ask the Lord to search your heart for any desires for self-focus instead of God-focus. Ask Him to forgive you and to renew your thoughts in His Word. Ask God to remind you daily that only what we do for His glory will last for eternity.

For further reading: Matthew 6:1-18, 1 Corinthians 10:31, Colossians 3:17, Revelation 4:11

DAY 138

"I love the LORD, for he heard my voice; he heard my cry for mercy. Because he turned his ear to me, I will call on him as long as I live"
(Psalm 116:1-2).

These verses are some of my favorites in all of Scripture. These words are my testimony in two short sentences. I was lost in sin, drowning in a sea of rejection, confusion, and self-loathing. Then I cried out to the Lord for mercy. He turned to me and heard my cry. He lifted me out of my darkness and brought me into His light.

And that's why I love Him.

I love Him because He first loved me (1 John 4:10, 19).

I love Him because He died for me while I was still lost in my sin (Romans 5:8).

I will call on Him as long as I live because He did for me what I couldn't do for myself. He took away my rejection and accepted me. He delivered me from confusion and gave me a sound mind. He showed me how to love myself because I was made in His image—beautifully and wonderfully!

I love the Lord, because when I cried out to Him, He heard my voice. He didn't turn me away as others had. He didn't reject me because I was unworthy. He loved me in spite of my unworthiness. I love Him and I will serve Him forever because of all that He has done for me.

Why do you love the Lord? What has He brought you out of and what has He blessed you with? How would your life be different today had He not heard your voice and turned His ear to you?

Celebrate the love of the Lord today and call on His name.

For further reading: Psalm 139, Romans 5:8, 1 John 4:10, 19

DAY 139

"Praise the LORD, all you nations; extol him, all you peoples. For great is his love toward us, and the faithfulness of the LORD endures forever. Praise the Lord" (Psalm 117:1-2).

I love this short little psalm! It sums up why we are on this earth—to praise the Lord for His love and faithfulness. It applies to all the people of the earth.

"For God so loved the world that he gave his one and only Son, that whoever believes in him shall not perish but have eternal life" (John 3:16).

Many people today claim that Christianity is exclusive and biased. Because the Word of God establishes for us truth—right and wrong—many people see Christianity as a religion that excludes those who don't agree with God's version of truth. Truth is seen as relative; therefore, many believe that just because their truth is different, they shouldn't be excluded from heaven.

What they fail to understand is that God *is* truth. There is no such thing as different versions of truth—there is only one truth. Christianity is very inclusive. Salvation is offered to "whoever believes." There is no bias, no rejection based on nationality, gender, race, or even religion.

Many Muslims, Buddhists, and Hindus have come to faith in Christ Jesus. People from every color, language, and tribe of the world have been welcomed into the family. The only prerequisite is faith in Jesus Christ and His finished work on the cross.

And that is available to every single person on the planet.

Jesus Christ offers relationship to everyone because "great is his love toward us." It isn't biased, privileged, or exclusive. Salvation in Jesus Christ is for "whosoever believes."

Share the love of Jesus with someone today who doesn't look or believe like you.

For further reading: John 1:29, 3:16-17; Romans 3, 10; 2 Corinthians 5:19

DAY 140

"This is the day the LORD has made; let us rejoice and be glad in it"
(Psalm 118:24).

On the surface I think we can all agree that not every day seems worthy of rejoicing in. There are hard days, bad days, sad days, and days we wish we could forget. Not every day seems to offer a reason for celebration.

But if we look a little deeper, we can see that every day is ordained by the Father. Nothing happens that doesn't first pass through His fingers. Every sunrise is evidence of a faithful God. And even though we may see nothing in our circumstances that makes us glad, we can still be glad.

You know why?

Because the One who makes each day is also in complete control. As we surrender our lives to His authority and spend more time in His Word, we come to realize that what constitutes a good day to us is not necessarily what makes a day good to God.

In God's economy, nothing is wasted. He can feed five thousand with a few fish and loaves and still pick up the broken pieces. And He can take what's left of our broken lives and still feed a few hungry souls. We may feel that all we have done is survive a season of pain and suffering, but God sees a much bigger picture—one that often involves using our pain for His glory.

Are you in a season of more bad days than good?

Don't despair of rejoicing. God can take even our hardest days and give us a reason to rejoice. Don't focus on your pain. Focus on the One who is Lord even over your pain.

This may be a hard day, but it's another day that the Lord has made. In that, we can rejoice and be glad.

For further reading: Psalm 84:10, Matthew 14:13-21, Luke 11:3, 2 Corinthians 4:16

DAY 141

Psalm 119:1-8 ~ Aleph
"I will praise you with an upright heart as I learn your righteous laws. I will obey your decrees; do not utterly forsake me"
(Psalm 119:7-8).

Psalm 119 is an acrostic of the Hebrew alphabet, with every stanza devoting eight verses to each letter. Each of the 176 verses of this psalm refers to God's Word—commands, laws, decrees, statutes, precepts, ordinances, word, ways, or promises. We will look at each of these over the next few weeks.

The first letter of the Hebrew alphabet is *aleph.* In Hebrew culture, each letter had an actual meaning. *Aleph* means "father." How appropriate at the beginning to start with the head. The ancient pictograph for *aleph* was an ox, representing strength and leadership. That is what a Hebrew father was expected to be, and that is what God is to us. He is our Father, giving us His strength and leading us day by day.

This is the same word translated *alpha* in the Greek. So when Jesus said three times in Revelation, "I am the Alpha and the Omega," He was essentially saying, "I am the Aleph and the Tav." *Tav* is the last letter of the Hebrew alphabet. So, yes, He is literally the Beginning and the End.

Do you start and end every day with time set aside to spend with Jesus? The Hebrew word *aluph*, which was derived from *aleph*, means master or lord. He is the Head, the Master, the Lord of all.

The letter *aleph* is the first letter used in "El," "Elohim," and "Adonai"—all names for God. This letter is also the first letter in the Hebrew words for fire, light, and love.[28]

If we make Jesus our beginning and end, look to Him as our strength to lead us throughout our day, allow Him to be a fire within us, light for our path, and the love of our life, we *will* walk in His Word, His very presence, with obedience and faithfulness. And, no, He will not forsake us—not ever.

For further reading: John 1:14, Hebrews 12:29, 1 John 1:5, 4:16

DAY 142

Psalm 119:9-16 ~ Bet
"I have hidden your word in my heart that I
might not sin against you" (Psalm 119:11).

Today's verses all begin with the Hebrew letter *bet*. *Bet* or *beth* means "dwelling" or "house." The ancient pictograph looked like a tent.[29] The very first letter of the Bible is *bet*. In the beginning, God created the heavens and the earth because He wanted to create a people with whom He could dwell. From the Garden to the Tabernacle, God's desire has been to dwell among us.

"Then have them make a sanctuary for me, and I will dwell among them" (Exodus 25:8).

"The virgin will be with child and will give birth to a son, and they will call him "Immanuel" —which means, 'God with us'" (Matthew 1:23).

Not only does God desire to dwell among us, but if we accept Jesus as our Savior and Lord, He comes to dwell within us. "Don't you know that you yourselves are God's temple and that God's Spirit lives in you?" (1 Corinthians 3:16). So what does all of this have to do with Psalm 119:9-16, you may ask?

The psalmist begins with a question: "How can a young man keep his way pure?" That's a good question, and it applies to each of us—man, woman, and child. He answers his own question—by living in the Word and the Word living in us.

That's why the Word became flesh. Colossians 3:16 tells us to let that Word dwell richly within us. I love that! Because now it's up to us to let that Word dwell in us. We get to choose how much of us we let Him have. We get to choose how much of His Word we soak up on a daily basis, how much of His presence we seek in our life.

My prayer is that you are falling more deeply in love with Christ and allowing His Word to dwell in you every day.

For further reading: Exodus 25:8, Matthew 1:23, John 1:14, 1 Corinthians 3:16, 2 Corinthians 6:16, Ephesians 2:22, 3:16-17, Colossians 3:16

DAY 143

Psalm 119:17-24 ~ Gimel
"Open my eyes that I may see wonderful
things in your law" (Psalm 119:18).

As we look at the Hebrew acrostic of Psalm 119 today, remember that Jewish children are taught these meanings as they learn their letters. *Gimel* has a couple of meanings, but I believe they are related. The pictograph is a camel, which kneels low to receive its rider and then rises to lift up the one upon it. The classic letter itself looks like a man walking forward, facing the next Hebrew letter, *dalet*. *Dalet* can mean "poor" or "impoverished," so traditionally *gimel* has represented a rich man bowing low to lift up a poor man.[30] What an amazing picture of what God has done for us! He is the rich man, lifting us out of our poor estate and raising us up by His grace (Psalm 40:2).

There is a beautiful connection here between our low estate and His lifting us up. We are the poor and needy without Christ. We are destitute, hopeless, helpless, like sheep without a Shepherd, until Jesus comes and rescues us from the mud and mire of sin. We have to come humbly to the Lord, agreeing with Him about our sin, and then out of His great mercy, He lifts us up and gives us a firm place to stand. Will we extend grace to the needy around us? That is what a Hebrew child would have been taught about this letter.

The root word that *gimel* comes from is *gamal*, which means "to deal out, to give, or wean."[31] As believers, we have been dealt grace, time and time again. Now what will we give out to others?

We are free to choose what we will chase. Look at the psalm passage again. The psalmist knows the value of running after the Word of God. He asks God to do good to him—to show him grace. And he prays that God will open his eyes to the wonderful truths of Scripture.

The more we chase after the things of God, the more grace we will bestow on others. That's just the way it works. So, let's be generous with grace today, even if they don't deserve it. Neither do we.

For further reading: Psalm 40:2, 113:7, James 4:10, 1 Peter 5:6

DAY 144

The Hebrew letter *dalet* is my favorite. *Dalet* means door.[32] A door is an opportunity—to shut ourselves in or to take a step out. Look at these words of Jesus:

"But when you pray, go into your room, close the door and pray to your Father, who is unseen. Then your Father, who sees what is done in secret, will reward you" (Matthew 6:6).

"Ask and it will be given to you; seek and you will find; knock and the door will be opened to you. For everyone who asks receives; he who seeks finds; and to him who knocks, the door will be opened" (Matthew 7:7-8).

The first door we need to concern ourselves with is the one that we close when we enter into the secret place with the Lord. We have to close the door on every distraction, including those within our own thoughts, our own will, our own desires, so that we can pray to the Father and hear His voice. We need a quiet place to read the Word and meditate on God's thoughts. He is there in that secret place, and the Word promises that He will reward us for the time we spend behind that door.

How does He reward us? What we ask, He will give; what we seek, He will provide; and when we knock on that door, He will open it and lead us into opportunities we never thought possible.

The key to the open door is the closed door. God may not grant every single prayer request, but He surely honors those requests that are seeking His face, His will, His kingdom. And when we shut ourselves in with Him, that's the direction He leads our hearts. So if you are seeking an open door in your life right now, maybe it's time to close the door. And if you have been in the room for a while now, keep knocking. Jesus said the door would be opened. And when it does, you'll be ready.

For further reading: Matthew 6:6, 7:7-8, 1 Corinthians 16:9, Revelation 3:20

DAY 145

Psalm 119:33-40 ~ Hey
"Turn my eyes away from worthless things; preserve
my life according to your word" (Psalm 119:37).

This stanza of Psalm 119 is based on the fifth letter of the Hebrew alphabet *hey*. The early pictograph for *hey* was a man with his arms raised, while the word is actually translated to mean "look," "behold," or "lo" in Scripture.[33]

It's a word that signifies amazement, revelation, and wonder. *Hey* can also mean "breath" or "sigh." Have you ever stood on the shore and marveled as the waves broke, one after another, in power and strength and continuity? Or maybe you have gazed on the multitude of stars on a clear night and felt the sheer vastness of the galaxies. Maybe you have held the tiny foot of a newborn baby in the palm of your hand, and the moment took your breath away.

That is *hey*—the wonder of God. Perhaps that was what John the Baptist felt in that moment when he exclaimed, "'Look, the Lamb of God, who takes away the sins of the world!'" (John 1:29).

Those are the moments that should cause us to not only miss a breath, but then to respond with hands lifted in worship and surrender, just like the man in that ancient pictograph. Wouldn't it be awesome if we could just see more of those moments in our day instead of those that cause us to worry or fear or be angry?

The psalmist prayed that God would turn his eyes away from worthless things and turn his heart toward His Words instead. Of course, we can't hide from the world and pretend ugliness doesn't exist. But there are plenty of moments in which we can choose to turn away from the "worthless things" that consume us, and instead choose to focus on the glory of God.

Sigh. Hands to the sky. That's my God.

For further reading: Daniel 3, John 1:29, 1 John 3:1

DAY 146

Psalm 119: 41-48 ~ Vav
"May your unfailing love come to me, O LORD,
your salvation according to your promise" (Psalm 119:41a).

This portion of the acrostic is based on the Hebrew letter *vav*. The pictograph for *vav* is a tent peg or nail. The translation for the word *vav* can mean "hook" (as in the hooks used to secure the curtains in the tabernacle), "secure," or the word "and."[34]

In Genesis 1:1, the Word says "In the beginning God created the heavens and the earth." The word "and" between heavens and earth is *vav*. God created the heavens, where He reigns over all creation. He created the earth where He would dwell with man. Then mankind brought sin into the world, which separated us from God. The only thing that could connect heaven and earth was represented in a nail.

God is holy and perfect and pure. In our sinful state, none of us can come into a relationship with Him. The nails that pierced His hands and feet have connected heaven to earth and made a way for us to know Him and live forever with Him in heaven. How do we become connected or secured in a relationship with Jesus?

Salvation is a matter of receiving the gift of God into our hearts and lives by faith. The grace of God in sending His perfect Son from the splendor of heaven to the dirt of earth to be nailed to a cross is what saves us—the *vav* connecting heaven and earth. The psalmist penned these words over 2000 years ago, probably 400-500 years before Jesus came, and yet he chose these eight verses for *vav*. Truly, God's unfailing love has come to us through His Son—His salvation according to His promise.

Jesus is the Divine Hook between us and the Father. He can secure your future as surely as those nails secured Him to a rugged cross. That's the promise of God.

For further reading: Genesis 1:1, Isaiah 64:6, Romans 3:23, 10:9-10, Ephesians 2:13, Colossians 2:13-14

DAY 147

Psalm 119:49-56 ~ Zayin
"Remember your word to your servant, for you have given me hope"
(Psalm 119:49).

Zayin comes from an ancient pictograph that looks like a sword, but the root of the word is *zan*, which means "food, cut, or nourish."[35] God says His Word is a sword (Ephesians 6:17).

In the context of this passage, these words are about our battle with the enemy, Satan, and not against other people. All of God's armor against our enemy is defensive so that we can protect ourselves from his evil attacks against us. But the sword of the Spirit, which is God's Word, is our only offensive weapon. With it we can take our stand against the enemy.

"For the word of God is living and active. Sharper than any double-edged sword, it penetrates even to dividing soul and spirit, joints and marrow; it judges the thoughts and attitudes of the heart. Nothing in all creation is hidden from God's sight. Everything is uncovered and laid bare before him to whom we must give account" (Hebrews 4:12-13).

The best way to defeat the devil with the Word of God is to use it to search our own hearts. Let it penetrate. Let it judge. Let it reveal to us those things that are not pleasing in His sight, even when it hurts. A sword is painful, but God's sword will bring healing. We must take time to let God's Word reveal the truth in us, and then do something about what we find.

In today's passage, the psalmist is being mocked by the arrogant, and he is full of indignation because they have forsaken God's Word. And yet, he takes no action against them. Instead, he looks to God's Word for comfort and hope. He praises God with song, and he obeys His Word. That, my friends, is how we defeat the enemy. And that is how we nourish our own souls.

No devil in hell can stop a man or woman of God who will read the Word, search his or her own heart, and do what the Word says. That's how God's Word can be both a sword and bread. Let it be food. Let it nourish. Let it cut. Sharpen your sword by spending time in God's Word.

For further reading: John 6:35, Ephesians 6:13-17, Hebrews 4:12-13, James 1:22-25

DAY 148

Psalm 119:57-64 ~ Chet or Heth
"You are my portion, O LORD; I have promised to obey
your words. I have sought your face with all my heart; be
gracious to me according to your promise" (Psalm 119:57-58).

The above passage is based on the eighth letter *chet*. The ancient pictograph for this letter looks like a fence; the word itself is derived from *chayim*, which means "life."[36] A fence is normally used for protection. We fence in animals to keep them from wandering away and being hurt or lost. But the fence also keeps the animal from having the freedom to choose his own path.

We may be tempted to think we are better off without the fence.

"Therefore Jesus said again, 'I tell you the truth, I am the gate for the sheep. All who ever came before me were thieves and robbers, but the sheep did not listen to them. I am the gate; whoever enters through me will be saved. He will come in and go out, and find pasture. The thief comes only to steal and kill and destroy; I have come that they may have life, and have it to the full'" (John 10:7-10).

Jesus is saying that the enemy, Satan, will tempt us to leave the safety of the fenced-in pasture, but if we will stay in the fence, there we will find life. He is not trying to keep us in and never let us find freedom; on the contrary, if we follow Him, we can come in and go out, and find pasture there with Him. There is no life without the fence. When we ignore the fence and go our own way, we end up bound with the ropes of the wicked (Psalm 119:61).

So don't be fooled by the enemy's illusion of freedom outside the fence. He lures us there to bind us in chains that we cannot break alone. The Great Shepherd, however, will lead us right through the gate and into an abundant life we never dreamed was possible from here inside the fence. He is the Gate. He is the way to freedom. He is life.

For further reading: Psalm 5:11-12, 32:10, 37:3-4, Matthew 9:36, John 10:3-10

DAY 149

Psalm 119:65-72 ~ Tet
"Do good to your servant according to your word, O Lord. Teach me knowledge and good judgment, for I believe in your commands"
(Psalm 119:65-66).

These verses of Psalm 119 all begin with the Hebrew letter *tet*. The ancient pictograph for *tet* is a snake coiled in a basket. The word *tet* is connected in meaning to the word *tov*, which means "good." We first see the letter *tet* used in Genesis 1:4.[37] "God saw that the light was good, and he separated the light from the darkness." The word *good* begins with *tet,* but here we see that although the light was good, there was also darkness. So in Hebrew tradition, children learning their "aleph-bet" would have been taught the connection between good and evil with this letter.

Paul also addresses this concept in Romans 7:18-19: "I know that nothing good lives in me, that is, in my sinful nature. For I have the desire to do what is good, but I cannot carry it out. For what I do is not the good I want to do; no, the evil I do not want to do—this I keep on doing." Have you ever felt like Paul? You know the basket could contain the snake, but you still want to open the lid. That's the nature of sin, which is evil and leads to death. But Paul tells us in Romans, that there is a good answer.

"Because through Christ Jesus the law of the Spirit of life set me free from the law of sin and death. For what the law was powerless to do in that it was weakened by the sinful nature, God did by sending his own Son in the likeness of sinful man to be a sin offering (Romans 8:2-3a). Paul goes on to say that because we are controlled by God's Spirit, we can choose what is good over what is evil. See, that's the nature of the basket: You and I choose whether or not we will open it.

The psalmist asks God to give him good judgment—the ability to know through the Word and through the Spirit whether or not to open the basket. There are many baskets before you today. Choose well.

For further reading: Genesis 1:4, Romans 7-8

DAY 150

Psalm 119:73-8- ~ Yodh
"Your hands made me and formed me; give me
understanding to learn your commands" (Psalm 119:73).

The 10th letter of the Hebrew alphabet, the *yodh*, was originally represented as a pictograph of the arm of God reaching down to us. The letter itself means both worship and work. The *yodh* is the first letter that we translate into Yahweh, literally "yodh-heh-vav-heh." It's the first letter in Yeshua (Jesus), Yerushalayim (Jerusalem, city of God), and Yisra'el (Israel, nation of God).[38]

Each of these words shows us the hand of God reaching down to us through His Son, Jesus, and drawing us to worship Him. Out of our worship, we are led to work for Him.

Yodh also represents humility because it is the smallest letter in the Hebrew alphabet. I love how all of these meanings fit together. When I come humbly before Him and recognize that I am a sinner in need of His grace, He reaches down His hand through the life, death, and resurrection of His Son, whose blood paid the price for my sin. I am humbled at His love and mercy towards me. I am drawn into His presence in worship. I am compelled to serve Him.

That is the heart of worship—when our hearts can trust in the One who formed us, no matter what. Worship is a lifestyle, an attitude of the heart, a song sung with our lives every day. Like the songbird, I want my heart to sing a melody to Jesus, even as I work to care for my young—just a permanent place at the altar of God, nestled down in His goodness and grace.

What about you? What is leading your heart to worship God today?

For further reading: Psalm 84, Psalm 95, Romans 8:18, 12:1

DAY 151

Psalm 119:81-88 ~ Kaf
"My eyes fail, looking for your promise; I say,
'When will you comfort me?'" (Psalm 119:82).

Have you ever felt like the psalmist—frustrated and persecuted by the enemy and seeking relief? It is no coincidence that this portion of Psalm 119 is based on the Hebrew letter *kaf*. You see, the original pictograph for this letter looks like an open palm or the crowned head of a king who is bowing down. The word *kaf* comes from the root word *kafah*, which means "to bow down, bend, open, or allow."[39]

What is so interesting about this letter is the connection between bowing and the open palm. In Hebrew culture, a son would bow down to receive the blessing of his father, which came through the laying of his hands upon the son's head. This letter is clearly about receiving the blessing. In ancient Hebrew culture, the blessing or *berakah* was a legally binding statement given to the firstborn that involved his inheritance and promise of future provision, grace, and favor.[40] Remember the story of Jacob and Esau? Once Isaac had given the blessing to Jacob, no provision was left for Esau. Thankfully, if we belong to Jesus, He has enough blessing for each of us! And that is the key to the above passage in Psalm 119.

The only prerequisite to blessing is bowing. Just as *kaf* symbolizes both bowing and blessing, so we must bow in humility before the King of kings in order to receive the blessings of His hand. Once we become followers of Jesus, we are blessed by our faith in Him.

So when we are going through trials and troubles like the psalmist in the above passage, how should we respond? The psalmist put his hope in God's Word, and he clearly understood that meant humbling himself before the Lord.

When we humble ourselves, God can lift us up. How about you? Are you in need of lifting up? Try bowing down.

For further reading: Psalm 40:4, 112:1, Colossians 1:12-14, 1 Peter 5:6

DAY 152

Psalm 119:89-96 ~ Lamed
"Your word, O LORD, is eternal; it stands firm in the heavens"
(Psalm 119:89).

These eight verses all begin with the 12th letter, *lamed.* The ancient pictograph for *lamed* looks like a shepherd's staff. The letter itself is the tallest in the "aleph-bet" and is also in the middle, so Hebrew children were taught that *lamed* is looking around at all the other letters, keeping watch over them. The word *lamed* comes from the Hebrew word *lamad,* meaning "teach, prick, sting, incite, or goad."[41]

Most of us don't like the word *authority,* unless we are the one in authority. We don't always want to be taught, pricked, stung, incited or goaded. We want to be our own authority. That is human nature. Even for those of us who say we love the Lord, sometimes we still try to hold onto our own way of doing and being. Trusting in an authority that we can't see can be scary and difficult, especially when we are being tossed on the waves of confusion, strife, or discontent.

But let me tell you just a little about the authority of Jesus. Jesus has authority over demons, sickness, disease, sin, and death. His message has authority. His presence has authority. His power takes authority over all. There is no higher, no greater, no better authority in all of heaven or earth. You know why? Because the word *authority* begins with author, and He is the Author of it all.

Satan has limited authority on this earth, and that is why you and I sometimes feel the sting of demons, sickness, disease, sin, and death. There is one, and only one, remedy for the limits to perfection in our world—the boundless Word of God, made flesh, crucified, resurrected, and living forever at the right hand of God. He is the Great Shepherd. That staff of His Word may sometimes sting, prod, and goad, but it is always for our good. We *can* trust Him. We can *trust* Him. We can trust *Him.*

For further reading: Luke 4:32, 36, 5:24-25, John 10:17-18, Colossians 1:16-17

DAY 153

Psalm 119:97-104 ~ Mem
"How sweet are your words to my taste, sweeter
than honey to my mouth!" (Psalm 119:103).

The preceding verses each begin with the letter *mem*. The ancient pictograph for *mem* looks like a wave of water and comes from the word *mayim*, which means "water, stream, or fountain." Traditionally this letter was associated with the "fountain of wisdom" found in the Torah, the Hebrew name for God's Word.[42] "The words of a man's mouth are deep waters, but the fountain of wisdom is a bubbling brook" (Proverbs 18:4).

So, how do we get God's Word to become that fountain of wisdom that we read about in Proverbs? I think the answer is in the passage from Psalm 119. The psalmist didn't just read God's Word in the morning during his quiet time. He meditated on God's Word throughout the day. He kept the Word always before him and allowed God's truth to guide him in all his decisions, like a fountain continually pouring out wisdom.

We need more of God's Word and God's wisdom continually being poured out into our lives. And He promises all that we need. "If any of you lacks wisdom, he should ask God, who gives generously to all without finding fault, and it will be given to him" (James 1:5).

Do you need more of the wisdom of God throughout your day? Ask Him. His wisdom will guide us into what is right and true. Don't doubt, but believe God to give you what you need. Find Scriptures that speak to your situation and write or print them out and read them often during the day. Memorize a new verse each week. Memorization can be challenging, but God will help us with it. We can review verses while sitting in traffic or waiting in lines.

His Word is the key to wisdom and direction for the decisions we face every day. Do you want to spin your wheels all day, making decisions that don't really acknowledge Him? Or do you want the Spirit of God to lead you in every little decision you face? Like the psalmist, His Word can be "ever with you." That's the fountain of wisdom.

For further reading: Proverbs 18:4, 1 Corinthians 1:17-31, Ephesians 1:17, James 1:5

DAY 154

Psalm 119:105-112 ~ Nun
"Your word is a lamp to my feet and a light for my path"
(Psalm 119:105).

The verses in this passage each begin with the Hebrew letter *nun*. The ancient pictograph for *nun* looks like a sprouted seed or sperm, both indicating the meaning of this letter, which is "life, continuity, or heir."[43]

In the parable of the sower, Jesus clearly told His listeners that the seed represents the Word of God (Matthew 13:1-23). Right after that, He told them that the kingdom of God is like a mustard seed, that although it is tiny, will produce a large plant (Matthew 13:31-32). Likewise, our faith, though it is small, when placed in Jesus, can move a mountain (Matthew 17:20).

Are you getting this picture? A seed is something small that has the potential to produce something beautiful and life-giving under the right conditions. Just as a sperm cell guided by the hand of God will find an ovule and create life in the womb, so God's Word will find its place in our hearts and create meaningful life for us.

In order for a seed to sprout, the right conditions must be present: soil, light, and water. In the same way, God's Word must find fertile soil in our hearts in order to take root and produce a harvest of righteousness in us. That's what the parable of the sower is all about. The secret to a meaningful life is having a heart that receives the seed of God's Word and lets it grow. Because when life on this earth ends, eternal life begins.

That seed in the form of the gospel, when met with the right conditions in a believer's heart, becomes a tree of life in which others can come and find shade. Then when that person believes, the seed is reproduced, and what a mighty harvest comes forth! Through the continuity of His Word, we are heirs to His Kingdom.

And that, my friends, is what life is all about.

For further reading: Matthew 13:1-23, 31-32, 17:20, John 12:23-25, 1 Peter 1:23-24

DAY 155

Psalm 119:113-120 ~ Samekh
"Sustain me according to your promise, and I will live;
do not let my hopes be dashed" (Psalm 119:116).

Each of the preceding verses begins with the letter *samekh* whose ancient pictograph first resembled a thorn and had the meaning of "pierce" or "sharp." As the letter morphed over time it came to look like a shield and is one of only two Hebrew letters that is closed (like an o), so the letter also came to represent the idea of a circle with no beginning or end. Interestingly, the word *samekh* comes from the root word *samech,* which means "lean upon," "uphold," or "support."[44]

Notice what the writer said in Psalm 119 about dealing with the rejection of the world: He knew who was his shield and who upheld him, and that's where he placed his hope.

Our security is in the Lord. He shields us from the hurts we face. And that pictograph of the thorn? I recently read that thorn bushes were used by shepherds to create a shield that would enclose their flocks at night to protect them from predators. That thorn pictograph evolved into the shape of a shield which was rounded like a circle—no beginning and no end. Are you getting this picture?

"The soldiers twisted together a crown of thorns and put it on his head" (John 19:2a). The thorns that pierced His head and the nails that pierced His hands and feet ushered in the salvation and deliverance that is our shield from the world—our faith.

The world and the enemy will seek to destroy you with flaming arrows, and many times these come in the form of words, accusations, and rejection. You need not fear as long as you fear the Lord and His Word. He will sustain you, uphold you, defend you, strengthen you, and support you.

For further reading: Deuteronomy 33:12, Psalm 3:3, Isaiah 41:10, John 19:2a, Ephesians 6:16

DAY 156

Psalm 119:121-128 ~ Ayin
"I am your servant; give me discernment that I
may understand your statutes" (Psalm 119:125).

These verses all begin with the letter *ayin*. The ancient pictograph for *ayin* looks like an eye, and the word itself means "eye," "to see," or "to understand," and carried with it the idea of spiritual discernment.[45]

In Old Testament language, the concept of "failing eyes" was often used to describe failing strength, grief, or longings unfulfilled and hopes deferred.

"My eyes grow weak with sorrow; they fail because of all my foes" (Psalm 6:7).

Do you ever feel this way when you pray and pray for some situation to change, but what you see with your physical eyes stays the same—or gets worse? That is the concept the psalmist expressed in these verses, but look carefully at his conclusion to the matter. While he waits on God to act, he continues to love God's Word and hate what is wrong.

I want to encourage you today, as the Lord has encouraged me. Begin to pray with your eyes open—open to the possibilities of what He can do. Ask God to give you discernment and spiritual understanding of your situation. Some things take time and others require action. But all things need faith, not just with our words, but with our hearts.

So today let's pray, not just believing what God can do, but seeing it with our eyes of faith. Picture your loved ones accepting His forgiveness and grace. See with your heart the revival coming to your church. Envision a move of God unlike anything you've ever seen. And then remember that He is able to do above and beyond anything we can imagine!

One day we shall see Him face to face, because He is coming in the clouds and every eye will see Him! Until then, may the eyes of your heart truly see.

For further reading: 2 Chronicles 16:9, Psalm 6:7, 1 Corinthians 2:9-10, 2 Corinthians 4:18, Hebrews 12:2

DAY 157

Psalm 119:129-136 ~ Pey
"The unfolding of your words gives light; it gives understanding to
the simple. I open my mouth and pant, longing for your commands"
(Psalm 119:130-131).

These eight verses all begin with the letter *pey*. The ancient pictograph for *pey* looks like a mouth, and the word *pey* means "mouth, word, or speech." Remember our last letter, *ayin*, which means "eye" or "understanding"? Hebrew children were taught that *ayin* comes before *pey* because we need to watch and learn before we speak.[46]

The Bible has much to say about words, speech, and the tongue. Most of us know these verses, but how many of us struggle to make these truths a reality in our everyday lives? Let me share three tips for wise speech.

Check your heart: "For out of the overflow of the heart the mouth speaks" (Matthew 12:34). The first step to wise speech is to search our hearts before God and ask Him to show us anything that is not of Him. If we have repressed anger, unforgiveness, bitterness, jealousy, envy, pride, or discontent, these sins will spew forth out of our mouths.

Check your lips: "Set a guard over my mouth, O LORD; keep watch over the door of my lips" (Psalm 141:3). Ask God to stop your tongue and give you time to think and understand before you speak.

Check your worship. "I will extol the LORD at all times; his praise will always be on my lips" (Psalm 34:1).

Remember, when your heart is right with God, He can close your mouth and teach you to wait and gain understanding and insight before you speak. Then open that mouth and declare His praise.

For further reading: Psalm 19:14, 40:3, 71:8, Proverbs 10:19, 13:3, Matthew 12:34

DAY 158

Psalm 119:137-144 ~ Tsade
"My zeal wears me out, for my enemies ignore your words"
(Psalm 119:139).

These eight verses all begin with the Hebrew letter *tsade*. The ancient pictograph for this letter looks like either a man lying on his side or a trail. *Tsade* comes from two root words: *tzod*, which means "hunt, capture, or catch" and *tsad*, which means "side or stronghold."

A stronghold was built on the side of a mountain as a place fortified against attack, a place of protection from which one could be defended. The letter *tsade* was generally associated with being on a hunt and following a trail that leads to a stronghold.[47]

But consider the fact that *tsade* was also associated with a man lying on his side, which would signify need. So if we stay in a place of needing God and running after Him, He will lead us along a trail that ends in a stronghold—not an enemy stronghold, but a place of refuge *from* the enemy.

The world will taunt us with numerous things to chase, most of which seem important. But only one will lead to the stronghold. Only in the stronghold can you be defended from the enemy. We like to think that we can handle things on our own and defend ourselves, but, honestly, that's a lie from Satan. We'll just be on the wrong trail, chasing the wrong things.

And zeal for the wrong things will wear us out. But if we, like the psalmist, run after Jesus and His Word, He will lead us along the trail that offers a place of rest and defense from the enemy. The enemy may be chasing us. Trouble and distress may come. But we can run after a God who loves us fiercely and will hide us under His wings.

So, I ask again: What are you chasing? Are you stressed and overwhelmed from running after many things? Run to Jesus and find rest in His stronghold.

For further reading: Proverbs 18:10, Romans 10:1-2, 12:11, Galatians 4:18

DAY 159

Psalm 119:145-152 ~ Qoph
"I rise before dawn and cry for help; I have put my hope in
your word. My eyes stay open through the watches of the night,
that I may meditate on your promises" (Psalm 119:147-148).

The above verses all begin with the letter *qoph,* whose ancient pictograph is a line with a half circle on top, representing the sun on the horizon. *Qoph* means "divide, time, or circle."[48] The sun has always served as our indicator of the passing of time, for it divides day from night. The movement of the earth on its axis and around the sun is what marks our "seasons, days, and years" (Genesis 1:14). Before clocks, one had to look up at the sky to tell the time.

Likewise, the Son of God divides time. Just as the sun "sleeps" every night and "rises" every morning, so the death and resurrection of Jesus marked the rising of hope for each of us and the promise of the resurrection to new life. Every sunrise is the promise of God's love and faithfulness through Christ.

"Sow for yourselves righteousness, reap the fruit of unfailing love, and break up your unplowed ground; for it is time to seek the LORD until he comes and showers righteousness on you" (Hosea 10:12).

Friend, if you do not have a personal relationship with the Lord Jesus Christ, it is time to seek the Lord. The letter *qoph* has another meaning: "to call or gather." Jesus will once again divide time for all eternity. He is coming again, and He will call and gather those who belong to Him. These Hebrew letters and the Words of God have survived thousands of years, because the Word of God is eternal—God exists outside of both time and space.

Jesus is Lord over time, space, creation, and all eternity. No one knows the day or hour, but we are told to keep watch. Keeping watch implies readiness. Are you ready? Because at the end of the day, the only time that truly matters is now.

For further reading: Lamentations 3:22-23, Hosea 10:12, Romans 13:11, 2 Corinthians 6:2, Hebrews 9:28

DAY 160

Psalm 119:153-160 ~ Resh
"See how I love your precepts; preserve my life, O LORD,
according to your love. All your words are true; all your
righteous laws are eternal" (Psalm 119:159-160).

These verses each begin with the Hebrew letter *resh*. The ancient pictograph for *resh* looks like the head of a man, and the word *resh* means "head, first, top, chief, or beginning."[49]

Many of us suffer stress because of so many obligations and responsibilities. I truly believe that if we put God first in our lives, He will give us grace and favor to move through our day with peace.

"But seek first his kingdom and his righteousness, and all these things will be given to you as well" (Matthew 6:33).

So what does putting God first look like in your life? For me, it means spending time with the Lord as soon as I get up. That time with the Lord is non-negotiable. Numerous activities and plans can fall by the wayside during my day but not my quiet time with Jesus.

I encourage you, if you don't already, to set aside time at the beginning of your day to make Jesus the first and most important thing in your life.

Ask God during your time with Him to help you prioritize your day. Trust me, He can do that. He can also remind you of obligations you may have forgotten. When we choose to make Him first and love His Word more than television social media, and other daily distractions, He brings us peace, joy, and order.

Busy, stressed, and feeling anxious? Persecuted and harassed by the enemy? Here's my prescription for the day: Seek Him first.

For further reading: Psalm 27:4, Matthew 6:33, Luke 10:38-42

DAY 161

Psalm 119:161-168 ~ Shin
"Rulers persecute me without cause, but my heart trembles at
your word. I rejoice in your promise like one who finds great spoil"
(Psalm 119:161-162).

The above verses each begin with the Hebrew letter *shin*, whose ancient pictograph resembles two front teeth or two flames of fire, both which carry the meaning of "consuming."[50]

Shin is the first letter of the words Shaddai (Almighty), Shabbat (Sabbath), shalom (peace), and shekinah (glory). This letter represents the awesome and consuming power of the almighty presence of God.

Look back at the psalmist's understanding of God. His heart trembled at God's Word, but he knew that peace comes to those who love God and His laws. The fear of the Lord is the reverence and awe with which we consider Almighty God. He is all-loving, but He is also all-powerful. He is equally a God of compassion and a God of judgment. He loves His people, but He hates sin, and so should we.

It seems that in our attempt to draw people to the God of mercy and grace, we have created a politically correct god of our own making who is without judgment and wrath. And that's just an idol.

We fear God, not because we are afraid of Him, for perfect love casts out fear (1 John 4:18), and His love is perfect. But we should fear being separated from Him by our own sin. That is the reverent fear of God that should drive us to our knees.

I'm not talking about a religious spirit that reveres tradition and church politics above Jesus. I'm not talking about a Pharisaical spirit that values rules over relationships. I'm simply referring to a holy reverence and fear of the Almighty that will bring us to our knees in worship and service and love.

Fear God and give Him glory. That's true wisdom.

For further reading: Deuteronomy 4:24, Hebrews 12:28-29, Revelation 14:6-7

DAY 162

Psalm 119:169-176 ~ Tav
"May my cry come before you, O LORD; give me
understanding according to your word" (Psalm 119:169).

We have come to the end of Psalm 119, all of which is an acrostic of the Hebrew alphabet. These last eight verses all begin with the letter *tav*. The ancient pictograph for *tav* is two sticks in the shape of a cross. Remember, this "aleph-bet" was given to the Hebrews thousands of years before Christ came to earth. The meaning of the word *tav* is "mark, sign, or covenant." So in this letter we see that thousands of years ago, God gave us the cross as a sign of covenant. Isn't that beautiful?

The word *truth* in Hebrew is *emet. Emet* is spelled with the letters *aleph, mem,* and *tav. Aleph* is the first letter of the Hebrew alphabet and means "father." *Mem* is in the very middle of the alphabet and means "water" or "Spirit." And *tav* is the last letter, meaning "cross." How cool is it that the very word truth contains the idea of the Trinity!

Tav is the first letter of the word *tikkun*, which means "redemption," *teshuvah*, which means "repentance," and *Torah*, which means "teachings," referring to the Word of God. The cross is literally the beginning of redemption, repentance, and the Word of God.[51]

Jesus triumphed over the enemy and He canceled all our debt. That is the power of the cross. Two beams of wood that represented death and shame have come to represent forgiveness and freedom.

Sometimes the cross gets heavy and seems too much to bear, but remember that for the joy set before Him—that joy was you and me—Jesus endured it. So can we, with our eyes fixed on Him, the Author and Finisher of our faith, the true Aleph and the Tav.

For further reading: Matthew 16:24, 1 Corinthians 1:17-18, Colossians 2:13-15, Hebrews 12:1-3

DAY 163

"I am a man of peace; but when I speak, they are for war"
(Psalm 120:7).

Have you ever been lied about and falsely accused of something? It really hurts to have others think less of us, especially if it's someone we trusted. As much as we want others to be happy with us, there will be times that we have to stand for God's truth, even if it puts others at odds with us.

The psalmist called on God to protect him from those who spoke deceitfully about him. Instead of trying to defend himself, he trusted the Lord to defend him (Psalm 120:1-2).

While Jesus promised inner peace for those who trust in Him (John 16:33), he also warned His followers that His truth will sometimes divide.

"'Do not suppose that I have come to bring peace to the earth. I did not come to bring peace, but a sword. For I have come to turn "a man against his father, a daughter against her mother, a daughter-in-law against her mother-in-law—a man's enemies will be the members of his own household'" (Matthew 10:34-36).

When we follow Jesus, we have peace with God and peace with others in the Body of Christ. Our relationship with Jesus will not be understood by some, however. Choosing to live by God's standards in His Word will actually cause conflict with unbelievers, even within our own families. The forces of darkness seek only war, even if we are for peace. So, as believers, we seek peace as much as we can, but when God's truth causes conflict, we stand on God's Word and trust Him to defend us.

"If it is possible, as far as it depends on you, live at peace with everyone" (Romans 12:18).

Seek peace, but where your faith in Jesus brings conflict, trust Him to deliver you from the attacks of the enemy.

For further reading: Matthew 10:34-36, John 16:33, Romans 5:1, 12:18, Ephesians 2:14

DAY 164

"I lift up my eyes to the hills—where does my help come from?
My help comes from the LORD, the Maker of heaven and earth"
(Psalm 121:1).

As I write this devotion, we are preparing for one of the worst hurricanes in recent history on the East coast. Many are fearful, worried about their homes, families, and possessions. While a storm of this magnitude can certainly cause fear and concern, I'm so glad that I know where my help comes from.

The Maker of heaven and earth is our source of help. The One who created the ocean waves is Lord over those waves. When we look to Him for help, we are acknowledging that He alone has the power to stop a storm or to keep us safe in the storm.

He alone is the source of all that we have, and therefore, we can look to Him in times of uncertainty. Do you know where to look for help in times of distress? Do you know where to turn when circumstances threaten your well-being?

Turn your eyes away from the source of fear and look to your source of help.

"So we say with confidence, 'The Lord is my helper; I will not be afraid. What can man do to me?'" (Hebrews 13:6).

Man cannot deliver us from the storms of life. We need not turn to self-help books, television personalities, or social media, because man is not our source of help. The world cannot give us the deliverance, peace, or comfort that we seek.

The world cannot provide wisdom or instruction for how to navigate the struggles we face. Only God can truly give us the help we need in any circumstance.

So lift your eyes to the hills today and know that your help comes from the Lord, the Maker of heaven and earth.

For further reading: Psalm 33:20, 46:1, 108:12, Hebrews 13:6

DAY 165

*"I rejoiced with those who said to me,
'Let us go to the house of the LORD'" (Psalm 122:1).*

I know many have been hurt in church, which can leave us feeling that church is more of a place of suffering than one of rejoicing.

The church is the body of Christ, which is made up of sinful people. No church body is going to be perfect. All people in a particular church gathering will not necessarily be Christ followers. Even those who are will be at different stages of discipleship and growth.

As hard as it is, we have to give others the grace and the space to grow in their relationship with Jesus. We also have to be willing to forgive those who hurt us, to communicate in love, and to talk through conflict within the church.

If we study the early New Testament church, we will see that there was often sin, conflict, forgiveness, and grace all flowing through the body of Christ.

The bottom line is that Jesus loves the church. He died for the church, He established the church, and He is coming again for the church. My encouragement for you today is to find a church in which truth is proclaimed, and then learn to love it.

Prepare your heart before you go. Keep your focus on Jesus and lifting Him up in worship. Look for ways to encourage others in their walk with the Lord. When misunderstanding arises or personality conflict shows its face, seek God for the love and peace to walk through those times with grace.

Each church body is a fellowship of believers who are growing and striving to be more like Jesus. Community is an important part of how we do that. We need each other for accountability and support. So don't give up on church!

Learn to love the body of Christ as He does, and rejoice to go up to the house of the Lord.

For further reading: Matthew 16:18, 18:17, Colossians 1:18, 24

DAY 166

"As the eyes of slaves look to the hand of their master, as the eyes of a maid look to the hand of her mistress, so our eyes look to the LORD our God, till he shows us his mercy" (Psalm 123:2).

When we come into relationship with Jesus, we acknowledge His authority over us. We have to humble ourselves before Him and submit to that authority on a daily basis. He is God and we are not. We have to seek His way for our lives and not our own way. Oftentimes, we get comfortable in our relationship with the Lord and subtly begin to walk in our own ways. We forget that He is sovereign and we need to surrender to His authority over us daily.

One great prayer to pray each morning is to acknowledge our dependence on the Lord and tell Him we are submitting to His authority. Just as a slave looks to his master or a maid looks to her mistress, we should look to the Lord for His direction and instruction for each day.

The good news is that our Lord will show us mercy. He blesses those who seek Him daily and submit to His will for their lives. We can trust His ways for us are good. Do you struggle to submit to God's authority for your life?

Think about how much control you actually have. For instance, we can each make our own schedule each day, but circumstances beyond our control can keep us from carrying out our plans. We can decide how we are going to spend our money, but unexpected expenses can change that plan quickly.

So if we can't really control our schedule or our circumstances, then why do we strive to do things our way? Our sinful human nature is naturally self-centered and wants to be in control, but it's just an illusion.

We can't make one hair on our heads black or white (Matthew 5:36). So, why not let go of that control that's causing you stress anyway and let God lead you. Surrender to His authority and His way and trust Him with the outcome.

He is God and we are not. So let's submit to His authority over us.

For further reading: Matthew 5:36, Acts 5:29, James 4:7, 1 Peter 5:5

DAY 167

"If the LORD had not been on our side...the raging waters would have swept us away" (Psalm 124:2-5).

Do you truly believe that the Lord is on your side?

Sometimes we go through such devastating circumstances—grief, loss, heartache—that it's hard to believe God is with us. In seasons of darkness and doubt, our faith in God's goodness can waver.

David could certainly identify with such circumstances. He spent most of his life on the run—first from Saul and then from his own son who wanted to kill him and usurp the throne. He experienced times of great guilt and deep grief, the loss of a child, and the pain of watching his own children suffer the consequences of sin.

Yet David was able to testify that if the Lord had not been on his side, all would have been lost.

Even when it seems as though we have little good to hang onto, we can always find that God is still on our side. Romans chapter 8 is a great example of Scriptures that promise God's presence during difficult times. God is for us and not against us. He's working all things together for our good. Nothing can separate us from His love.

If you are in a season of disappointment, darkness, or despair, please be assured today that Jesus is still for you. He is with you, and He is cheering you on. Turn to Him as David did and trust Him to bring you through it.

Look to the Word to strengthen and encourage you. Pray for the Holy Spirit to surround you. Worship the Father who loves you.

You will make it. He's on your side.

For further reading: Isaiah 41:10, Romans 8, 2 Corinthians 4:8-9

DAY 168

"Those who trust in the LORD are like Mount Zion,
which cannot be shaken but endures forever" (Psalm 125:1).

Trust is hard to come by these days. We think we know others, but then they let us down, and we lose our faith in them. Trust lost is hard to regain. Sometimes we become distrustful of everyone.

If we open ourselves up to trust others, we make ourselves vulnerable. We put ourselves at risk of being hurt again. Instead, many of us put up walls, not allowing ourselves to get close to anyone, lest we have to suffer the pain of rejection or betrayal once again.

If we are not careful, we can allow that distrust to spill over into our relationship with God. We don't want to risk getting hurt, so we never really surrender all that we are to Him. We hold onto our hearts, our will, or our relationships, and we don't allow the Lord to penetrate those areas of our lives. We are afraid of letting go.

But this verse today tells us that those who trust in the Lord are like Mount Zion. Mount Zion represented the holy hill, Jerusalem, the City of God. The temple was there, where the very presence of God dwelt in the Old Testament. To the psalmist, Mount Zion represented the power and presence of God—His majesty, strength, glory, and splendor. It was secure, defended from all enemies, a place surrounded by God Himself.

And that is the image described of those who put their complete trust in the Lord. The Hebrew word for *trust* means "to trust in or have confidence in; to be bold, to be secure"[52] When our trust is in the Lord, we hold nothing back. We are all-in, surrendering everything to Him and trusting Him with every area of our lives.

We can trust Him, knowing that we are secure in Him. He will never let us down, never reject us, never betray us. In Him, we will never be shaken. Put your complete trust in the Lord today and allow Him to prove His love to you.

For further reading: Proverbs 3:5-6, Isaiah 30:15, John 14:1, Romans 15:13

DAY 169

"Those who sow in tears will reap with songs of joy. He who goes out weeping, carrying seeds to sow, will return with songs of joy, carrying sheaves with him" (Psalm 126:5-6).

This series of psalms (120-134) is known as the songs of ascent. They are songs that would have been sung by the Israelites as they made their yearly pilgrimage to Jerusalem for the Feast of Tabernacles. This song in particular is a celebration of returning from captivity back to the land of Zion.

For the Israelites, many had sown in tears, never knowing if they would return to their inheritance. We often sow many prayers for our friends and family who don't know the Lord. We don't know if they will ever receive salvation, but we continue to faithfully sow the Word into their lives, often with tears.

When the harvest comes, what a time of rejoicing! When our friends or loved ones return from captivity to sin and come to faith in the Lord, we celebrate with songs of joy.

Maybe you have been interceding for someone for a long time, and she is still bound, still being held captive by her sin. Don't give up! Though you sow in tears, you will reap with joy. Your prayers are not in vain. The witness and the Word that you sow into others' lives are bringing forth a harvest.

The Lord has seen each tear you have shed on her behalf, and He is working in her heart. Others have the right to choose whether or not they will answer His call, but you can trust that nothing you have sown into their lives is wasted.

Confess your faith in God to hear your prayers and work on their behalf. Continue to sow and trust God with the harvest. When the time comes, you will go forth with joy, celebrating what God has done!

For further reading: Acts 26:18, Romans 10:1, 1 Timothy 2:4, 2 Peter 3:9

DAY 170

"Unless the LORD builds the house, its builders labor in vain"
(Psalm 127:1a).

If you have a family, you have an enemy. The devil hates marriage and strong families. His weapon is division—divorce, strife, enmity, confusion, causing parents to feel judged for having family worship or putting their children in a Christian school or homeschooling them; that they are "old-fashioned" to only listen to Christian music or not allow certain movies or video games; that they are "too-sheltering" to keep their teens close to home and not allow them to go out and do whatever they want, whenever they want.

But Jesus is for marriage and home and family. Jesus wants husbands and wives to stay together. He wants to bless our children. He wants us to build our homes on His foundation. So I will fight for my family. I will use the weapons of warfare that God has given me, and I will stand my ground. Armed with truth coming out of my mouth, faith in what my God can do, prayer that agrees with God's Word, I will fight. You should, too.

So, what are some strategies for fighting this battle?

Pray over every room of your home. Walk around outside your house and pray for God's spiritual, emotional, social, and physical protection over your family. Make a list of Scriptures that you can confess over your spouse and children. Pray those verses aloud over your family. Pray together with your spouse and with your children. Have family dinner at the table as many nights of the week as possible. Read a devotional together and talk about it. Don't allow cell phones at the dinner table or the television to be on. Just be with each other. Connect emotionally with your children. Ask about their day and listen to them actively with your full attention.

Remember who the enemy is. When the devil seeks to bring division, be quick to recognize his tactics and join together in prayer rather than fighting one another. Satan is crafty. Be wise to his strategies to divide and conquer. Commit that nothing will come between you and your spouse or children.

Build your home on the foundation of Jesus, the Cornerstone.

For further reading: Exodus 20:12, Joshua 24:15, Proverbs 22:6, Ephesians 6:4, Colossians 3:13

DAY 171

*"You will eat the fruit of your labor; blessings
and prosperity will be yours" (Psalm 128:2).*

The Protestant work ethic flowed out of America's beginnings, when our forefathers came to this land for freedom to worship and to work. They knew that in order to prosper, they had to work the land and each man had to do his part. They started out with a communal garden, but quickly realized that the sin nature of man would lead some to be lazy while others toiled to produce food. So each family was given a plot of land on which to grow their own food. The early settlers soon learned the value of hard work and the consequence of laziness. As America grew under this work ethic, the land began to flourish and prosper.

In the natural, this process of sowing and reaping can be seen through seedtime and harvest and through the prosperity of capitalism, as America has grown and prospered under the Protestant work ethic. But just as that work ethic has waned over the years and socialism has become a buzzword, so too have we begun to grow lazy in spiritual things.

In the spirit realm, we also "eat the fruit of our labor." In other words, we reap the consequences of what we sow, whether for good or bad. If we grow weary in prayer, we will suffer the consequences. If we sow selfishness and pride, we will reap accordingly. We will indeed eat the fruit of our labor; therefore, we need to consider how we plow and what we sow. Do we put in the effort to fast, pray, and spend time with the Lord? Do we sow love and grace toward others? Are we putting down roots in the Word of God and sowing seeds in the lives of lost people around us?

I want to sow righteousness and reap eternal rewards. I want to do the hard work of prayer and making disciples. I long to see spiritual prosperity and blessings in my life. Just as hard work brings a paycheck and financial blessings, our efforts to build God's kingdom will bring payback.

What are you sowing today?

For further reading: Job 4:8, Hosea 8:7, Luke 6:38, 2 Corinthians 9:6, Galatians 6:7-10

DAY 172

"They have greatly oppressed me from my youth,
but they have not gained the victory over me" (Psalm 129:2).

From the time Israel became a nation, the people have been oppressed by their enemies. From the time you gave your life to Jesus, you have become a target of the enemy. Think about Jesus. The enemy tried to take Him out as a child when Herod put a bounty on the head of every boy under two in an effort to kill Him (Matthew 2). The enemy was threatened by the rise of King Jesus, and he is threatened by the Spirit of Christ in you.

Just as Jesus was constantly confronted by evil—tempted in the wilderness, provoked by the religious leaders, and eventually tortured and hung on a cross—we, too, have become the enemy of Satan. From the time you gave your life to Jesus, your enemy has sought to oppress you and cause you to stumble. He wants to ruin your witness or fill you with fear and doubt.

Israel has survived, Jesus has overcome, and so will you. Don't give in to the pressure to conform to the ways of the world or listen to the lies of the enemy. Jesus died for you to have victory over sin and Satan.

"Be self-controlled and alert. Your enemy the devil prowls around like a roaring lion looking for someone to devour. Resist him, standing firm in the faith, because you know that your brothers throughout the world are undergoing the same kind of sufferings" (1 Peter 5:8-9).

"Submit yourselves, then, to God. Resist the devil, and he will flee from you. Come near to God and he will come near to you" (James 4:7-8a).

Our victory is in Jesus. Both of these Scriptures tell us to resist the enemy. He was defeated at the cross, and he is defeated in you. Don't fall prey to his deception. You belong to Jesus.

"And having disarmed the powers and authorities, he made a public spectacle of them, triumphing over them by the cross" (Colossians 2:15).

You may have been opposed and oppressed since your youth, but praise God, you have the victory. Walk in it.

For further reading: Matthew 2, Colossians 2:15, James 4:7-8, 1 Peter 5:8-9

DAY 173

"I wait for the LORD, my soul waits, and in his word I put my hope"
(Psalm 130:5).

We all hate to wait. We want everything now, especially answers to our prayers. We know God is good. We know He has the power to answer. So why does He sometimes seem quiet, even though we are crying out to Him for answers?

I surely can't answer that question—I've asked it enough myself. But what I can tell you is that He is working when we are praying. We may not see it, but His Word tells us.

"Ask and it will be given to you; seek and you will find; knock and the door will be opened to you. For everyone who asks receives; he who seeks finds; and to him who knocks, the door will be opened" (Matthew 7:7).

We have to ask according to His will and His Word, so we must seek to know what pleases Him.

"...and find out what pleases the Lord" (Ephesians 5:10).

God wants to give good gifts to His children. Are we asking according to His pleasure or our own desires? How do we know what pleases the Lord? We learn His ways in His Word.

"If you remain in me and my words remain in you, ask whatever you wish, and it will be given you. This is to my Father's glory, that you bear much fruit, showing yourselves to be my disciples" (John 15:7-8).

While waiting can be so hard, if we are staying in the Word and seeking God's will, then we can pray and wait on the Lord to answer, knowing that He is at work. We stand on His promises and hope in His Word, and we can wait—our minds, will, and emotions at rest in Him.

What are you waiting to see God do in your life? Stay in His Word, pray according to His will, and wait on Him with hope.

For further reading: Isaiah 30:18, Matthew 7:7-12, John 15:7-8, Ephesians 5:10

DAY 174

"But I have stilled and quieted my soul; like a weaned child with its mother, like a weaned child is my soul within me" (Psalm 131:2).

Our soul is comprised of our minds, wills, and emotions. Most of the time, our minds are so busy, our emotions so frazzled, and we rarely have moments that our soul is quiet. Like the psalmist, we need to take time to still and quiet our souls before the Lord. What does it mean to be "Like a weaned child with its mother"?

Think about a baby still on the breast. When I was nursing my babies, they were hungry all the time. They couldn't be satisfied but instead wanted to nurse every couple of hours. There was little rest for either of us. When they were hungry, they were distressed, crying, and upset.

Once they were weaned, however, they were at rest. They trusted that if they needed to be fed, I would feed them. They didn't have to cry every few hours to get what they wanted. Instead, they knew how to drink from the cup I gave them and be satisfied. Oh, that we could trust God like that!

He wants us to come to Him and be at peace, resting in His presence, not striving, content in knowing that He will give us what we need. We can be satisfied with the cup that He gives us.

The secret for the psalmist was in having a humble heart (Psalm 131:1). He knew that if he humbled himself before the Lord, his needs would be met. He didn't concern himself with how the needs would be met. He just rested in the Lord and put his hope in Him.

Today, if you are frazzled, worried, or struggling to figure things out, know that God wants you to come to Him and quiet your soul like a weaned child with its mother. Rest in His capable arms, knowing that He cares enough to take care of you.

Be still and know that He is God (Psalm 46:10).

For further reading: Psalm 23:2, 46, Isaiah 30:15, Zephaniah 3:17, Mark 4:39

DAY 175

"May your priests be clothed with righteousness;
may your saints sing with joy" (Psalm 132:9).

In the Old Testament, priests carried out the functions of worship, sacrifice, and atonement for the sins of Israel. They were all Levites who were chosen by God to serve Him in the tabernacle and later in the temple. They were also called to sacrifice to the Lord on the Day of Atonement for the sins of all the people. The Bible teaches that Jesus is our Great High Priest. He alone was able through His sacrifice to make atonement for our sins once for all.

"And by that will, we have been made holy through the sacrifice of the body of Jesus Christ once for all" (Hebrews 10:10).

He serves as our Priest by making intercession for us.

"Therefore he is able to save completely those who come to God though him, because he always lives to intercede for them" (Hebrews 7:25).

Christians are also called to be priests.

"But you are a chosen people, a royal priesthood, a holy nation, a people belonging to God, that you may declare the praises of him who called you out of darkness and into his wonderful light" (1 Peter 2:9).

We are priests, the saints of God, and we have been called to clothe ourselves with His righteousness and sing for joy. The word *saint* comes from a Greek word meaning "faithful, kind, godly, holy one, pious."[53] Since we are priests of God and saints, we should carry ourselves with the anointing of a priest of God. This psalm was a prayer for the favor and anointing of God to be on those whom He has chosen.

Well, my friend, that's you and me. So, let's ask the Lord today to anoint us with favor and power to walk in His Spirit, to intercede for others, and to teach the truths of God's Word.

You're a saint.

For further reading: Leviticus 16, Hebrews 7-10, 1 Peter 2:9

DAY 176

"How good and pleasant it is when brothers live together in unity! It is like precious oil poured on the head, running down on the beard, running down on Aaron's beard, down upon the collar of his robes. It is as if the dew of Hermon were falling on Mount Zion. For there the LORD bestows his blessing, even life forevermore" (Psalm 133:1-3).

The Hebrew word translated *unity* in this passage is *yahad*, meaning "together, along with, in close proximity or concord either in space or time; by extension; close association in relationships."[54]

Unity brings anointing: The oil poured over Aaron the priest was to anoint him. It signified "his total consecration to holy service."[55] Without unity in the body of Christ, we lose the anointing of God to do the things He has called us to do. We can't have revival or impact our communities for God apart from his power and anointing.

Unity brings fruitfulness: *The NIV Study Bible* proclaims, "A dew as profuse as that of Mount Hermon would make Zion richly fruitful."[56] Unity brings life, growth, and fruitfulness. Without it, we can't have a fruitful ministry.

Unity brings blessings: "For there the Lord bestows his blessing" (Psalm 133:3b). Where there is unity, there is the blessing and favor of God, which are essential to do anything of value for the kingdom.

So what does unity look like? It's believing God and praying together in one accord—one heart, one mind, united in our purpose to see God's Kingdom come, His name glorified, His church revived, and His world reached with the gospel.

That's the kind of unity that will bring anointing, fruitfulness, and blessings on our lives.

For further reading: John 17:20-23, Ephesians 4:1-16, Colossians 3:14

DAY 177

"Praise the LORD, all you servants of the LORD who minister by night in the house of the LORD. Lift up your hands in the sanctuary and praise the LORD" (Psalm 134:1-2).

We already established a few days ago that as Christians, we are all called to be priests. A priest is a servant of God, called to minister in the house of the Lord.

Priests were responsible to carry out their duties both day and night. As we serve Him in our local churches, we need to be dedicated to the work He has called us to. Whether we are serving in the nursery, in the kitchen, in the classroom, or in the choir, we should be faithful to fulfill our duties.

Mother Teresa once said, "God didn't call me to successful. He called me to be faithful."

Are we being faithful to our commitments in the church?

When we lift our hands to the Lord in worship, we are signifying that we let go of control and surrender to Him. As we surrender, we give up our way of doing and being and we submit to God and His ways. I have often wondered as I sing "I Surrender All" if I should be singing "I Surrender Some."

Complete surrender to God and His ways is paramount to our being faithful. We struggle with faithfulness when we don't get our way or when we don't like someone else's ways. But when we surrender to the Lord and His will for our lives, we can be faithful to what He has called us to do because it's all for Him.

We don't serve for our own glory or to please others, but we do it for our Lord. When our hearts align in ministry with the Lord's heart for us, we can truly lift our hands to Him in surrender and praise the Lord!

For further reading: 1 Samuel 12:24, Luke 9:23-24, 16:10, Galatians 6:9, Colossians 3:23

DAY 178

"The idols of the nations are silver and gold,
made by the hands of men" (Psalm 135:15).

According to Kelly Minter in her book *No Other Gods,* anything we set our heart on, that motivates us in life, that controls us, or that we serve with our energy and resources, other than God is an idol.[57] As I studied her book, I came across this verse: "Even while these people were worshiping the Lord, they were serving their idols" (2 Kings 17:41).

Since becoming a Christ-follower, my heart's desire has been to have a family that lives for Jesus and represents Him well to the world. I have always wanted to be in full-time Christian ministry. But God is showing me that if I can't be content, peaceful, and joyful unless I can control those outcomes, then I have placed my hope in something other than Jesus. Worshiping the Lord—but serving my own desires.

You see, I can encourage my family to seek the Lord and raise them in a Christian environment, but as they become young adults, I can't control their choices any longer. They have to make decisions for themselves. I am learning to let go, stop trying to control, and trust God with my family. My hope has to be in Him and not in my dreams.

The same is true of having a Christian ministry. I love Jesus with all my heart, and I want to serve Him and tell others how good He is. I want to share the gospel and disciple others and intercede for them. But I can't let my idea of how that should look be greater than my trust in Him. I have to let go and let God have His way.

And I can't take the gifts He's given me and turn them into tools for my own glory. When the desire for ministry is greater than the desire to minister, I'm serving an idol, all while I keep worshiping my God.

I don't know where you are today. But if you, like me, have been worshiping God but still serving some idols of your own making, then perhaps it's time to lay it all down.

For further reading: Exodus 20:1-4, 2 Kings 17:41, Colossians 3:5, 1 John 5:21

DAY 179

"Give thanks to the LORD, for he is good. His love endures forever"
(Psalm 136:1).

When I started my jog this morning, I smelled smoke in the air. Kenneth had burned some brush the night before, and the pile was still smoldering. As I continued down the road, I noticed the sweet fragrance of honeysuckle, mingling with the smoke. Even among the weeds and brush that grow beside the road, I noticed tiny yellow and white blossoms—beauty in the midst of brush.

"Give thanks in all circumstances, for this is God's will for you in Christ Jesus" (1 Thessalonians 5:18).

I always thought of this Scripture as Superwoman level of spirituality—something to be attained at some point in my life, but I'm just not there yet. As I studied it a little more, I began to understand. *Joyful* can be translated "to rejoice, be glad, delighted."[58] The Hebrew for the word actually means "calmly happy."[59] We all know that inner joy isn't dependent upon circumstances, but it's still really difficult to laugh when we're going through a trial.

When we can maintain a sense of calm, even in the midst of trying times, we are being joyful always. Only the Holy Spirit can make us "calmly happy" in difficult circumstances. Maybe we can't pray all the time with words, but we can stay in an attitude of prayer and worship. This process will only come about for us as we seek the Lord and spend time in His presence. When I studied "in everything," I learned that it doesn't necessarily mean every individual thing, but being collectively grateful all the time—just an attitude of thankfulness to God no matter our circumstances.

So, whatever you may be going through today, just know that God is with you. You may not feel joyful, but you can thrive if you choose to seek Him, call on Him for help, and be grateful for His presence in your life. When life smells like smoke, find the honeysuckle. In the overgrowth of weeds, look for the blossoms.

For further reading: 1 Corinthians 15:57, Colossians 2:6-7, 1 Thessalonians 3:9, 5:16-18

DAY 180

"By the rivers of Babylon we sat and wept when we remembered Zion. There on the poplars we hung up our harps" (Psalm 137:1-2).

Have you ever felt as if you had no song left in you? You followed the path you thought was God, but somehow you ended up in a foreign land with no reason left to sing? Let me encourage you today that you still have a song in you.

I'll admit, things looked pretty dark for the Israelites. They had been overtaken by the Babylonians and forced into captivity. The Jews were literally in a foreign land. Remember their worship centered on the temple, which had been destroyed. When their tormentors asked them for "songs of joy," perhaps they were just taunting them. So the response of God's people was "If we can't worship God in the temple, and we can't be free in our own land, then we have no reason to sing the songs of Zion."

I understand the allegiance they felt to their native land and to the way of worship God had instituted through the temple. But their hearts were focused on what they had lost rather than on the God who gave them all they had. I'm sure after all the Israelites had been through—facing the slaughter of their family and friends, being taken captive, dwelling in a foreign land with no access to their place of worship—hanging up their harps sounded like a good idea.

When we give up our worship out of fear, discouragement, disappointment, or despair, we are actually revealing what is in our hearts. We've given up hope in our God. We've looked at our circumstances and forgotten that God is almighty, omniscient, all-powerful, sovereign, and supernatural! Just as He was able to lead the Israelites out of captivity and return them to their homeland, He can turn around our circumstances and use them for great good and for His glory in our lives.

Don't look at your circumstances. Look at the One Who is above your circumstances, and sing with all your heart. So go ahead, sister. Play that harp.

For further reading: Mark 12:30, 2 Corinthians 4:1-16, Colossians 2:2, Acts 16:16-40

DAY 181

*"I will praise you, O LORD, with all my heart; before
the 'gods' I will sing your praise" (Psalm 138:1).*

Even in the face of opposition and pagan gods, David was determined to worship and sing. David knew something that we don't always get: worship will lead us into the presence of God, where there is freedom, joy, and peace.

He didn't have it easy. He faced opposition from Saul and even his own sons. He spent a majority of his life on the run. Yet, he knew the secret of real joy and freedom: worship.

"I will bow down toward your holy temple and will praise your name for your love and faithfulness, for you have exalted above all things your name and your word. When I called, you answered me; you made me bold and stouthearted" (Psalm 138:2-3).

You see, we have two things that we can call on in the face of opposition: The name of Jesus and the Word of God. There is power in the name of Jesus to tear down strongholds and set the captive free. There is power in His Word when we confess it over our situation (Psalm 138:5-7).

And yes, our worship can be an awesome witness to those around us when they see that our hearts are on our mighty God. May even those who don't believe be drawn to "sing the ways of the LORD."

Here's the end of David's psalm:

"The LORD will fulfill his purpose for me; your love, O LORD, endures forever—do not abandon the works of your hands" (Psalm 138:8).

Praise God, He will not abandon us, but He will fulfill His purpose for us, no matter what life looks like today. So call on the name of Jesus and the power of His Word.

For further reading: 2 Chronicles 20, Isaiah 35, Acts 16:16-40

DAY 182

*"You know when I sit and when I rise; you
perceive my thoughts from afar" (Psalm 139:2).*

You are known. To some, that can be a scary thought, but to others, it's very comforting. To be known means that God created you and He knows you intimately. He knows the number of hairs on your head (Matthew 10:30). He knows your thoughts. He knows your words before you even speak them (Psalm 139:4). And He loves you still.

In John 10, we learn that Jesus is the Good Shepherd who knows His sheep. "I am the good shepherd; I know my sheep and my sheep know me" (14).

Jesus chose to lay down His life for us. "I am the good shepherd. The good shepherd lays down his life for the sheep" (11). "No one takes it from me, but I lay it down of my own accord" (18a).

Fully known. Fully loved.

"But God demonstrates his own love for us in this: While we were still sinners, Christ died for us" (Romans 5:8).

There's no need to run and hide from God because He knows our deepest, darkest, vilest sin, and still chose to die for us. That's what it means to be known. That's what it means to be loved.

Our lives are valuable to God, not only because He knit us together in our mothers' wombs, but also because we are made in His image and made to know and love Him back. Everything God has done in sending Jesus to die for us has been so that we could know Him in return.

God is holy. But through Jesus we can know Him. Personally. Intimately. Relationally. Fully.

"Now we see but a poor reflection as in a mirror; then we shall see face to face. Now I know in part; then I shall know fully, even as I am fully know" (1 Corinthians 13:12).

Fully known. Fully loved. That's who you are.

For further reading: Matthew 10:30, John 10, Romans 5:8, 1 Corinthians 13:12

DAY 183

"Search me, O God, and know my heart; test me and know my anxious thoughts. See if there is any offensive way in me, and lead me in the way everlasting" (Psalm 139:23-24).

The truth is we don't really know what is in our hearts. Jeremiah told us so:

"The heart is deceitful above all things and beyond cure. Who can understand it?" (Psalm 139:17:9).

We want to love God with all our hearts, but our hearts can betray us and be easily led astray. God knows what is in our hearts at all times, though. We can ask Him, as David did, to search our hearts. I often hear people pray a blanket prayer of confession. Something like this: "Lord, please forgive me for all my sins."

I know the Lord hears our prayers for forgiveness, but I think true repentance (turning away from our sins) requires acknowledging our specific sins. Since we may have blind spots about some of the sin in our lives, it's a good practice to daily ask God to search our hearts and show us our sin. Only then can we truly repent and turn away from it.

Do you want to know and love God with all your heart? Are you serious about repentance and purity in your life? The more we seek God, the more we will want to love Him with all our hearts. The more we love Him, the more we will seek purity and holiness. God knows us better than we know ourselves. We can start each day asking God to show us our sin, reveal to us what is in our hearts, and give us the desire to turn away.

The Holy Spirit can reveal to us the things that are offensive to Him. He has the power to lead us in what is right and true and everlasting. What a privilege to have the power and presence of the Holy Spirit in our lives to lead and guide us, to convict and correct us, and to know and search us!

For further reading: Jeremiah 17:9, Matthew 22:37, 2 Corinthians 13:5, Galatians 6:3-5

DAY 184

*"I know that the LORD secures justice for the poor
and upholds the cause of the needy" (Psalm 140:12).*

We often look around at those who suffer and wonder why God allows such injustice on the earth. It's hard to watch other people go through starvation, persecution, and disaster. Yet we know our God is good.

In times of intense suffering, we can remember two things: God loves us enough to give us free will, and God is just.

Because God loves us, He has given us the freedom to choose right and wrong. Nobody forces us to serve God; likewise, no one forces us to choose evil. Sin entered this world through the first man and woman, who were given the freedom to choose. And mankind has been choosing ever since.

Some people will choose to follow the way of evil. Bad things happen in this world. That's a given, but our God is just. He will not let the evil go unpunished or the suffering go unheeded.

Our God will bring justice to those who are poor and needy. Those who are evil will face eternal punishment for their sin. Those who are suffering will have every wrong made right.

Our response to the suffering we see in this world is to pray and then to take action. God often chooses to meet needs in this world through us. Where we see hurting people, we can choose to act. We can feed the hungry, clothe the naked, and stand up for the rights of those who are abused and persecuted.

So, the next time you see suffering and wonder where God is, look in the mirror. He wants to use *you* to be His hands and feet in this world. Instead of questioning God's intentions, ask Him how He wants you respond.

Then go and make a difference in Jesus' name.

For further reading: Genesis 3, Deuteronomy 30:19, Joshua 24:15, John 7:17

DAY 185

"Set a guard over my mouth, O LORD; keep watch over the door of my lips" (Psalm 141:3).

Nothing can cause us to sin quite like our two lips. James said if we could control our mouths, we would be perfect (James 3:2). The fact is that if we have the self-control it takes to keep our mouths in check, we would have what it takes to control every area of sin in our lives.

"The tongue also is a fire, a world of evil among the parts of the body. It corrupts the whole person, sets the whole course of his life on fire, and is itself set on fire by hell" (James 3:6).

We can use our lips to praise God, and then turn around and curse people (James 3:9). We can use our mouths to lie, curse, complain, or criticize. We can be negative, hateful, or boastful. The mouth can start wars, ruin relationships, and destroy lives.

It's that powerful.

How seriously, then, should we take the command to watch our mouths?

"Do not let any unwholesome talk come out of your mouths, but only what is helpful for building others up according to their needs, that it may benefit those who listen" (Ephesians 4:29).

We have the responsibility to control our tongues, but we need the Holy Spirit to empower us to do so. We can begin by praying a prayer like David did, asking the Lord to guard our lips each day. Then we need to exercise the self-discipline to keep our tongues from evil speech.

Ephesians tells us to not only stop speaking what is unwholesome, but also to start speaking what is helpful. Ask the Lord to give you speech that is holy and helpful to those around you. The more we focus on what is good, the more God will help us avoid what is evil.

Guard your tongue today.

For further reading: Matthew 12:34-37, Ephesians 4:29, James 1:26, 3:1-12

DAY 186

"I pour out my complaint before him; before him I tell my trouble"
(Psalm 142:2).

Yesterday we looked at the power of the tongue to cause us to sin. One way our mouths cause us to sin is by complaining. When we complain, we focus on what is negative in our lives. Then we spread that negativity to others.

We learned that we can ask God to guard our lips, but we also have to take steps to exercise self-control. Another way we can do that is by pouring out our complaints to the Lord.

We all have problems that we could choose to focus on, becoming negative and bitter. If we choose to dwell on those thoughts, we will voice our complaints to those around us, spreading the poison of discontent.

Rather than spreading our complaining spirit, we can go to the Lord. We can tell Him what's on our hearts and ask Him to show us the way. In this psalm, David wasn't complaining to the Lord because he was disappointed with God as the Israelites did in the Old Testament.

When they complained and became bitter towards the Lord for their problems, God sent snakes into their camp as punishment. They were ungrateful for all God had done (Numbers 21:4-9).

Instead, David was voicing to God his complaint over those who were seeking his life. Rather than taking matters into his own hands, he prayed and turned to God for help, seeking the Lord's way rather than his own.

Surely we will have circumstances in our lives that cause us to want to complain, but rather than voice our complaints to others, we can take our problems to the Lord in prayer—not blaming Him, but trusting Him with our needs.

What difficulties are you facing today? Tell it to Jesus alone.

For further reading: Numbers 21:4-9, Philippians 2:14, 1 Peter 4:9, Jude 16

DAY 187

*"Let the morning bring me word of your unfailing love,
for I have put my trust in you. Show me the way I
should go, for to you I lift up my soul" (Psalm 143:8).*

Mornings, right before the dawn, hold such promise and freshness. No matter what we are going through, tomorrow has the potential to be a better day (Lamentations 3:22-23).

God is so tender and merciful toward us. That's what compassion means. His heart is for us. Every time the sun comes up, we experience new mercies, fresh compassion, renewed hope. God is true and faithful, and His love towards us is unfathomable, without question, and unconditional.

When we awake to a new day, we have the opportunity to seek Him first. We can begin each day with God as our priority. Time spent with Him is never wasted; in fact, it will make our day more productive. When we choose to put God first and spent time in His presence, He gives us an eternal perspective that can renew our hope and make even the darkest day seem brighter.

We can begin each day with the Lord, seeking His presence through worship, prayer, and His Word. As we do, He will show us the way we should go. He will teach us how to prioritize our day and give us hope and strength for whatever we face. When we choose to go about our business and not seek Him first, we are showing where our priorities lie. We are putting our trust in ourselves instead of in our God. David knew that no matter what he faced in life, he was better off trusting God and seeking His ways.

What about you?

We all have the same twenty-four hours, and we each have a choice in how we start them. Will you start your day with God and trust Him with your plans? The mornings can bring you word of His unfailing love, if you let them.

For further reading: Lamentations 3:22-23, Psalm 5:8, Matthew 6:35, Mark 1:35

DAY 188

"Praise be to the LORD my Rock, who trains my hands for war, my fingers for battle" (Psalm 144:1).

If you are serving Jesus, you are either in a battle, coming out of a battle, or heading into a battle. So you better be learning how to fight your battles the Lord's way! The best way to handle the challenges we face in life is with God as our Rock.

"Therefore everyone who hears these words of mine and puts them into practice is like a wise man who built his house on the rock. The rain came down, the streams rose, and the winds blew and beat against that house; yet it did not fall, because it had its foundation on the rock" (Matthew 7:24-25).

We are still in the midst of Hurricane Florence as I write this. Our power just came back on after a long, hot night and half a day. As I look out my window, the rain is still coming down, the floodwaters are still rising, and the wind is still blowing and beating against our house.

Some of you are in the midst of battles just like that. This hurricane, unlike ones we've weathered in the past, is a slow mover. We've been pelted with wind and rain for over twenty-four hours, and she's still not finished. Sometimes it seems our battles will never end. The good news is that if you have built your faith on the Rock of Jesus Christ, you will be able to stand. God trains our hands for war through His Word. With our faith firmly grounded in Him and our hands trained for battle, we can go forth into our battlefield, armed and ready.

Even if the battle seems to linger, we have spiritual armor to help us stand. Stay in the Word. Stay in prayer. Stay in praise. Stay in obedience. Let God teach you how to fight His way. Remember that Jesus said we have to put His Word into practice. It's not enough just to know what the Bible says—we have to walk in it. Whether you are coming out of a battle, in a battle, or headed towards a battle, know that God will train you to fight if you will build your life on Him.

For further reading: Matthew 7:24-25, 2 Corinthians 10:3-6, Ephesians 6, 1 John 4:4

DAY 189

"The LORD is gracious and compassionate,
slow to anger and rich in love" (Psalm 145:8).

When I was growing up, I didn't know God. I wasn't in church or familiar with God and His ways. Consequently, I didn't understand the grace and compassion of God. I only understood Him to be harsh and cruel. I thought that He just had a bunch of rules for me to follow that would cause me to be miserable. Since surrendering my life to Jesus, I have found the opposite to be true. See, I spent the first part of my life as a people pleaser. I was under the impression that I had to do something to earn other people's love. I never felt that I quite measured up. As a result, I transferred that understanding to God

When I finally gave my life to Jesus and began to understand His Word, I was set free from people-pleasing. I have come to know God as One who is gracious and compassionate to me. He sees my sin, which He hates because it brings pain to my life. But He looks beyond that to see me, and He loves me. I have learned to understand that He is a God of justice who does not turn a blind eye to sin, but for those who are in Christ, He is slow to anger and rich in love. Because I feel secure in His love, I am free to love Him back through my obedience. Following Him no longer seems burdensome. I obey out of love rather than a fear of retribution.

The truth is that I could never measure up to God's standard of holiness. He is God, and His standard is perfection. His grace is not a license to sin, but neither is His standard something I can't attain. Through Him I am free from all of that. Instead, I follow the One who loves me and I love Him back. When I mess up, I go to Him for forgiveness and correction, secure in His love for me. And I no longer feel the need to try to please others, because I am pleasing to my Father—not because of who I am, but because of who Jesus is in me.

Do you struggle with feelings of insecurity or not measuring up to the expectations of others? Find your security in your relationship with God through His Son Jesus. You don't have to please others when you are seeking to please God. And He is rich in love towards you.

For further reading: John 15, Galatians 2:20, 1 John 3:1, 5:3

DAY 190

*"I will praise the LORD all my life; I will sing
praise to my God as long as I live" (Psalm 146:2).*

Commitments don't mean much anymore. Contracts can be dissolved. Agreements can be dismissed. Marriages can be broken. Promises can be ignored. But if we truly put our trust in the Lord, we are not turning back. Those who fall away never really trusted in Him in the first place. If we truly have a heart for God, we will worship Him as long as we live. I often see people who were once active in church, serving and showing up on a regular basis. But then something happened and they walked away from it all, turned back to their former ways, and never darkened the doors of a church again.

Jesus talked about the seed of the Word falling on different types of soil, which represents the heart. He said that some hear the Word but don't understand it. 1 Peter 2:3 tells us that we have to grow up in the Word by learning, studying, and obeying it. If we don't, the evil one comes and snatches away what was sown (Matthew 13:18).

Then Jesus said there are those who hear the Word and receive it with joy, but they have no roots, so they only last a short time (Matthew 13:20-21). Colossians 2:7 says that when we receive Jesus, we have to "continue to live in him, rooted and built up in him, strengthened in the faith."

Jesus also said that sometimes the Word would be choked out by the worries of life and deceitfulness of wealth, making it unfruitful (Matthew 13:22). Those are the hearts that don't put Jesus and His Word first.

Only those who truly understand who Jesus is will produce fruit for Him. They aren't playing church or looking for a get-out-of-hell card. They are sincerely seeking the ways of the Lord and are committed to following Him all the days of their lives. Real commitments aren't broken. True relationships aren't dissolved. If you have surrendered your life to Jesus, it's for keeps. He's not turning His back on you. And if you truly love Him, you aren't turning your back on Him.

For further reading: Matthew 13, Colossians 2:7, 1 Peter 2:3

DAY 191

*"He determines the number of the stars
and calls them each by name" (Psalm 147:4).*

It's hard for us to fathom just how tremendous the universe really is. In the scope of all eternity, we are a tiny blip in time. In the realm of all creation, we are just a speck here on earth.

Yet we serve a God who knows the number of stars in the universe and calls them each by name. How crazy is that?

It is estimated that there are somewhere around 100 billion stars just in the Milky Way galaxy.[60] The Hubble estimates 100 billion galaxies in the universe.[61] My brain can't even compute that kind of math.

Then we read Scriptures such as this one, telling us that God knows each of them by name. How much more then, does He know us?

"Lift your eyes and look to the heavens: Who created all these? He who brings out the starry host one by one, and calls them each by name. Because of his great power and mighty strength, not one of them is missing" (Isaiah 40:26).

"When I consider your heavens, the work of your fingers, the moon and the stars, which you have set in place, what is man that you are mindful of him, the son of man that you care for him?" (Psalm 8:3-4).

God not only created all this vast beauty, but He created you and me in His image and called us to rule over all He created (Psalm 8:5-8).

He gave humanity alone the ability to think, to reason, to develop language, and to be saved. We were created to know and love Him in a way no other creation can.

And He knows you by name.

Nothing about you has escaped His eyes. You are not just noticed. You are seen. You are called. You are loved. You are known.

For further reading: Psalm 8, Isaiah 40:26, Matthew 10:30

DAY 192

"Let them praise the name of the LORD, for his name alone is exalted; his splendor is above the earth and the heavens. He has raised up for his people a horn, the praise of all his saints, of Israel, the people close to his heart. Praise the LORD" (Psalm 148:13-14).

I love the nature psalms—probably because I love nature. I love to be outside, to take walks in the woods, to sit on the beach, to hike a mountain trail. I delight in simple things—butterflies, weeds with tiny flowers, a star-filled night, a huge harvest moon. We humans thrill at using a camera or a paintbrush to capture a moment of the spectacular in nature. We were made in the image of our Creator with hearts that beat to create, yet the most we can do is imitate the beauty of our God. All creation on earth praises Him, along with all the heavenly hosts. We were all created to worship God and bring Him glory. That's why Christians don't worship created things—we worship the Creator in all of His magnificence.

And we praise Him because He has raised up for his people a horn. The word *horn* means "the Lord's anointed," referring to the Christ.[62] The Father sent His Son to this earth, to walk where we walk, to feel what we feel, to live as we live, yet to overcome sin and death for our sake.

My daughter-in-law recently visited Israel with a group of college students. As she recounted her experiences with us, she shared how visiting the places Jesus walked was significant and meaningful, but nothing moved her as much as the time she spent worshiping together with the others on the trip. It wasn't the sites—the Mount of Olives, the Jordan River, or the Upper Room that caused her heart to erupt in worship. But when she joined hearts with other students—strangers before, but now one in Christ—her heart was poured out in love and devotion to her Creator. That's what moved her heart.

As you praise the Lord today for all the beauty you see in nature, don't forget to praise Him for the greatest gift of all—salvation through His Son.

For further reading: Romans 1:20, 8:19-22, 2 Corinthians 5:17, Colossians 3:10

DAY 193

"Praise the LORD. Sing to the LORD a new song, his praise in the assembly of the saints" (Psalm 149:1).

Have you ever thought about the fact that a new song is one no one has ever sung before? Okay, I guess that's a no-brainer, but when you think about it, it's rather amazing. A new song is a creative expression of an inner voice, an emotion, a longing, a passion for something.

Moses burst into song after the Israelites were led out of Egypt and through the Red Sea on dry ground. Can you imagine the miracle he had just witnessed? Moses couldn't contain his praise and celebration over all that Yahweh had done. Think of all his struggles with God, with Pharaoh, and with the Israelites up to that point. Moses was so in awe of the works of God. As he shared his song, Miriam was inspired to join him in praise. His worship was contagious.

David, too, sang a new song (Psalm 40:1-3). David cried out to the Lord from the pit of despair and God heard Him. He lifted him up and settled him down, and David couldn't help but praise Him. Because David sang a new song, others put their trust in God, too. His worship was a witness. Several times the psalmists call forth new songs from the hearts of God's people.

I find it interesting that there are numerous Scriptures about singing songs, and then there are a few that pertain to singing a *new* song. I think God knows that we love to keep singing the old songs that touch our hearts, but we sometimes need a new song.

Sometimes we are crying out from the pit and other times we are in awe of His presence *in* the pit, Regardless, God just brings a new song to our hearts that allows us to worship from a new place. Can you remember the first time you heard a particular song that came at just the right moment to express what was in your heart? That's the power of a new song. It really doesn't matter if you sing an old song or a new song, as you express the cry of your heart to God, your praise is contagious. And your worship is a witness.

For further reading: Exodus 15, Psalm 40, 96:1, 98:1

DAY 194

"Let everything that has breath praise the LORD. Praise the LORD (Psalm 150:6).

As we come to the end of the psalms, I find it so fitting that we began Psalm 1 with instructions about how to follow the ways of God and not the world. We end the psalms with instructions to praise Him.

- We praise Him in the sanctuary.

- We praise Him for His power and greatness.

- We praise Him with music and dancing.

- We praise Him with as long as we have breath.

Friend, if your heart seeks after the things of God and not the ways of the world, you will soon find that you can't help but praise Him. You won't be able to contain your praise. The more you know Him, the more you will love Him. The more you witness His power and provision and presence in your life, the more you will want to praise Him.

You will praise Him in the sanctuary, and you won't care who sees your lifted hands or hears your off-key voice. You will praise Him for His power and greatness, even when your prayers don't get answered the way you want. You will praise Him in your home, on your job, in your church, and everywhere you go. You will have to do a little jig every now and then because you can't be still when you think about how good He is.

Sister, you will praise Him with every breath. Because when you delight yourself in the Lord, He will give you the desires of your heart. As you meditate on His Word, He will show you rich and beautiful treasures of truth. When you are satisfied in Him, nothing can move you. That's why we worship.

So, let your praises out today. Don't let anything hold you back. Let everything that has breath praise the Lord!

For further reading: Deuteronomy 10:21, 1 Chronicles 16:35, Psalm 8:2, Ephesians 1:3, 1 Peter 4:11

DAY 195

*"The fear of the LORD is the beginning of knowledge,
but fools despise wisdom and discipline" (Proverbs 1:7).*

As we begin our journey through the Proverbs, we start with a truth that is similar to Psalm 1. It's also a truth that will be repeated often in this book: true wisdom is found in God and His Word, not in the world. As we look at Hebrew poetry, we must remember that it is characterized by parallelism. In Proverbs we will often see this poetic structure: A truth stated and then repeated as its opposite, as in the verse above.

Sometimes the best way to learn something is by knowing both what it is and what it is not. We will also see much repetition, but as a teacher I can attest to the fact that repetition is how we learn. Wisdom is to fear the Lord; despising wisdom is foolish. To fear the Lord means to have a reverential awe and respect for God and His ways. The *NIV Study Bible* defines the fear of the Lord as "a loving reverence for God that includes submission to his lordship and to the commands of his word."[63]

Paul affirms the truth of Proverbs in 1 Corinthians where he tells us that the "message of the cross is foolishness to those who are perishing, but to us who are being saved it is the power of God" (1:18). This philosophy is probably a good place for us to start. There are many highly intelligent people in this world, to whom God has given great understanding, yet they are fools because they reject Him.

We place much value on education, but all the degrees in the world can't compare with the wisdom of knowing God and His ways. Paul goes on in 1 Corinthians to tell us that some things are only spiritually discerned. In other words, no matter how much worldly wisdom we have, we won't understand the ways of God unless we have the Spirit of God within us. So, our search for wisdom is actually a search for God. God is wisdom. There is no true wisdom apart from His Spirit. The book of Proverbs is full of God's wisdom, guidance, and instruction for life. It's a very practical book with instructions for how we should handle everyday life—family, finances, friendships, parenting, business, ministry, and so on. We all need more wisdom. The choices we have to make every day demand it. And God has it.

For further reading: Romans 11:33-36, 1 Corinthians 1:18-25, Ephesians 1:17, Colossians 2:3, James 1:5

DAY 196

"The Proverbs of Solomon son of David, king of Israel:
for attaining wisdom and discipline" (Proverbs 1:2a).

Most of us cringe when we hear the word *discipline*. We tend to have a negative view of it, thinking of punishment, or at the very least, a lifestyle that is difficult to maintain.

The word *discipline* in this verse means "discipline, instruction, correction." It can also mean "wisdom and teaching that imply correcting errant behavior."[64] The book of Proverbs contains instruction for how to live our lives God's way. These are words of instruction that are meant to be followed.

They are also words of correction, so if we are convicted when we read them, that's good! We are learning and growing into what God wants us to be. When we read something that convicts us, it should be an encouragement that God loves us and only wants what is best for us.

"Endure hardship as discipline; God is treating you as sons. For what son is not disciplined by his father? If you are not disciplined (and everyone undergoes discipline), then you are illegitimate children and not true sons. Moreover, we have all had human fathers who disciplined us and we respected them for it. How much more should we submit to the Father of our spirits and live!" (Hebrews 12:7-9).

When we are corrected and disciplined by God's Word, we are being treated as His children. Just as we discipline our children for their good, God disciplines us because He loves us.

Let the correction and reproof fall on a soft heart. Don't harden your heart to His discipline. Let His Word draw you to Him with grace and truth. Yes, sometimes discipline hurts, but that's how we learn and how we grow.

We need God's wisdom and God's discipline to make good decisions in life. Let's surrender to both.

For further reading: 1 Corinthians 11:31-32, 2 Thessalonians 1:4-5, Hebrews 12:7-9, Revelation 3:19

DAY 197

"...for acquiring a disciplined and prudent life,
doing what is right and just and fair" (Proverbs 1:3).

If we want to understand what it means to "acquire a disciplined and prudent life," we need to understand the meaning of *prudent*. To be honest, I never really understood this word correctly.

The word in Hebrew means "to have success; to have insight, wisdom, understanding; to prosper, successful; the potent capacity to understand and so exercise skill in life, a state caused by proper training and teaching, enhanced by careful observation."[65]

All the books and degrees and education in the world can't give us the insight and understanding we need to follow God and make good decisions. Notice that to be prudent is not to just know what it takes to have success, but to be successful. It's not just having the capacity to understand, but also exercising those skills. In other words, a truly disciplined and prudent life is not that of one who knows the Word, but of one who puts it into practice.

"Do not merely listen to the word, and so deceive yourselves. Do what it says. Anyone who listens to the word but does not do what it says is like a man who looks at his face in a mirror and, after looking at himself, goes away and immediately forget what he looks like" (James 1:22-24).

As we study God's Word and see where we fall short, we need to make a change. Proverbs is the perfect book for helping us to do that.

So, as we continue in the introduction to this book, let's remember this: We need to seek God's wisdom as found in His Word. We need to receive His discipline, even when it hurts. And when we learn what is right, we need to put it into practice.

If we are going to follow the ways of God, we have to be constant learners. After all, that's what being a disciple is all about. Let's ask the Holy Spirit to give us teachable hearts today.

For further reading: Proverbs 15:5, Matthew 7:24-27, James 1:22-24, 2 John 9

DAY 198

*"...for giving prudence to the simple, knowledge
and discretion to the young—"(Proverbs 1:4).*

Have you ever met people who are really naïve and simple? They will believe anything you tell them. They aren't well-acquainted with the ways of the world. Those who prey on the simple will take advantage of their vulnerability. When our children are young, we want them to be innocent and pure, but we also try to teach them how to be wise and not swayed by evil.

When Jesus sent the disciples out two by two on a missionary journey, He told them to be "shrewd as snakes and as innocent as doves" (Matthew 10:16b).

Shrewd means to be "wise and sensible."[66] *Innocent* means to be "pure, not mixed with evil."[67] We need to have a healthy combination of both, and Proverbs teaches us how.

We already learned that *prudence* means understanding what it takes to be successful and putting it into practice. That takes maturity. Now, let's look at *discretion*, which means "scheme, plan, purpose, intent."[68] It comes from the word *discreet*, meaning "discernment or judgment."[69] Taken together, we see that these proverbs are helpful for teaching us how to be purposeful, intentional, and discerning—good qualities to have when dealing with the world.

We can see why Jesus told His disciples they would need a healthy dose of both common sense and good judgment. We may not be of the world, but we still have to live in the world. As we do, whether in business, education, parenting, marriage, or ministry, we will need to learn how to be innocent of wrong but not blind to it. We need to be wise to evil but not accepting of it.

So, as we begin each day in the Proverbs over the next few weeks, we have some characteristics to keep in mind: wisdom, discipline, prudence, and discretion. May we learn the meaning of each and how to apply them to our lives.

For further reading: 1 Chronicles 22:11-12, Proverbs 5:1-2, Matthew 10:16b, Romans 16:19

DAY 199

*"Listen, my son, to your father's instruction and
do not forsake your mother's teaching" (Proverbs 1:8).*

Solomon, who wrote these proverbs to his son, was the wisest man who ever lived apart from Jesus. God granted him whatever he asked for, and Solomon asked for wisdom (1 Kings 4:29-34). He then passed these instructions on to his son.

You may not have had godly parents. Or you may be struggling to be a godly parent. In either case, what a blessing that we have God's Word and these nuggets of wisdom in the Proverbs to live our lives by and to teach our children or the young people in our lives!

Solomon shared with his son a warning not to be led astray by so-called friends who would draw him into sin. He told his son not to give in to their enticement to follow them. He warned that following this crowd into evil would end in destruction, taking away the lives of those who seek after such things.

We can easily get caught up in following the wrong crowd. We want to be liked and accepted. We all desire friendships and connections. But to spend much time with those who don't share our values can be dangerous. Of course, we should befriend lost people in order to connect with them and share the love of Jesus with them. Those relationships should be kept at a level of association and conversation, but never taken into deep trust to the point that we begin to follow their culture and way of thinking.

Solomon warned his son not to follow the way of sinners, or he would be led astray into sin along with them. We, too, need to guard our hearts and our relationships. If we spend much time with those whose values don't align with God's Word, we can easily begin to compromise our beliefs for the sake of being liked and valued by them. We know this to be true for young people, but it is equally true for each of us. Let's ask God to give us Spirit-filled women to spend time with so that we can encourage one another to follow Him.

For further reading: 1 Kings 4:29-34, 1 Corinthians 15:33, 2 Corinthians 6:14, James 4:4

DAY 200

"For the LORD gives wisdom, and from his mouth
come knowledge and understanding" (Proverbs 2:6).

We can read entire libraries of books, search the internet, or watch Oprah, Dr. Phil, or Dr. Oz, but no where will we find true wisdom apart from God and His Word. He is the final authority on every topic we can think of. If we need truth, guidance, or direction, we can find it in God's Word. God's wisdom can be found in His Word. He calls us to search it out, to dig for it like hidden treasure.

"...if you call out for insight and cry out for understanding, and if you look for it as for silver and search for it as for hidden treasure, then you will understand the fear of the LORD and find the knowledge of God" (Proverbs 2:3-4).

If someone told us there was silver buried in our backyard worth millions, we would be out there right now with a shovel, digging for all we are worth to get to that treasure. But God tells us in His Word that His wisdom is a treasure worth far more. Imagine if we spent as much effort looking for truth in God's Word as we spend trying to gain money, status, or material things. Sometimes the world and all its stuff just seem more appealing to us than spending time in the Bible.

Don't believe the lies of the enemy. Get into God's Word. Get a hi-lighter or a pencil and start marking it up. Get a notebook and write down what God is showing you. If you are struggling with a particular area in your life, look that word up in a Bible concordance. A concordance will show you every verse in the Bible that contains that word.

For instance, if you are struggling with anger, look up all the Scriptures containing that word. Go back several verses or chapters and read the entire context of that Scripture. Ask God to show you His truth and how you can apply it in your life. Use the notebook to keep track of all the treasures of wisdom God is revealing to you. The more time we spend in God's Word, the more wisdom He imparts for our lives.

That's worth all the treasure in the world. So start digging!

For further reading: Matthew 6:19-21, 13:52, 2 Corinthians 4:7, Colossians 2:3

DAY 201

"Then you will understand what is right and just and fair—every good path" (Proverbs 2:9).

We all struggle from time to time with knowing what is right in any situation. We all want life to be fair and just. The truth is that life isn't always fair—but God is.

We can trust Him to be right and just and fair in every area of our lives. He will also show us how to be right and just and fair in our relationships with others and in the paths we choose.

Have you ever thought about how many decisions you make in a day? Various sources estimate that we make an average of 35,000 choices every day. That makes me tired just thinking about it! Imagine that every choice we make leads us down a particular path in life. How we choose affects our destiny.

Are you facing some difficult decisions now, my sister? Don't despair. Turn to God and His Word. Pray for the Holy Spirit to guide you with His peace. Know that God is for you (Romans 8:31) and has great plans for your life (Jeremiah 29:11).

There is a good path for you.

God's wisdom will lead you down the right path as you trust in Him (Proverbs 2:10). God's wisdom will protect you and guard you from the wrong path (Proverbs 2:11). His truth will save you from the wrong people and the temptation to go astray (Proverbs 2:12-13).

Trust God and His wisdom. Don't look to the world or to your lost friends for advice. Wisdom will lead you to make the right decisions and follow the path God has for you.

Seek Him now.

For further reading: Psalm 16:11, Jeremiah 29:11-13, Luke 1:79, Romans 8:31

DAY 202

"My son, do not forget my teaching, but keep my commands in your heart" (Proverbs 3:1).

Our heart is the seat of our emotions but to the Israelites, it also represented the mind, the character, and the motives of a person. Our sinful nature will always seek the selfish way or the easy way, so we need God's truth in our hearts to seek His way.

Solomon told his son to keep God's commands in his heart—the place of his thoughts and desires and attitudes. Often we think that as long as we aren't hurting someone else, it doesn't really matter what we think or what our inward life is like.

But God looks at our hearts, our moral character, our motives and attitudes. Only by keeping His Word in our hearts can we reflect His character to a watching world. What's in our hearts and on our minds will come out eventually in our words and actions.

I know sometimes in my life, I get confused or distracted. I love that Proverbs is so practical in how we are to live. In Proverbs chapter 3, we are told to do several things that we can apply to our lives:

Study the Word and keep it in our hearts. Be loving and faithful. Trust God. Don't be wise in our own eyes. Honor the Lord with our wealth. Submit to God's discipline. Don't withhold good from someone if it's in your power to act.

All these commands are straightforward. They may not all be easy to do, but they are easy to understand. Let's ask God today to help us put these truths into practice in our lives. God sees our inward moral character. But, really, so does the world.

For further reading: 1 Samuel 16:7, 1 Chronicles 28:9, James 4:3, Hebrews 4:12

DAY 203

*"Trust the LORD with all your heart and lean
not on your own understanding" (Proverbs 3:5).*

There's a reason we're not to lean on our own understanding. What you and I understand is deeply flawed and incomplete. We like to think we know it all (at least I do), but the truth is that we know very little compared to God's vast knowledge. This verse is a great sound bite until we realize that we have to give up control in order to trust God. Leaning on our own understanding is a lot like trying to protect our children. We would move heaven and earth to protect our babies, because we think we know what is best for them.

Sometimes we can hold on too tightly, though, and try to control their lives. We don't want them to make bad choices or go down the wrong path, so we do our best to make them go the way we want them to. That's okay when they are little, but when they get older, we have to trust the Lord with them. Sometimes letting them make mistakes is the best way for them to learn. Our desire to control is linked to our love for them. We want what is best for them, but true love will let go and let them make their own choices once they are old enough to do so.

We sometimes lean on our own understanding when our prayers don't get answered the way we think they should. We question and doubt God, but maybe we should realize that our own understanding of things is so limited. God sees beyond what we see. He is able to do so much more when we let go and trust Him.

To trust means "to rely on, put confidence in, to be confident, to lead to believe, make trust."[70] As Christian women, will we put our trust in God rather than our own understanding? Will we rely on the Lord and put our confidence in His way as opposed to our own way? Will we be led to believe that God's way is the best way, no matter how we may perceive things?

Put your trust completely in God today. He holds your life in His hands. No matter how things appear, don't lean on your own understanding. Be confident in your God.

For further reading: Psalm 112:7, Isaiah 26:3, 55:8-9, John 14:27

DAY 204

"Wisdom is supreme; therefore get wisdom.
Though it cost all you have, get understanding" (Proverbs 4:7).

What do you value most in life? To be supreme means to rank first.[71] Whatever comes first in our lives is what we value most. It's what we spend most of our time, effort, resources, and energy pursuing.

In the Proverbs we will see that wisdom is often a personification of Jesus. Solomon equates wisdom with the commands of God. John tells us that Jesus is the Word made flesh (John 1:14). So when we talk about seeking wisdom, we are essentially referring to a relationship with Jesus Himself.

In the parable of the pearl, Jesus described the kingdom of heaven as being worth all we have.

"'Again, the kingdom of heaven is like a merchant looking for fine pearls. When he found one of great value, he went away and sold everything he had and bought it'" (Matthew 13:45-46).

The kingdom of heaven or the kingdom of God is everywhere that Jesus rules and reigns. When we choose to follow Jesus and make Him our Lord, we are submitting to His reign over our lives. We begin living within His kingdom.

This parable along with this proverb is not implying that we can buy our way into heaven; rather, they both are teaching us that if it costs all we have to pursue Jesus, it's worth it. He's worth it.

Let's take some time today to think about what we treasure most in life. Is it our family, friends, career, or ministry? Or is it our relationship with Jesus, our supreme source of wisdom? What captures the majority of your thoughts, your time, your resources, and your energy?

Though it cost all we have, let us seek Jesus above all else. He is wisdom.

For further reading: Matthew 6:33, 13:44-46, John 1:14

DAY 205

"I guide you along the way of wisdom and lead you along straight paths. When you walk, your steps will not be hampered; when you run, you will not stumble" (Proverbs 4:11-12).

God has a path, plan, and purpose for each of us. If we will seek His will and His way for our lives, He will guide us along the right way—the way of wisdom (Jesus). When we are on the right path, we will run with faith and perseverance.

"Therefore, since we are surrounded by such a great cloud of witnesses, let us throw off everything that hinders and the sin that so easily entangles, and let us run with perseverance the race marked out for us" (Hebrews 12:1).

When we are focused on God and running our race for Him, we will not be distracted by things that could hinder our race. We will deal with sin in our lives quickly and get back on track with God. Easier said, than done, right?

I have found that if I start my day with Jesus and seek Him first, He will guide me down that path. He will open my eyes to things that could hinder my race as I spend time in His Word. He will convict me of sin so I can turn away from it if I am spending time with Him in prayer. As I keep my eyes on Jesus, He helps me run my race with grace. Are you struggling to stay in the race?

"Let us fix our eyes on Jesus, the author and perfecter of our faith, who for the joy set before him endured the cross, scorning its same, and sat down at the right hand of the throne of God" (Hebrews 12:2).

Turn your eyes to Jesus.

"Let your eyes look straight ahead, fix your gaze directly before you" (Proverbs 4:25).

You followed Him in faith; now stay with Him by faith.

For further reading: Isaiah 40:31, 1 Corinthians 9:24, Philippians 2:16, Hebrews 12:1-4

DAY 206

"Above all else, guard your heart, for it is the wellspring of life"
(Proverbs 4:23).

Remember that the heart represents the inner man or soul—the mind, will, emotions, attitudes, and motives of a person. We are told to guard our hearts. The word *guard* can mean "watch, protect, keep, preserve, to be kept secret, hidden."[72] Why are we to keep such diligence over our heart? Because it is the wellspring of life. In other words, everything we do flows from our heart. It represents who we are. We must guard and protect our heart from the world, the lies of the devil, and our own sinful nature. So how can we guard our heart?

I believe we guard our heart by protecting it from what we allow in. Our five senses are the portals to our souls. What we see, hear, smell, touch, or taste affects who we are. The greatest influences are what we watch and listen to. We have to feed our heart what it needs rather than what it wants. Remember, the heart is deceitful. In order to guard our heart from what is evil, we must protect our eyes and ears from wrong.

We must not allow impure images from television or internet into our heart. We must preserve our ears from what is not of God, including music that is ungodly, coarse joking, and conversation such as foul language or gossip. If we allow the world to dictate what we see and hear, our hearts will become corrupted. We also have to guard our thoughts.

"We demolish arguments and every pretension that sets itself up against the knowledge of God, and we take captive every thought to make it obedient to Christ" (2 Corinthians 10:5).

In order to guard our hearts, we must watch over what we allow in through our eyes, ears, and our thoughts. What we put in is what will flow out.

Put the Word of God, worship, wholesome books and music, and God-honoring conversation in your heart, and watch the goodness of God flow out of you!

For further reading: Job 31:1, Psalm 119:37, Jeremiah 17:9, 2 Corinthians 10:5, Philippians 4:8

DAY 207

"Drink water from your own cistern,
running water from your own well" (Proverbs 5:15).

Isn't it amazing how we always want what someone else has or what we can't have? Greener grass and all that, but the truth is that the enemy will always draw our attention away from our blessings and toward what appears to be something better.

We can easily become dissatisfied with what we have and start searching—at least in our hearts—for those greener pastures. That's why so many people fall into adulterous situations. The enemy causes them to become dissatisfied with their own spouse. Suddenly, somebody else's spouse looks like a better alternative.

Solomon knew the danger of adultery—perhaps his own father had shared his testimony of sin and the consequences it brings on our lives. So Solomon spilled a good bit of ink on warning his own son of the dangers of becoming dissatisfied with what he had.

Granted, some folks are in bad situations in their marriages. If you are in an abusive situation, please find help in a pastor, counselor, or shelter. But if you are simply no longer content with your marriage, you are in a dangerous place.

Solomon told his son to be satisfied with his own wife. Sometimes we need to look at what we have instead of dwelling on what we think we don't have. Often a matter of perspective can change everything. Try writing down everything about your spouse that you love and admire. Think of those characteristics that drew him to you in the first place.

Then begin to verbalize your appreciation to him. Your heart will follow your head as you make the right choice to drink from your own well.

I think you'll find the water is still sweet. Maybe even sweeter.

For further reading: Genesis 3, Matthew 4:1-11, Philippians 4:11-13, Hebrews 13:5

DAY 208

"For a man's ways are in full view of the LORD,
and he examines all his paths" (Proverbs 5:21).

We all know that God sees everything, but do we really *know* it? If so, do we really understand that God not only sees, but examines our paths? We will one day be held accountable for all we have said and done (Romans 14:12).

We sometimes think that because we are in Christ and all our sins are forgiven by His grace, we no longer are accountable for our sins, but the Bible says otherwise. While it's true that by faith we receive the righteousness of Jesus and are thereby saved from death, we still will have to give an account for what we've done with our lives as the Parable of the Talents and the account of the sheep and the goats in Matthew 25 both clearly show.

If our ways are in full view of the Lord, that means He knows our thoughts, attitudes, motives, and who we are when nobody else is around. He knows our character fully. He examines all we think, say, and do. The kindness and grace of God are not excuses to live sinful, sloppy lives. God calls His children to a higher standard.

"Make every effort to live in peace with all men and to be holy; without holiness no one will see the Lord" (Hebrews 12:14).

Holiness is a state of being set apart unto the Lord. We should seek to honor Him in all we say and do. Even though we know we will fall short, that should still be the desire of our hearts because we love Him and we want to serve Him out of gratitude for all He has done for us (John 14:23-24).

We can be blessed by His grace and thankful for His forgiveness, while also seeking to live lives of purity and holiness. It's not either/or; it's both/and.

Let's ask the Holy Spirit today to give us humble and obedient hearts, fully aware that He sees all our ways. And let us be thankful that He forgives when we fail.

For further reading: Matthew 25, John 14:23-24, Romans 14:12, Hebrews 12:14

DAY 209

"Go to the ant, you sluggard; consider its ways and be wise"
(Proverbs 6:6).

Isn't it amazing that something as tiny and insignificant as an ant can be used as an illustration for us in the Bible? Solomon uses the ant as an example of industry and diligence as opposed to laziness and folly.

Oh, how often we fall into folly, though, right? It's so easy to sit on the couch, eating and watching television. I know because I struggle with this. But the ant. Always busy, always working, always preparing. Ants are actually amazing creatures. They can carry up to 50 times their body weight.[73] They work together in colonies to build and to store up food, each one doing its part. Nobody has to give them instructions or encourage them to get to work. They just get busy and get it done. Me? Not so much.

But, as I am struggling to keep my house clean and keep up with marketing and keep up my blog posts and serve in my church, (oh! and finish this book!) I am encouraged that if an ant can do it, so can I.

Maybe I can't get everything done every single day, but I can work hard every day and choose to not be lazy. I can write three more devotions instead of watching a television show. I can work on my next blog post instead of scrolling through Facebook. I can clean my house instead of reading a magazine.

After all, God gave us Sunday for Sabbath rest and peace. How blessed we are that we serve a God who rested on the seventh day, not because He needed to but because He knew we need to. I can work hard this week, marking off the items on my schedule, because I know I will rest tonight, and I will rest on Sunday.

Even the ants don't get a day of rest! How much more, then, should we be encouraged to give it our best this week and then enjoy our Sabbath with Him!

For further reading: Genesis 2:2, Exodus 23:12, Matthew 25:26, 1 Corinthians 4:12, Colossians 3:23, 1 Thessalonians 4:11, 5:12, 2 Thessalonians 3:10, Hebrews 6:12

DAY 210

"When you walk, they will guide you; when you sleep, they will watch over you; when you awake, they will speak to you. For these commands are a lamp, this teaching is a light, and the corrections of discipline are the way to life" (Proverbs 6:22-23).

God has given us everything we need in His Word. We have guidance for how to walk and how to live our lives. His Word guides us in every area. His Word watches over us when we sleep, for His promises never fail. When we awake, God speaks to us through His Word.

I love to study, meditate, memorize, copy, and read the Words of my Savior. These Words are life and truth and blessing to us. The Bible is like a lamp, giving us light. The world is dark, and we can often lose our way. We can become confused with all the different opinions and philosophies of the world.

But God's Word illuminates our path and shows us clearly the way to go. His correction to us changes our course and sets us back on the right path when we stray. Even when we face discipline because we have chosen to disobey, God's discipline is both loving and firm. He helps us course-correct and find our way so that we can walk in His peace and His blessings.

His Word is the way to life. When we go days without consulting the Word, we set ourselves up for failure. If we don't spend time in the Word daily, the enemy will take the opportunity to direct us in the wrong way. We have the opportunity to know God's will in any situation. All we have to do is take the time to spend with God in His Word.

I am so thankful that we have the Bible in every translation, any size or color, whatever kinds of study notes or devotional reading or journaling pages we want. All we need is at our fingertips.

Are you spending time in God's Word every day?

For further reading: Deuteronomy 6:4-9, Joshua 22:5, Psalm 119:105, Isaiah 30:21

DAY 211

"I saw among the simple, I noticed among the young men, a youth who lacked judgment" (Proverbs 7:7).

This entire chapter of Proverbs is a warning to Solomon's son to avoid the adulteress. You would think I could have skipped this in a devotional written for women, but verse seven really jumped out at me. This "youth who lacked judgment" fell prey to the temptation of a woman who was dressed seductively, was loud and defiant, and whose feet never stayed at home. She tempted this young man and led him astray, down a path ultimately leading to death (Proverbs 7:27).

We will look at the attitude of the woman in chapter nine, but today I want us to think about the young man. The word translated *simple* means "naïve, someone easily deceived or persuaded."[74] Because this guy was simple-minded and lacked judgment, he was led astray by her persuasive words. Solomon tells us that she has brought down many victims (Proverbs 7:26).

Although the woman is at fault here in leading him astray, Solomon's warning is to his son to not be simple and lacking judgment, but to walk in the wisdom of God. As Christian women, we may likewise be seduced by men who do the same thing. We must heed this warning as well (2 Timothy 3:6). There are men who will try to take advantage of women, especially if they sense problems in a marriage. In order to be a woman who walks in wisdom and good judgment, we should be aware and guard our hearts from such men.

We should never share problems we are having in our marriage with another man. If you need to talk to someone, find a girlfriend you can trust who will pray with you and encourage you to follow God's Word. Never be alone with a man who is not your husband or relative in a car, an elevator, a room, or any other place that would make you vulnerable. And never allow thoughts toward another man that should be reserved for your own husband. Ask God to renew your mind in His Word and help you think right thoughts.

Yes, women can be led astray by men. We need to do our best to walk in wisdom and sound judgment as far as is possible with us. Let's not be weak-willed women, swayed by sin; let's be women of sound judgment and integrity who guard our hearts.

For further reading: Proverbs 4:2, Romans 12:1-2, Philippians 4:8, 2 Timothy 3:6

DAY 212

"Does not wisdom call out? Does not understanding raise her voice?"
(Proverbs 8:1).

Wisdom is personified in these verses as one calling out to us. Because all wisdom is found in Jesus and in His Word, we can also think of these verses as the Lord calling out to us. Everywhere we go, He is calling out to us to choose wisely.

When we are in our homes with our families, wisdom calls. When we are on the phone with a friend, wisdom calls. When we are posting on social media, wisdom calls. When we are driving down the road, wisdom calls. When we are in line at the grocery store, wisdom calls. When we are on the bleachers at the game, wisdom calls. When we are at our desk at work, wisdom calls. When we are in our Bible study, wisdom calls. When we are in the church parking lot, wisdom calls.

What is she saying?

"You who are simple, gain prudence; you who are foolish, gain understanding" (Proverbs 8:5).

We have a choice every moment of every day to choose wisdom above all else.

"Choose my instruction instead of silver, knowledge rather than choice gold, for wisdom is more precious than rubies, and nothing you desire can compare with her" (Proverbs 8:10-11).

We may not trade so much in gold, silver, or rubies, but we do trade in gossip, anger, and unforgiveness. We do trade in pride, selfishness, and pity. Those are currencies we understand well. God is calling us to something better.

So the next time you are faced with one of your 35,000 choices a day, and your heart is leaning toward a lesser thing, remember that wisdom is calling out. And choose well.

For further reading: Deuteronomy 30:20, Luke 10:39, John 10:27, James 1:19

DAY 213

"I love those who love me, and those who seek me find me"
(Proverbs 8:17).

As we seek to walk in wisdom, we need only to seek more of Jesus in our lives. God wants to be first in our lives. Are we giving Him what we have left over at the end of the day, or do we seek Him first? If we want to walk in God's wisdom, we need to spend time with God on a regular basis.

My daily quiet time consists of reading a devotional, much like this one, reading a psalm and journaling my response, confessing my specific sins, giving thanks, interceding in prayer for the needs of my family, friends, church, and community, and listening for God's voice to me.

I truly believe that the more we seek God and His ways, the more He pours out in our lives—peace, blessings, favor, provision, protection, and His presence. He wants us to come to Him.

"And without faith it is impossible to please God, because anyone who comes to him must believe that he exists and that he rewards those who earnestly seek him" (Hebrews 11:6).

"Come near to God and he will come near to you" (James 4:8a).

If we are seeking God, we will not be disappointed. When we put our hope in Him and trust Him for every area of our lives, He meets our needs and shows us the way.

If you need wisdom in some area of your life right now, I encourage you to seek the Lord, spend time in His Word, give Him the best part of your day, when you are at your best. Make your relationship with God your number one priority, and God will do the rest.

"But seek first his kingdom and his righteousness, and all these things will be given to you as well" (Matthew 6:33).

Seek Him first.

For further reading: Jeremiah 29:13, Matthew 6:33, Hebrews 11:6, James 4:8a

DAY 214

"Now then, my sons, listen to me; blessed are those who keep my ways...For whoever finds me finds life and receives favor from the LORD" (Proverbs 8:32, 35).

We all want the blessing and favor of the Lord on our lives, and Solomon tells us through the inspiration of the Holy Spirit how we can have them—through finding Jesus and keeping His ways. Jesus is wisdom; and wisdom is Jesus.

When we become Jesus followers, we take on the blessing and favor of the Lord. The Hebrew word for *blessed* means "blessed! happy! a heightened state of happiness and joy, implying very favorable circumstances, often resulting from the kind acts of God."[75] Don't you love the exclamation points they put in there?

Let's look at *favor*: "pleasure, acceptance, favor, will, pleased, delights."[76] When we give our lives to Jesus, we take on the pleasure and acceptance of God. We are no longer bound by sin, but we have been freed to walk in the power of the Holy Spirit, in purity and righteousness, which often result in favorable circumstances.

Think about it: When we were in sin, we were constantly living with the consequences of sin on our lives. We may have pretended things were okay, but inside we were really a mess. We reap what we sow, and sin brings a curse on our lives. Once we were freed from sin and learned how to walk in the Spirit, we began to reap the blessings of obedience. When we sow spiritual seed, we reap spiritual blessings.

Of course, we won't always be happy or undergo favorable circumstances, but as Christians, we walk in the peace and joy and grace of the Lord Jesus Christ. Those are blessings that far outweigh our circumstances. So, if you want to experience the blessing and favor of God, surrender your life to Jesus Christ and follow Him day by day. You will never be the same.

For further reading: Psalm 23:6, Matthew 4:19, John 10:10, 1 Corinthians 14:1, 1 Timothy 1:18

DAY 215

"Wisdom has built her house; she has hewn out its seven pillars. She has prepared her meat and mixed her wine; she has also set her table" (Proverbs 9:1-2).

Wisdom is personified in these passages as a woman who builds her house and sets her table. She then calls out an invitation for those who are simple to come to her house and join her for a meal. Wisdom has built her house. I like to think of this as a woman who takes the time to think about the materials with which she is building. Jesus had something to say about how we build.

"I will show you what he is like who comes to me and hears my words and puts them into practice. He is like a man building a house, who dug down deep and laid the foundation on rock. When a flood came, the torrent struck that house but could not shake it, because it was well built (Luke 6:47-48).

We can know what the Word says, but if we do not put it into practice, we are not building a house—we're just playing house. Unless the Lord builds the house, its builders labor in vain (Psalm 127:1).

We need to build on the Rock of our salvation, which is Jesus Christ. If we live a life that acknowledges God as only *part* of our lives, we are in trouble. When Jesus is the foundation of the life we are building, He is not part of our lives. He *is* our life.

Wisdom also builds with seven pillars. Seven is the number of completion in the Bible, so let's look at seven qualities of wisdom according to James (3:17-18).

Imagine if we built our lives and our homes on the foundation of the Word of God and our salvation, and then we framed it in with purity, peace, consideration, submission, mercy and good fruit, impartiality, and sincerity.

Now, that's a house worth living in.

For further reading: Psalm 127:1, Luke 6:47-48, James 3:17-18

DAY 216

"The woman Folly is loud; she is undisciplined and without knowledge. She sits at the door of her house, on a seat at the highest point of the city, calling out to those who pass by, who go straight on their way. 'Let all who are simple come in here!' she says to those who lack judgment" (Proverbs 9:13-16).

Wisdom sets her table and invites others to come, but Folly sends out invitations to the simple, too. Folly is an attention-seeker; she has to be the loudest voice. She may be popular, but she is leading others to destruction (9:18). Folly hasn't even set a table, because what she has to offer is not worthy of the table (9:17). It may seem that what she has to offer is delicious—sin is enticing. But the truth is that what is done in secret is usually revealed. Sin has consequences that are not so pleasant.

These passages in Proverbs are written to warn others to follow the ways of wisdom and not folly. But I think they also serve as instructions to us as women. Which woman do we want to be?

We can be the attention-seeker—loud and undisciplined, manipulative, and leading others astray. Or we can be the voice of wisdom and truth to those around us—to our families, friends, co-workers, and neighbors.

Let's build a home on the foundation of truth with the walls of wisdom. Let's set a table with food that will endure and drink that will quench every thirst. Let's invite others to the home we have built and the table we have set and offer them life. Our homes can become a place to share the gospel. Our table can be a place to disciple someone. So, how about it? Do you know someone, young or old, who needs an invitation?

"Come, eat my food and drink the wine I have mixed. Leave your simple ways and you will live" (Proverbs 9:6).

The house and table of wisdom lead to life. What's on your table?

For further reading: 1 Thessalonians 4:11-12, Titus 2:3-5, 1 Peter 3:4

DAY 217

"The LORD does not let the righteous go hungry but he thwarts the craving of the wicked" (Proverbs 10:3).

The youth recently led our church in a 30-hour fast to bring awareness to the problem of world hunger. As the fast came to an end, some of them ate too much and got sick. They waited all that time to eat, but then over-indulged in the wrong things! When we hunger for the right things, we will always be satisfied (Matthew 5:6).

We are really good at feeding our flesh, but the flesh is never satisfied. We are always hungry for more. When we are lost, we are controlled by the flesh; once we surrender our lives to the Holy Spirit, we are to be controlled by the Spirit. Our old sinful nature will wage war against the Spirit of God within us. We must surrender daily and crucify the sinful nature in order to walk in the Spirit. So how do we learn to live by the Spirit and not this sinful nature?

Stop feeding it! If we continue to feed the flesh with what it desires—whether that be food, alcohol, gossip, sex, whatever—it will continue to demand more. But if we starve the flesh and feed the spirit, that part of us that desires more of God, we will be satisfied. The problem is that starving the flesh is painful, and most of us don't like pain.

But the good news is that if we will endure it for just a little while, eventually our soul will learn to be satisfied with what pleases our spirit. And when our soul is satisfied, the flesh will stop hungering for more. For example, if I replace some of my bad habits with reading the Bible, listening to Christian music, or prayer, at first my flesh will still be screaming for pleasure. We will struggle for a little while, and it will hurt.

Whatever we feed grows; whatever we starve dies. The question is, "Do we trust God enough to endure the pain to our flesh?" I know from experience that I will often continue in a bad habit because of the comfort and pleasure, even if it is temporary. We have to make a daily decision to crucify the flesh.

Don't fill up on junk. Let Jesus satisfy you with the real thing.

For further reading: Psalm 103:1-5, 107:9, Matthew 5:6, John 6:26-27, Romans 8:5-9, Galatians 2:20

DAY 218

"The man of integrity walks securely, but he who takes crooked paths will be found out" (Proverbs 10:9).

I love just how practical the proverbs are. These are truths that we can apply to so many areas of our lives. They teach us how to live life God's way. If we want to grow as disciples, we need to learn what it means to follow Him. Learning to walk with integrity is one way we do that.

The word *integrity* used in this verse means "blamelessness, integrity, innocence."[77] If we seek to live our lives so that we are innocent of wrongdoing and blameless, we will be secure. But if we try to take crooked paths, we will get caught.

What do you think it means to take crooked paths?

Crooked in this sense actually means "perverse." [78] In other words, we know the right way, but we choose the wrong way.

I can remember before I became a Christian, I often made choices that I knew were wrong. I would later be so filled with anxiety, worrying about whether or not I would get caught. There is no security, no peace, when we live that way. We will be constantly looking over our shoulders.

Once I gave my life to the Lord and began trying to make decisions that would please Him, I began to enjoy the peace that comes from not worrying about getting caught. Being able to rest at night without fear and anxiety becomes a great incentive to walk in integrity.

We may fail at times, but if we will seek to be upright and blameless in how we live our lives, we will rest securely in our relationship with the Lord.

We will have no fear of getting caught, and that's a much better way to live.

For further reading: Matthew 7:13-14, Ephesians 6:18, 1 Thessalonians 5:2-9, 1 Peter 5:8

DAY 219

"Hatred stirs up dissension, but love covers over all wrongs"
(Proverbs 10:12).

Have you ever been around people that are always trying to stir something up? It's almost as if they thrive on the drama. The older I get, the less patience I have with drama, and the more I value peace.

Hatred is such a strong word, that most of us would probably say we don't hate anyone. But when I read this verse, it occurred to me that if I am stirring up dissension, there is hatred in me. Dissension means we are causing division and strife. Paul said in Galatians that it's an act of the sinful nature:

"The acts of the sinful nature are obvious: sexual immorality, impurity and debauchery; idolatry and witchcraft; hatred, discord, jealousy, fits of rage, selfish ambition, dissensions, factions and envy; drunkenness, orgies, and the like. I warn you, as I did before, that those who live like this will not inherit the kingdom of God" (5:19-21).

You know why these people aren't going to heaven? They are living a lifestyle that shows they haven't been changed by Jesus. When Jesus comes into our hearts, He changes us. If we still have a desire to stir up strife and dissension, we haven't been changed. But Proverbs tells us that love covers over all wrongs. That doesn't mean we cover up sin. It means that when someone does something to hurt us, we let love cover it, rather than letting hate stir it.

"But the fruit of the Spirit is love..." (Galatians 5:22).

The first sign in us that we belong to Jesus is that we love. It may not always be easy, but because we no longer live for ourselves and our own desires, we submit to God and do the right thing.

Are you struggling today to love someone who has hurt you? Surrender to the One who is able to make all things new. Let Him fill you with love, and then let His love cover every wrong.

For further reading: Proverbs 6:19, 15:1, 18, 16:28, Romans 13:13-14, Galatians 5:19-22

DAY 220

*"The wages of the righteous bring them life, but the income
of the wicked brings them punishment" (Proverbs 10:16).*

If you have a job, you go in and work—say 40 hours a week—and at the end of
that week you earn a wage. Your paycheck is your reward for the work you
have done. According to this proverb, you earn according to how you have live
your life. It's the same principle as sowing and reaping.

Old Testament believers put their faith in the promise of the Messiah to come.
We put our faith in the finished work of the Messiah who has already come.
We don't have to earn salvation by righteous living, however. Jesus already
paid the price for our sin. So we only have to receive His righteousness by
faith.

"But now a righteousness from God, apart from law, has been made known, to
which the Law and the Prophets testify. This righteousness from God comes
through faith in Jesus Christ to all who believe" (Romans 3:21-22).

"For the wages of sin is death, but the gift of God is eternal life in Christ Jesus
our Lord" (Romans 6:23).

Our sin earns us death and destruction, but Jesus paid the debt we owed. Now
eternal life is not something we earn but a gift we receive by faith.

"God made him who had no sin to be sin for us, so that in him we might
become the righteousness of God" (2 Corinthians 5:21).

Walking by faith in the righteousness of God is made attainable through the
Holy Spirit who lives within us. It's not a wage. It's a gift. So open it, receive it,
and enjoy it.

For further reading: Romans 3, 6:1-14, 2 Corinthians 5:21

DAY 221

*"When words are many, sin is not absent, but
he who holds his tongue is wise" (Proverbs 10:19).*

Does your mouth ever get you in trouble? I love to talk! But, boy, can my mouth get me in trouble, too! Sometimes, I am misunderstood; sometimes I am too honest; sometimes I speak before I think. Sometimes I am just plain critical and negative. Sometimes my pride gets the better of me. Sometimes my feelings direct my words. And sometimes I just get stupid and say things that I don't even really mean.

Like David, we need to spend time being quiet before the Lord every day, asking God to search our hearts and show us anything that is not of Him. The Lord can reveal those areas of pride, insecurity, judgment, or even hate that would lead us to unholy speech. We can pray a prayer like this one:

"Set a guard over my mouth, O Lord; keep watch over the door of my lips. Let not my heart be drawn to what is evil" (Psalm 141:3-4a).

If we know that we have a problem with a hasty tongue, then we can find Scriptures that encourage us to think before we speak and put them on note cards. We can then work on memorizing them, for Psalm 119:11 says that we can hide God's Word in our hearts that we might not sin against Him. We can tuck these Scripture cards in our Bibles as bookmarks, in our purses to read while standing in the checkout or waiting at the doctor's office. We can post them on our mirrors, microwaves, and bulletin boards—any place where we can see them daily.

Having God's Word in our hearts and on our minds will transform us so that our mouth will reflect the truth: We are saved by grace, and God is able to work in us to make us what He wants us to be—witnesses of His glory. Let's grow in wisdom by learning to control our tongues. Just because we have an opinion doesn't mean we have to share it. Join me in asking God to help us think before we speak. Or just be quiet.

For further reading: Psalm 119:11, 139:4, 141:3-4, James 3:9-10, Matthew 12:34-36

DAY 222

*"The way of the LORD is a refuge for the righteous,
but it is the ruin of those who do evil" (Proverbs 10:29).*

I live in the South in what we call the Bible Belt. There is literally a church on every corner. In our small county of 27,000 people there are about 100 churches.

Church is a way of life for many in our community. They grew up in church. It's what they've always done. It is culturally and socially acceptable.

But many attend church out of obligation, tradition, or for social status. And they do so without having a heart for God. They are in the "way of the Lord" but not sincere in their devotion to the Way.

The danger is that they are hearing the Word of God without responding to it. And once we have heard truth, we are accountable to that truth.

The way of the Lord is a refuge of the righteous. Those who attend these churches because they love Jesus and want to be part of a community of faith find refuge within those walls.

The way of the Lord is the ruin of those who do evil. For those who use the church for their own personal gain, only judgment and ruin await them.

But for those who truly love the Lord and seek His face, His ways are a refuge. The Word is a refuge, the church is a refuge, the community of believers is a refuge to those who love Jesus.

May we each seek the way of the Lord and find refuge there.

For further reading: Matthew 15:8, 23, Acts 2:42-47, Romans 12:9, Hebrews 10:22

DAY 223

"The LORD abhors dishonest scales, but accurate weights are his delight" (Proverbs 11:1).

I'm guilty. I have tasted the grapes in the grocery store before paying for them—you know, by the pound. I hate to get home and have grapes that aren't good. But really, if I eat them, am I not stealing? I know one grape is probably not really a big deal. How much could one little grape cost? But God convicted me about it. He is holy and He calls us to be holy, above reproach in all that we do.

In the days of King Solomon, I doubt they were worrying over grapes. Yet, as in any civilization, they dealt with the sin nature. And one area in which that nature will rear its ugly head is money. A merchant couldn't just weigh his produce on a fancy scale and sell it accordingly. There was no standard of measurement. Instead, each merchant had his own stone weights for comparison, so it was easy to cheat. That's why the Israelites were warned in Leviticus "Do not use dishonest standards when measuring length, weight, or quantity. Use honest scales and honest weights" (19:35-36a).

As Jesus-followers, we should be reflecting the character of Christ in all that we do and say. We should pay our taxes, purchase songs that we download, pay for movies we watch, and not try to cheat someone out of their hard-earned money. A child of God should be someone that others know they can trust.

If we aren't honest in dealing with money, chances are that we will not be honest in other areas of our lives as well. If we have a reputation for dishonest dealings, we bring reproach to our God.

Honestly, the reason I was convicted about grape-stealing is because I did it one day in the grocery store and then turned to see someone watching me. She knew who I was—that I write Christian books and speak in churches. I was so embarrassed. I made a joke about testing the grapes to make sure they were sweet, but I felt so ashamed.

A Spirit-filled woman of God doesn't steal even a grape. She is above reproach in all that she says and does so the name of her God will never be maligned because of her.

For further reading: Leviticus 19:35-36a, Deuteronomy 25:13-15

DAY 224

*"When pride comes, then comes disgrace,
but with humility comes wisdom" (Proverbs 11:2).*

I never intended to be a writer. I was a high school teacher and enjoyed my job. But God had different plans and began to open doors that led to where I am now. As the books began to sell and more opportunities to speak came my way, I started praying that God would keep me humble and focused on serving others.

One day, I had some issues that sent me to the urgent care. It turned out to be a kidney stone, and I was beginning to feel some discomfort. The nurse that was taking care of me was so kind and concerned. After taking all of my vitals and samples, she said, "I know you don't feel well, and I didn't want to say anything, but it's so cool to meet you! I love your books! In fact, I'm reading one of them right now. It's in my car!"

I had never had a total stranger recognize me before, and I'll admit that even though I felt bad, inside I was feeling pretty good about myself. You know what I mean? We talked for a minute and then she left while I waited on the doctor. While I waited, the pain was getting worse, so by the time the doctor came, I was in distress. She ordered one shot for pain and one shot for nausea. So a few minutes later, my fan girl walked back in the room with two needles, one for each cheek.

There's something about baring your bottom to a total stranger that brings your sense of self right back down where it needs to be. God reminded me in that moment that all I do is to serve Him and others. I had to laugh because Jesus knows me so well. He knows the second I entertain a thought that is not of Him, and He loves me enough to guard me from that thinking. Pride leads to disgrace. There's nothing worse than thinking you are something and having God expose you. Literally.

But praise God, He will expose our sin and draw us back to Him in humility. With humility comes wisdom. Wisdom helps us see ourselves in light of God's glory and goodness..

For further reading: Philippians 2:3, Colossians 3:12, James 3:13, 1 Peter 5:5

DAY 225

"The integrity of the upright guides them, but the unfaithful are destroyed by their duplicity" (Proverbs 11:3).

I love the story of Joseph in the Old Testament. He was the son of his father's favorite wife (Well, there's our first clue to the problems in this family), which made him the favorite son. Joseph began to have dreams of his brothers bowing down to him, which he shared with them (clue number two). His brothers saw that he was the favorite, so they hated him all the more.

One day they decided to sell him into slavery, and Joseph ended up in Egypt. But the Lord was with Joseph and he prospered. He found favor in the eyes of Potiphar, one of Pharaoh's officials, and was put in charge of his household. One day Potiphar's wife made advances on Joseph, but he refused to fall into sin with her. Although he escaped her clutches, she claimed *he* had tried to seduce *her*. So Potiphar had Joseph thrown in jail where he remained for some time.

Even while in prison, the Lord was with him and showed him favor. Eventually, Joseph was remembered for interpreting dreams and released from prison to interpret a dream for Pharaoh. Joseph made clear that *he* could not interpret a dream, but his God could. Because he depended on the Lord, God used him to such an extent that Joseph was promoted to second-in-command over all of Egypt.

Joseph was a Hebrew placed in an official position in the royal administration of Egypt. God blessed Joseph and guided him to such a place of power because he was a man of integrity. Had Joseph compromised his faith with Potiphar's wife, his story probably would have been very different, but Joseph took the higher road. He walked with integrity, which means he acted according to a proper standard. Duplicity is a characteristic of those who claim to be one thing, but given a choice, are really something else. Joseph proved that he was the man Potiphar initially believed him to be.

We all have the opportunity to choose to do what is right. Let's seek to be guided by integrity—following the moral standard found in God's Word.

For further reading: Genesis 37-50, Titus 2:7

DAY 226

"A gossip betrays a confidence, but a trustworthy man keeps a secret" (Proverbs 11:13).

Have you ever shared something in confidence, only to find out later that your secret wasn't kept? I once was in a relationship that I later ended. I shared with a friend some of the details of that breakup, confident that my friend would keep it between us. Imagine my surprise when I received a letter from someone who was upset over how I handled the relationship—details I had shared only with my one friend.

The Scripture uses the word *betray* for when a gossip breaks our trust. That's exactly how we feel—betrayed. It's as though the other person's desire to spread that juicy morsel of information was more important to her than our thoughts or feelings.

What is it about gossip that makes people so susceptible to it? Why do we long to share information that is not ours to share? Perhaps we enjoy the feeling of being the first to know something or to have some insider information. Maybe it makes us feel important to the person we share it with. Or maybe we love being the center of attention.

Whatever the reason, we should consider the life and feelings of the person who would be hurt by our words. Is losing a relationship worth a few seconds of feeling important? So how do we know what is considered gossip and what is just a "concern" we want to share with someone to pray about? My first pastor used to say that if I wouldn't say something in front of a person, I shouldn't say it behind her back. I've always found that to be a useful guide to my words.

The next time you are tempted to share some news or information, ask yourself if you would share it in front of the person it is about. How would you feel if you were overheard? What would Jesus think of your words?

Just because something is true, doesn't mean we need to share it.

For further reading: Proverbs 16:28, 18:8, 20:19, 26:20, 26:22, 2 Corinthians 12:20

DAY 227

*"For lack of guidance a nation falls, but
many advisors make victory sure" (Proverbs 11:14).*

One thing I have learned over the last several years in the writing and publishing business is that I need guidance. Writers often tend to keep to themselves, but others writers and self-publishers have a wealth of information that I have learned to glean.

When a nation is led by one who thinks he needs no guidance, despotism results. Only with many advisors and counselors does a leader consider all the possibilities and ensure his leadership is based on more than just his own opinion and ideals.

The truth is that we need others to guide us in life as well. Sure, if we are following the Lord, we have the Holy Spirit as our Counselor. He will guide us into all truth. But we can too often fail to hear Him clearly or wait on His leadership.

I have learned that I need others in my life who are walking the same path of faith to guide me not just in ministry but also in my walk with the Lord. I have friends whom I trust completely to guide me when I am confused, to counsel me when I need help, and to advise me when I need direction.

If a nation fails for lack of guidance, so will our plans. Be sure to seek God for His will in all that you do, but don't be afraid to also seek counsel from others who love the Lord. Don't look to the world's ideals or trust in your judgment alone. Our hearts are deceitful and can lead us astray.

Seek one or two trusted friends whom you can turn to when you need advice or guidance. God can use their counsel to get you on the right track and help you stay there.

For further reading: 1 Kings 22:5, Psalm 1:1, Proverbs 8:12-14, 12:15, 20:18

DAY 228

"He who puts up security for another will surely suffer,
but whoever refuses to strike hands in pledge is safe"
(Proverbs 11:15).

Have you ever made a promise you couldn't keep? Whether in financial matters or not, we often obligate ourselves before thinking or praying about a situation. I'm raising my hand really high on this one. I'm bad about wanting to get involved in everything that seems like a great ministry or outreach for the Lord, but surely he has not called me to do everything and help everyone.

When we tend to overcommit ourselves, I think it's a pride issue. We foolishly believe that unless we intervene, nothing good will be done. We have to remember that God called the body of Christ to work together like a well-oiled machine—or like, well, a body. All the parts of the body work together, each doing its own part, for our bodies to function as they should and carry out the many complicated processes involved in respiration, circulation, digestion, and so on. When each part does its job, everything runs smoothly.

When I begin to think I need to be involved in everything, I run the risk of taking over someone else's job. In doing so, I often commit myself to more than I can handle or get myself in a bind that I can't get out of. We are told to let our yes be yes and our no be no. So, once we commit to something, we need to see it through.

If we jumped into something that was not God's will for us, we can miss out on the things we were supposed to be doing. When it comes to finances, we can be quick to want to help others out, especially if it involves our own family. But often in the wisdom of the proverbs, we are told to guard against taking on someone else's debt because we will suffer for it.

The same is true of our time. Let's pray over every request that we will only commit our money and our time to those things the Father tells us to. Let's refrain from being quick to agree—especially when it comes to taking responsibility for someone else's duty. We will miss out, and so will they.

For further reading: Proverbs 6:1-5, Matthew 5:37, 1 Corinthians 12

DAY 229

*"A kindhearted woman gains respect, but
ruthless men gain only wealth" (Proverbs 11:16).*

We all know that reputation is important. While we don't want to be overly concerned with what man thinks of us as opposed to what God thinks, we do need to maintain a good witness so that we represent Jesus well.

Within our families, vocations, churches, and communities, we are gaining a reputation by what we say and do.

How we conduct ourselves when our children need discipline will speak volumes to them about the God we claim to serve. Do we deal with our children with kindness and love, even when we are correcting them?

When we encounter difficulties with a co-worker, our attitude in how we respond will label us quickly within that workplace.

When things don't go our way at church, will we react with gossip and complaining or with silence and prayer?

If the clerk at the market is slow or the umpire doesn't call the game according to our favor, will our response gain us a reputation that honors Christ?

This Scripture tells us that a kindhearted woman gains more respect than even a wealthy man. Let's be women who seek to bring honor to God through the respect we gain by being kindhearted towards others. Who knows that someone else may be drawn to Jesus when they see His heart in us?

For further reading: Proverbs 22:1, 1 Thessalonians 4:12, Titus 2:2

DAY 230

*"Like a gold ring in a pig's snout is a beautiful
woman who shows no discretion" (Proverbs 11:22).*

Do you ever look at women who age well and think "How do they still look so beautiful?" We all want to maintain our youthful appearance and present the best version of ourselves to the world, but the wisdom of Proverbs tells us that there is more to beauty than appearances. The Hebrew word translated *discretion* is *ta'am*, meaning "taste, discretion, discernment, judgment."[79] A woman can be gorgeous, but if she lacks good judgment, the beauty is wasted. Good taste, discretion, discernment, and judgment have to do with the decisions we make about what is right and wrong.

The Bible is our source for truth. While the world can often vacillate between standards of righteousness, the Word of God never changes. If we want to know God's principles of right and wrong, we can turn to the Scriptures. We have the opportunity to grow in our knowledge and understanding of God's Word through careful study, the teaching of our pastors, and commentaries on the Bible.

We also have the Holy Spirit, who guides us into all truth (John 16:13). So as women, we need never fear that we won't have direction from God about our choices. We must study the Word and seek to understand God's principles through careful study of passages in their contexts.

When we study the Bible with its entirety in mind, not taking verses out of context to say what we want them to say, God will give us the direction we need to walk in His truth. As women of God, we should walk in the beauty of discretion, both knowing and doing the right thing. We make judgments based on the Word of God. Real taste and class are the result of walking in integrity— that's what makes us beautiful.

So the next time you compare yourself to some gorgeous model or actress, just remember that true beauty comes from walking in the Spirit with taste, discretion, discernment, and good judgment.

For further reading: Proverbs 31:30, John 16:13, 1 Peter 3:3-5

DAY 231

"One man gives freely, yet gains even more;
another withholds unduly, but comes to poverty.
A generous man will prosper; he who refreshes
others will himself be refreshed" (Proverbs 11:24-25).

In God's upside-down economy, the more we give, the more we will receive; yet those who withhold from others out of greed will in the end lose it all.

Our world tells us to look out for ourselves first. If we earn it, we have the right to decide what to do with it. While it is true that God has given us free will, and we can choose how much we keep and how much we give, the reality is that all of it belongs to God. We are only stewards of what He has blessed us with.

Should we lose our health or job, we wouldn't have an income. God owns everything. I had on older friend, a lady who was a real prayer warrior in our church, who had been asking God for a fruit basket. She was a shut-in, only leaving the house when someone took her somewhere. She got meals from a program that delivered them to seniors, but she rarely had fresh fruit.

Mrs. Ruby started praying and asking God to send someone by her house with a fruit basket. She prayed and believed for weeks, but the fruit basket never came. Finally, she said to the Lord, "Why didn't you tell someone to bring me a fruit basket?' The Lord answered her, "I did, but they didn't listen."

When I heard that story from her, how I wish I had been the one to have had the privilege of taking Mrs. Ruby a fruit basket when she prayed for it! The more we give to others, the more joy and blessings God pours out into our lives.

And the more we try to hold onto what we have, the more we lose. That's how God's kingdom works. He calls us to give when it's in our power to do so. Whatever we let go of, we can trust Him with. As we refresh the lives of others, the Lord will refresh our lives and meet our needs.

And you'd better believe, we got Mrs. Ruby her fruit.

For further reading: Matthew 10:8, Luke 6:38, Acts 20:35, 2 Corinthians 9:7

DAY 232

"The fruit of the righteous is a tree of life,
and he who wins souls is wise" (Proverbs 11:30).

In the Garden of Eden, God placed the tree of life, giving immortality to Adam and Eve. They were created to live forever, but because they ate from the tree of the knowledge of good and evil that they were commanded not to eat, they were banned from access to the tree of life.

Sin brings death. But Jesus made a way for us to be saved through His death on another tree at Calvary.

"God made him who had no sin to be sin for us, so that in him we might become the righteousness of God" (2 Corinthians 5:21).

"He himself bore our sins in his body on the tree, so that we might die to sins and live for righteousness; by his wounds you have been healed" (1 Peter 2:24).

Through faith in Jesus Christ we now have access to the tree of life. Revelation tells us that the tree of life is in the paradise of God (Revelation 2:7). We will live forever on the New Earth where we will freely eat the fruit of the righteous.

As we walk in the wisdom of God, we will share that opportunity with others. We want them to live, too! Our family, friends, and neighbors all have the same chance to live forever, if they know the truth. It's our job to tell them.

"Remember this: Whoever turns a sinner from the error of his way will save him from death and cover over a multitude of sins" (James 5:20).

Spend time with a lost friend or family member and love on her until she asks you why.

For further reading: 2 Corinthians 5:21, James 5:20, 1 Peter 2:24, Revelation 2:7

DAY 233

"A wife of noble character is her husband's crown, but a disgraceful wife is like decay in his bones" (Proverbs 12:4).

The expression "health or decay to the bones" is a metaphor to describe the condition of the life or strength of a person. So when we read that a disgraceful wife is a like decay in her husband's bones, we can be put off by the idea that our choices can bring death and rot to the lives of others.

Yet, as a wife, I know there have been times that my disgraceful actions sapped the life and strength right out of my husband. On the other hand, we have the opportunity to be our husband's crown.

A crown or wreath in the days of the writer symbolized victory and leadership. Instead of sapping our husband's strength, we can be the source of his ability to lead well and walk in victory.

When he has the confidence to lead, our whole families will benefit, but he needs our noble character to give him that confidence. If we correct, belittle, or nag, we will sap his strength as surely as a virus confines one to the bed, weak and powerless.

How much influence we have in our husband's lives!

Whether you are married, single, divorced, or widowed, this verse has power to teach us about our influence on others. A noble or virtuous woman is one who walks with "strength, capability, skill, and valor."[80] She is not one who just quietly submits and never expresses her thoughts or opinions. She just knows how to do it with a gentle spirit that encourages others and brings life.

I don't know about you, but I have no desire to bring rottenness to anybody's life. Let's agree together today that we will be women of noble character who bring life and strength to those around us.

For further reading: Proverbs 3:18, 31:11, 23, 1 Peter 3:1-7

DAY 234

"From the fruit of his lips a man is filled with good things as surely as the work of his hands rewards him" (Proverbs 12:14).

We all know the value of a word well-spoken. We at times are lifted up by the encouragement of another as surely as we sometimes are torn down in like manner. Today's proverb shows us that we can expect a return on the investment of our words. Just as the negative words we speak can cause pain and heartache, our positive words can bring great reward.

For instance, if a farmer plants tomato seeds, then with the right conditions of soil, sunlight, and rain, she will soon reap tomatoes for her salad. Likewise, when we speak words of life, with the right conditions of obedience, prayer, and the will of God, we will see a harvest as well.

Negativity, complaining, and gossip are all examples of speech that only serve to bring despair, discouragement, and disunity. If we use our lips to speak forth what is not of the Spirit, our lives will be filled with the same.

Hard work brings a reward, but it's not easy. We have to invest time, energy, and effort on our job or in our homemaking in order to see a profit or a payday. Likewise, speaking words that are positive, uplifting, and encouraging requires intentionality, patience, and wisdom.

Most good things in life only come with effort. But they're worth it. Our families are worth it. Our own well-being is worth it. Our friendships are worth it. His kingdom work is worth it.

Take the time today to think before you speak. Are your words kind, uplifting, and positive? Do your lips produce fruit that is lasting and pleasing?

Ask God to guide you today to be "quick to listen, slow to speak, and slow to become angry" (James 1:19). Let's seek to speak words that bring good things into our own lives and into the lives of others.

For further reading: Psalm 37:30-31, 49:3, Ephesians 4:15, 29, 2 Corinthians 8:7, James 1:19

DAY 235

"The way of a fool seems right to him,
but a wise man listens to advice" (Proverbs 12:15).

I can't count the number of times I set out to do something that I just knew was the right thing, but in the end, I realized it wasn't. I think I know why the fool jumps out into something that just "seems" right. She doesn't have the patience to find out. Do you know what keeps us from slowing down and seeking advice? Pride.

We think we know it all and don't need anyone else's opinion. Or we think we hear from God just fine on our own—why would we need to check with someone else?

What we tend to forget is that we have an enemy who would love to deceive us into stepping outside God's plan so we can be side-tracked, delayed, and discouraged. He may be using a false sense of confidence to lure us away from the will of God. We need the advice of others for several reasons:

First, we need to slow down long enough to consider that we may be wrong. The time we take to consider another's take on things may be just the moment we need to reconsider. If it's of God, we aren't going to be delayed by seeking advice first.

Second, that pride thing. By admitting that we need advice, we are humbling ourselves before God and showing that we care more about His will than our own desires.

Third, a trusted friend or associate may know more about the situation than we do. Having the advice of someone who has gone before us may be just the wisdom we need to make the right decision.

Just because something seems right doesn't mean it is. When faced with a decision, let's prayerfully seek the advice of one we trust to seek the Lord and to be honest with us. That's what a wise person does.

For further reading: Proverbs 10:8, 11:14, 13:1, 34:6, 2 Timothy 2:15, James 1:5

DAY 236

"An anxious heart weighs a man down,
but a kind word cheers him up" (Proverbs 12:25).

Anxiety is fear manifested through our senses. We fear trouble, pain, suffering, or embarrassment, and therefore we experience stress. This stress can be felt in our racing heart, headache, worry, upset stomach, or mental anguish. How we process that stress is deeply felt at the seat of our emotions—our hearts.

When our hearts are anxious, it's like a huge boulder in the pit of our stomachs. We can't move it and we can't get around it. It affects every part of us. It weighs us down and keeps us from walking in joy and peace.

But God has the answer for our anxiety.

I used to struggle with anxious thoughts at night that kept me wide awake. I couldn't rest for fear of something bad happening to one of my children. During the day I would be busy and my mind occupied, but at night, I couldn't get the thoughts out of my head.

Finally, I started quoting Scriptures in my mind, focusing on the words and trying to remember the correct order of things I had memorized. Each time, my mind would be at peace and I would fall asleep. God's Word has the power to overcome our fears and bring us relief from our anxiety.

As children of God, we too have the ability to speak words that cheer others up. When we know someone is struggling with anxiety, we can offer a kind word of encouragement or a Scripture verse for them to hold onto.

We don't have to be weighed down by anxiety and fear, and neither do our friends. We can speak the Word of God to ourselves, and we can offer words of encouragement to others. Let a kind word be on your lips today as you encounter those who may be weighed down by the cares of the world.

For further reading: Matthew 6:25-34, John 14:27, Philippians 4:6-7, 1 Peter 5:7

DAY 237

*"A righteous man is cautious in friendship, but the
way of the wicked leads them astray" (Proverbs 12:26).*

I've never been good at making friends. Most people think I'm social, but I really prefer to be alone. I feel awkward around others and struggle to make conversation with people I don't know. I've also been rebuffed so many times that my fear of rejection keeps me from reaching out and making new friends. Can anybody relate?

Scripture actually warns us to be cautious in our friendships though. The reason is that friends can so quickly lead us astray. Peer pressure can cause us to make poor decisions that will lead us away from God, and that doesn't just apply to kids. Even as adults, we sometimes go along with the crowd in order to be accepted. Do we ever really grow up?

If we look at the life of Jesus, we will see that He had lots of associates, people He knew and ministered to (kind of like our thousands of "friends" on social media). Then He had at least seventy-two that He discipled and sent out on mission trips. He had twelve that He brought into His inner circle and trained to follow Him and serve Him.

And then there were three close friends—Peter, James, and John—whom Jesus engaged more intimately and shared spiritual things the others weren't privy to.

Jesus was open to associating with lost people. He went to their homes, ate with them, and taught them the way of the kingdom of God. But when it came to sharing His deepest thoughts and asking for prayer, He sought out those closest to Him. And when He revealed the depths of who He really was on the Mount of Transfiguration, only His three closest friends were there.

As we spend time with others and build friendships, we should also be cautious about whom we really let in. Spend time with unbelievers and show them the love of Jesus. But only open your heart to those whom God has given to you as sisters in the Lord, who will pray for you and seek God's best for you.

For further reading: Matthew 17:1-2, Luke 8:40-56, 9:28-36, 10:1-24

DAY 238

"The sluggard craves and gets nothing, but the desires of the diligent are fully satisfied" (Proverbs 13:4).

When I was growing up in the 70s and 80s, my grandparents owned and operated a gas station/country store. I grew up in that store. Most of my summers were spent there, as well as mornings and afternoons during school.

My sister and I were taught how to run the cash register and count back change. We learned to sweep and wash windows and do inventory and bag groceries. It was fun! We enjoyed working, learning the value of hard work, and being rewarded for our diligence.

Both my sister and I have had many jobs, starting in high school, working sometimes multiple jobs during college. We both pursued careers—mine in teaching and hers in business. We both have a strong work ethic: We believe in being diligent and giving our best; as a result, we enjoy the fruits of our labor.

Many today don't have that same work ethic that we were taught to value. Many believe life is about their comfort and convenience. If they don't feel like working, they don't. They feel everyone owes them something. Being on time, dressing professionally, and respecting authority seem to be ideas of the past.

But these values were founded on Christian principles, such as this one in Proverbs. Wisdom teaches us that the sluggard—one too lazy to value hard work—will crave but get nothing. There's no such thing as a free lunch. Everything has to be worked for by someone.

But those who are diligent will find their desires satisfied. They will work and find satisfaction in a job well done, even if their vocation doesn't bring great wealth.

No matter what your job is—whether you are a student, a professional, or a stay-at-home mom—be the best you can at what God has called you to be. Your diligence will reward you.

For further reading: Ecclesiastes 5:18-19, 1 Corinthians 3:9, Colossians 3:23, 1 Thessalonians 4:11-12, 5:12, 2 Thessalonians 3:10

DAY 239

"The light of the righteous shines brightly, but the lamp of the wicked is snuffed out" (Proverbs 13:9).

You know, we get to choose what kind of life we will live. God sets before us life and death—we can live for self or we can live for Him. One leads to eternal life and one leads to eternal separation from everything that is good.

The righteous are those who are in right standing with God, not those who are perfect. We are all sinners, but we can be in right standing with God by surrendering to the Lordship of His Son Jesus. When we come to God in faith and trust in the life, death, and resurrection of Jesus to pay for our sin debt, He gives us His righteousness.

By faith, we can walk in that righteousness, even though we are sinful creatures. We can get up every day and choose to surrender to the authority of God in our lives. We can spend time with Him in His Word and choose to obey Him to the best of our ability and with the help of His Spirit.

Salvation isn't exclusive or only for those who look right or act right or always have it together. The Bible says, "whoever believes in Him shall not perish but have eternal life" (John 3:16). We all have the same opportunity to let our light shine for Jesus.

Those who choose to put self above the Savior and reject Jesus as the Lord of their lives are those whose lamp will be snuffed out. They will not get to enjoy life and love for all eternity—not because God is mean but because that is what they chose.

When we live for sin and self, we are choosing a life of wickedness and pain. God knows how much our sin will hurt us and those we love. He wants us to choose His way because love is better than hate, peace is better than strife, and truth sure beats lies.

Choose to follow Jesus and walk in the light of His love. Shine brightly today.

For further reading: Deuteronomy 30:19, Joshua 24:15, Luke 10:42, John 7:17

DAY 240

"He who walks with the wise grows wise, but a companion of fools suffers harm" (Proverbs 13:20).

We all need people in our lives whom we can look up to. We need those who are more spiritual than we are who can be an example to us and encourage us to come up higher in our walk with the Lord.

I have women in my life who seek the Lord, who have walked with Him for many years, and whom I have seen live out the Christian life they profess. They aren't perfect, but their hearts are sincere. These are the women I turn to when I need prayer or direction for my life.

I want to know Jesus more and grow in my faith, so I look for other women who are seeking Him too. I look to see how they handle situations. I watch how they interact with their husbands and children. I ask them for advice when I'm uncertain in a situation.

If all we do is spend time with the same people we did before we were saved or other women who are less serious than we are about their relationship with God, we will slowly become like them. We will get slack in our time with the Lord. We'll lose our excitement for the things of God.

Because let's face it: it's easier to sin than to walk with God. Choosing to live for the Lord requires diligence, resisting temptation, and surrendering our will to His. Without people to encourage us to come up higher, we are more likely to fall away from our dedication to God.

Whom do you have in your life who is a spiritual mentor to encourage you to seek and serve the Lord? And who can you be an example to as well? Someone may need to look up to you, so walk with the wise and you will grow wise.

Then share that wisdom with others.

For further reading: Ecclesiastes 4:9-12, 1 Corinthians 15:33, 1 Thessalonians 5:11, James 4:4

DAY 241

*"He who spares the rod hates his son, but he who
loves him is careful to discipline him" (Proverbs 13:24).*

Whether or not you believe in spanking, if you have children, be careful to discipline them. We may read this verse today and think it is outdated. After all, with so many children being abused by parents, we definitely wouldn't want to encourage parents to hurt their children. The principle here, though, is that a parent who loves a child will discipline him.

Children learn behavior by what they see and hear. When kids are little, they seek what benefits themselves. We are all born with a sinful nature, and self is at the center of that nature. We will lie, steal, and pitch a fit to get what we want.

If a child behaves in an inappropriate way that is encouraged or not thwarted, he will learn to continue in that behavior, especially if it gets him what he wants. We don't stop wrong behavior without a deterrent. Discipline is the deterrent.

For children to learn right behavior, parents need to discipline with two things intact: love and consistency.

If we yell or spank our kids when we're angry, we're just teaching them how to deal with their anger—by yelling or hitting. Instead, we need to count to ten, and firmly deal with the behavior in a way that is consistent with the offense.

Each time the child shows that behavior, our response should be the same. Children are easily conditioned to understand what will be the result if they continue to misbehave. When the discipline is over, we should take them in our arms and tell them we love them. Discipline and love should go together so our kids understand our heart for them.

If you struggle in the area of discipline with your children or grandchildren, there are some great books that can help you. But the best place to start is in the Word of God.

For further reading: Ephesians 6:4, Colossians 3:21, Hebrews 12:5-11

DAY 242

"The wise woman builds her house, but with her own hands the foolish one tears hers down" (Proverbs 14:1).

How many Chip and Joanna fans do we have out there? I am amazed at what they can do to bring life to a dark, depressing home with some shiplap and subway tile. We too can bring life and light into our homes by thinking about how we are building. Because the truth is we're all either building or tearing down. The wise woman builds, so let's think about how she builds.

First, she builds on the right foundation. Jesus said in Matthew 7:24 that the wise person builds his house on the rock. As women, we can choose to make our homes a place where relationship with Jesus is the primary reason for all that we do. We can have devotions at the dinner table, use opportunities throughout the day to instill biblical principles, and pray with our family each night.

Second, she builds with the right materials. Proverbs 9:1 tells us that wisdom builds with "seven pillars." These pillars have often been compared to the seven aspects of wisdom seen in James 3:17—purity, peace, consideration, submission, mercy and good fruit, impartiality, and sincerity. When we walk in the Spirit and not the flesh, we exhibit the characteristics that match what we are teaching our families. We may not always do it perfectly, but we can strive to be an example and ask forgiveness of our families when we fail.

The foolish woman is the one who builds on the world's standards and then walks according to what her own flesh desires. She may love her family, but she is tearing her house down, brick by brick. When the storms of life come (and they will), her family will suffer because a house on shifting sand cannot stand.

Be the wise woman who builds her house on the Rock of Jesus Christ and with the pillars of wisdom that come from His Word. The best place to start is where you are right now—spending time with God every day.

For further reading: Matthew 7:24-27, 1 Corinthians 3:10-15, James 3:13-18, 1 John 2:15-17

DAY 243

"All hard work brings a profit, but mere talk leads only to poverty"
(Proverbs 14:23).

When I was about eleven or twelve, I found a book called *The Making of a Woman Surgeon* by Elizabeth Morgan. I was absolutely captivated by her stories of medical school and her experiences in surgery. Sure that I wanted to follow in her footsteps, I began to watch documentaries of operations and became fascinated with the human body.

I laid out my plan for college, medical school, and residency. That is, until I hit advanced biology and chemistry in high school. That dream ended quickly.

Have you ever set out to do something and then given up because you realized how difficult it would be? We can talk about our plans all day long, but only the hard work of putting those plans into action brings real fruit in our lives.

We live in a fast-food society in which most of us prefer what is convenient and quick to what is challenging and long-suffering. Even when it comes to going to college or learning a trade, many young people seek the easiest and shortest route rather than putting in the time, hard work, and effort it takes to earn a degree or learn a skill.

Hard work leads to profit, whether that profit comes in the form of wealth and material prosperity or wisdom and intellectual gain. Nothing worth having in life comes without effort, but the effort is worth it.

What have you put off or given up on because it just seemed too hard? Don't let challenges keep you from being all God created you to be. Set your mind to do the hard thing. You and God together have what it takes to do whatever He is calling you to do.

Turns out God wasn't calling me to be a surgeon after all. My new dream to be a teacher was fulfilled, but only with much hard work—including biology and chemistry!

For further reading: Romans 14:19, 1 Timothy 4:15, 2 Peter 1:5, 3:14, Hebrews 6:11

DAY 244

*"A patient man has great understanding,
but a quick-tempered man displays folly" (Proverbs 14:29).*

You've heard it said, "Don't pray for patience; you'll be tested."

Well, that's great advice if you don't want to grow. But if you know you need more patience in your life, you *should* ask God. Yes, you will probably be tested, but when you pass your test, you will have learned and grown into a more patient person.

Isn't that our goal as Christians—to be more like Christ? Patience is a character trait so needed in our lives. We need patience with our spouses and children, with our co-workers, and with our church family. In fact, we need patience in all of our relationships, but most of all, we need to learn to be patient and wait on the Lord.

When we don't walk in patience, we are showing that what we want is more important than how we treat others. A quick temper is evidence of one who is walking in the flesh and not the Spirit. Patience is a fruit of the Spirit because we need the Holy Spirit to lead us and comfort us when we start to feel out of control.

I have found that when I am struggling to be patient, it's usually because I have to wait on someone else or deal with a situation that is out of my control. But the more I understand that God is truly in control and can be trusted with those things I can't control, the more patient I become.

As we grow in patience, God will develop our character and make us more like Him—more loving, kind, and understanding toward others. He will use us to minister to the needs of others because we are able to wait on Him and trust Him with our lives.

So, if you need patience, don't be afraid to ask God. It's better to be tested and grow than to avoid the test and remain.

For further reading: Psalm 26:2, Romans 12:12, 1 Corinthians 13:4, 2 Corinthians 1:6, Galatians 5:22

DAY 245

"A heart at peace gives life to the body, but envy rots the bones"
(Proverbs 14:30).

There's nothing like having a heart at peace. When we are constantly looking around at what others have that we don't, we set ourselves up for disappointment and discontent.

I remember a time when I was home schooling my children. I didn't have an income, so we went without a lot of extras. One way I stayed content with what we had was by spending time with God every day and writing down what I was thankful for. Another way was by staying away from shopping centers and department store sales papers and not watching HGTV. I know that may sound foolish, but because I didn't look at those things, my heart wasn't drawn to them. And I was content with what we had.

I felt so blessed to be able to stay at home with my children. We were well-fed, clothed, and sheltered. We were warm in winter and cool in summer. Whenever I began to feel the pull toward things of the world, I would remind myself of these truths.

Paul said he knew what it was like to have plenty and he knew what it was like to be in need. He had learned the secret of being content in any situation: Finding his strength in Christ (Philippians 4:12-13). We too can do all things through Christ who gives us strength. He gives us strength to withstand the temptation to be envious and jealous of those who may have what we think we want or need. Jesus has the power to make our hearts be at peace.

Maybe you have been looking at someone's greener pastures, causing your heart to envy. Look to Jesus who meets all your needs. Turn your eyes away from worthless things, even if you have to turn off the television and drive away from the mall.

You just may find that time alone with the Lord and with your family is all you really need. That peaceful heart will bring life to you today.

For further reading: Philippians 4:11-13, 1 Timothy 6:6-8, Hebrews 13:5

DAY 246

"Righteousness exalts a nation, but sin is a disgrace to any people"
(Proverbs 14:34).

Righteousness is doing the right thing. A biblical principle that we can learn here is that doing the right thing will cause us to be lifted or raised up. This principle has been seen in many Scriptures, but here it is applied to nations.

When a nation as a whole does what honors God, He will cause that nation to be exalted. We see that in the Bible with the nation of Israel, and we can see that truth here in America as well. America has experienced God's blessing in the past. Unfortunately, much of America's former glory has been rewritten in order to highlight her former shame.

A nation is made up of people, and people are sinners. So along with times of righteousness, we have also made grievous errors in the past. If we would teach historical truth, we would see that when America did the right thing, she was blessed. When she chose to do evil, she was disgraced.

Our part as citizens of the Kingdom is to live our lives in such a way, that no matter what nation we hail from, we contribute to the righteousness that brings honor. If we live in a nation with democratic principles, we should let our votes be guided by our prayers and the Word of God. Life begins at conception and abortion is wrong. Marriage is between one man and one woman and should be honored and the marriage bed kept pure. The poor, widows, and orphans should be cared for by the church. Work is honorable and those able to work should support their families and give generously to others.

When we believe God's Word and hold to His standards through those we elect to represent us and in how we serve others, we will experience the honor and blessing of God on our nation. Conversely, when we choose to honor sin and walk in rebellion to the truth of God's Word, we will suffer shame and disgrace as a nation.

For further reading: Genesis 2:24, Psalm 139:13-14, 1 Thessalonians 4:11-12, 1 Timothy 6:17-19, Hebrews 13:4, James 1:27

DAY 247

"A gentle answer turns away wrath,
but a harsh word stirs up anger" (Proverbs 15:1).

Have you ever been having a perfectly good day, when someone says something to you that just stirs up anger and ruins your mood? I'm not sure why we creatures can be so easily affected by the words of others, but, oh, how we can!

A harsh word, a word spoken out of turn, the wrong thing said at perhaps the wrong time—all these can spark a firestorm of emotions that have that potential to not just ruin a day but a relationship.

Words have such power they can stir or stop, magnify or minimize. The tongue is hard to tame, yet a gentle answer has the power to soothe an angry heart or a wounded spirit. Our words can both harm and heal, comfort and condemn.

How our words affect those around us will depend upon our ability to think before we speak. Words that wound usually come from mouths that are quick to speak and slow to listen.

What if we begin to slow down, think about our responses, and measure our words more carefully? What if we consider what our words sound like to those around us? What if we pray and ask God to give us anointed lips that have the power to comfort, encourage, and mend?

Let's guard against words that stir up anger and instead speak words that will turn away wrath. Who knows how God might use our lips to bring peace, love, and joy to those around us.

For further reading: Psalm 37:30, Proverbs 31:26, Isaiah 50:4, 1 Corinthians 13:1, Colossians 4:6

DAY 248

"The house of the righteous contains great treasure, but the income of the wicked brings them trouble" (Proverbs 15:6).

What do we find in our homes? Are they characterized by love, joy, and peace; or strife, bitterness, and anger?

The house of the righteous contains great treasure. Oh, they may not have lots of material wealth, but they abound in the riches of the Spirit. When we strive to do what is right, we will experience the treasures of heaven.

Even in financially hard times, we can experience the provision of God. Even in times of sickness, we can have peace. In the times of our deepest need, we can experience the very presence of God. We can walk in His Word and find comfort in His care for us.

But those who seek to gain by deceit, rebellion, and selfishness, will suffer the heartache that comes as a result of sin. Even the wealth they gain will bring trouble on them and their households. What seemed to be right in their own eyes will become their downfall.

We can choose to walk with God and not rebel against His Word and the leading of His Spirit. Obedience may require sacrifice. It may cost us to surrender. But the cost is never as high as the price of sin.

Our homes can be filled with all the pleasant riches of the Spirit when we choose to make Jesus the center. As we clean, cook, and tend to our little ones, our hearts can be in prayer. Worship music can always be in the background. The Word can be posted everywhere we turn.

Let us be those who choose to do the right thing, even when it hurts, even when it may seem that we are losing. Let's trust God and His Word, that He makes all things beautiful in His time (Ecclesiastes 3:11).

For further reading: Ecclesiastes 3:11, Matthew 6:19-24, Luke 12:22-34, 1 Timothy 6:17-19

DAY 249

*"The discerning heart seeks knowledge,
but the mouth of a fool feeds on folly" (Proverbs 15:14).*

A discerning heart is one that seeks to understand, gain knowledge, grow, and be discipled. If we are followers of Christ, we should be always learning and growing and never think we have "arrived" as Christians. There is always more to learn about God and His ways.

A fool, however, thinks she already knows it all. She is always talking and rarely listening. The foolish woman is always in everybody else's business. She is very intolerant of anything that doesn't agree with her opinion, and you will definitely know her opinion if you are around her.

I know, because that used to be me. I was always frustrated with everyone who wasn't at the same level as I was (or thought I was). If someone didn't meet my expectations or do things my way, I was quick to "share" that information with others, whether it was in the disguise of a prayer request or not. How easily we forget we had to learn and grow to get where we are!

The older I get, the more I realize how little I actually know.

A discerning heart looks for opportunities for growth. She is seeking more of God and His ways and less of the world. She is never content with her spiritual life but always seeking to come up higher, to grow in her understanding of the Word of God, and to share what she has learned with others.

And a true, discerning heart looks for the best in others, seeking to help them grow rather than condemn their immaturity. She is tolerant of others and willing to overlook their opinions, even if she doesn't agree with their way of doing things.

Rather than folly, let's feed our hearts on the Word of God, growing in our understanding and sharing our faith with those around us.

For further reading: Proverbs 2:6, 1 Corinthians 8:1-3, Ephesians 1:17-18, 2 Peter 3:18

DAY 250

"Better a little with the fear of the LORD than great wealth with turmoil. Better a meal of vegetables where there is love than a fattened calf with hatred" (Proverbs 15:16-17).

What we choose to run after will define us. If we seek to keep up with the latest fads, fashions, and finances, chances are we won't have time for the things of God. The ways of the world will quickly turn our hearts away from God.

It's not wrong to have nice things, but when we let those things have us, we are in trouble.

The question is can we be content with what we have if following God means He calls us to a full-time ministry with little pay? Will we put off serving God until after we get married and settle down? Or after we have children? Or after our children leave the nest? Or after we retire?

When we truly fear God, we are willing to lay aside the trappings of the world and wealth in order to serve Him and do His will. Obeying God and being in His will bring such love and peace that once we experience them, we will never want to live for the world again.

Having a small, simple life may not seem desirable to the world, but this world is not our home. Those who put God and His will above their own wants and desires will find that they never really sacrificed at all. God is able to make all things abound to those who choose Him.

They may be those who have the most after all.

For further reading: 1 Samuel 12:24, Mark 10:45, 1 Corinthians 15:58, Colossians 3:23-24

DAY 251

"The LORD detests the thoughts of the wicked, but those of the pure are pleasing to him" (Proverbs 15:26).

Our thought life is an accurate indicator of our hearts. Who we are when no one is watching reveals the truth of our character. Are our thoughts in line with God and His Word, or do we entertain thoughts that are not of God?

Scripture tells us that we must be "transformed by the renewing" of our minds (Romans 12:2). Our minds are carnal or worldly in the natural. If we are to walk in the Spirit, our minds must be made new by the Word of God.

When we spend time reading and meditating on God's Word daily, we will begin to think in accordance with the Word. Our thoughts will be more pleasing to God. If we spend more time watching secular television, listening to secular music, and reading secular books, we will think more like the world.

Our thought life is so important because as we think, we will speak; and as we speak, we will act. Our thoughts direct the course of our day. And only we can choose what we think about.

Philippians 4:8 tells us what we should think about:

"Finally, brothers, whatever is true, whatever is noble, whatever is right, whatever is pure, whatever is lovely, whatever is admirable—if anything is excellent or praiseworthy—think about such things."

We also have the ability to redirect our minds when our thoughts are not in line with God.

"We demolish arguments and every pretension that sets itself up against the knowledge of God, and we take captive every thought to make it obedient to Christ" (2 Corinthians 10:5).

So, think about what you are thinking about. Let your thoughts be pure and pleasing to God.

For further reading: Romans 12:2, 2 Corinthians 10:5, Philippians 4:8

DAY 252

"All a man's ways seem innocent to him, but
motives are weighed by the LORD" (Proverbs 16:2).

We rarely judge ourselves and find us guilty. We are much more prone to consider ourselves innocent, but only God can truly judge our hearts.

Paul said this: "My conscience is clear, but that does not make me innocent. It is the Lord who judges me" (1 Corinthians 4:4).

Truly, we rarely know what is in our own hearts. Often our own sin is difficult to see. That's why we need to daily ask God to search us and reveal the motives and intents of our hearts. God cares about more than just what we say and what we do. He cares about the why. We can easily do the right thing for the wrong reason.

If we give so others will see, we give out of pride rather than generosity (Matthew 6:1-4). If we pray to get what we want, we pray out of selfishness (James 4:3). If we obey the letter of the law, but break the spirit of the law, we've become like the Pharisees. Jesus had some harsh words for them:

"'You are like whitewashed tombs, which look beautiful on the outside but on the inside are full of dead men's bones and everything unclean. In the same way, on the outside you appear to people as righteous but on the inside you are full of hypocrisy and wickedness'" (Matthew 23:27b-28).

God clearly looks at the "why" behind what we do. So, like David, we can ask God daily to search our hearts and show us anything that is not pleasing to Him. Then we can turn away from that sin by His help and walk in His purity and grace.

"Search me, O God, and know my heart; test me and know my anxious thoughts. See if there is any offensive way in me, and lead me in the way everlasting" (Psalm 139:23-24).

For further reading: Jeremiah 17:9, Psalm 139:23-24, Matthew 6:1-4, 23:27-28, 1 Corinthians 4:4, James 4:3

DAY 253

"Commit to the LORD whatever you do,
and your plans will succeed" (Proverbs 16:3).

The world's definition of success and God's definition of success are two different things. If we have in our minds that success means being rich and famous, then perhaps we will be left disappointed. But success in God's eyes means that we fulfill His call on our lives.

God calls us to be faithful. He calls us to walk with integrity. He calls us to make disciples. When we measure success by the Book, we are more likely to understand what it means to see our plans succeed. So, how do we make plans that line up with God's will for our lives?

I believe we do two things: Pray for God to lead us and then commit to Him whatever we do.

As we pray for God to lead us, He will open doors of opportunity we may have never even considered. When I was teaching high school, I had no idea that God would lead me down the path of writing and speaking. I could never have imagined how God is using me today. The key is that I was seeking God every day, praying for His will in my life, and open to whatever He called me to do.

As we seek His face and surrender to His will, the Holy Spirit will take us down the path God has for us. That path may sometimes seem unsure and even scary, but as we trust in the Lord, He will guide us with peace and confidence in Him.

When God begins to open doors, then we commit it all to Him. We get up every day and ask for His leading, and we strive to be faithful and walk with integrity. As we do that, we can be sure that our plans will succeed.

God may not always take us down the path of our own choosing, but He will guide in the path He has for us. We may face obstacles, but if we are following His lead, we will have success that is out of this world!

For further reading: 1 Samuel 18:14, Jeremiah 29:11, Matthew 6:33, Philippians 4:13

DAY 254

*"Pride goes before destruction, a haughty
spirit before a fall" (Proverbs 16:18).*

It's difficult to keep our hearts humble before the Lord. We are naturally self-centered creatures, and our thoughts easily turn inward. But as this Scripture warns us, pride eventually leads to destruction. So how can we avoid that haughty spirit?

What God wants is for us to cultivate a heart of humility. I'll admit: that's one of my biggest struggles. I read somewhere that humility doesn't mean that we think less of ourselves but that we think of ourselves less. In other words, for those of us who have struggled with insecurity, we don't have to think we are worthless, no-good failures.

That's what the enemy wants us to think. Jesus died to set us free from those lies. We can have confidence in our identity in Christ, yet walk in a spirit of humility by putting God first, others second, and ourselves last.

For example, instead of wanting to be the center of attention, we can focus on others when we walk into a room. Instead of thinking how great we are, we can meditate on how great God is. Instead of talking about ourselves all the time or always having to share our opinion, we can take the time to listen to others' opinions.

Instead of boasting of what we have, we can thank God for what He has provided. Rather than being proud of our education or skills, we can focus on using them to help others. Rather than looking down on others we can seek to build others up.

It's all a matter of what we choose to focus on. So the next time the Holy Spirit quickens your spirit about some haughty attitude, repent quickly and ask Him to redirect your heart to His goodness and how you can share it with someone else.

For further reading: Romans 12:16, Galatians 6:3, James 4:6, 1 Peter 5:5

DAY 255

"Pleasant words are a honeycomb, sweet to the soul and healing to the bones" (Proverbs 16:24).

What are some of the sweetest words that have ever been spoken to you?

Perhaps "I love you" or "I'm proud of you" from the lips of someone really special? Maybe a word of encouragement during a particularly difficult time? Think about how those words impacted you and why.

The right words can be healing to the broken, encouragement to the downtrodden, comfort to the grieved. Words can build us up and help us stand in faith.

But I think the sweetest words of all are those that tell the story of Jesus. When we share the gospel with those who don't know Him, we speak words of life that have the ability to impact eternity.

So why do we fail to share God's truth as often as we should? I think many times we fear that others will reject us, but Jesus made it clear that someone who rejects our message isn't rejecting us, but Him.

Who do you know that needs to understand the truth of God's love? Prayerfully consider sharing the gospel with her. She may be just waiting for someone to come along with the right words that will be sweet to her soul and healing to her bones.

Don't worry about the response. Remember our responsibility is to be faithful to share God's truth, but it's not our job to convince people or change their hearts. That's God's job.

Remember those life-giving words that have been spoken to you? Your words can have the same impact if you let them.

For further reading: Isaiah 52:7, Luke 10:16, John 15:18, Romans 1:16, 1 Corinthians 1:17

DAY 256

*"There is a way that seems right to a man,
but in the end it leads to death" (Proverbs 16:25).*

We love to be right, don't we?

Have you ever argued with someone just to prove your point, but later realized being right wasn't worth the strife? Or later discovered you were wrong?

In the Old Testament we learn of a time in the history of Israel when "everyone did as he saw fit" (Judges 17:6).

The Israelites had a covenant with God that was based on the Law. The Law gave them moral standards that would set them apart as a nation and guide them in what was right. But the people had decided they no longer needed to live by the standards of the Law, and everyone did what was right in his own eyes.

Today, we see that same pattern of thinking as truth has become relative in the minds of unbelievers. Many believe that what's right can change depending upon the situation. And many don't want a standard to live by; they would prefer to live by their own whims and wishes.

But often what we believe is right could actually be leading to destruction. That's why we need a standard for what is right and wrong, and we find that in the Word of God.

If we want to follow the way that leads to life, we need to surrender to God and follow Him. As we do, His Word will guide our lives into what is truly right so that we can show others the way. Let's not live by what just seems right to us; let's live our lives by what God's Word tells us is right.

Only then can we be an example that others want to follow and that will lead them in the right direction.

For further reading: Judges 17:6, John 8:12, Ephesians 5:1, 2 Timothy 3:16, James 4:17

DAY 257

*"Better a dry crust with peace and quiet than
a house full of feasting with strife" (Proverbs 17:1).*

This verse seems kind of funny at first, but if you've ever had to endure an atmosphere of strife, you realize how true it is. When we allow a spirit of strife in our homes, we open the door for heartache and broken relationships.

Even a steak dinner can't make up for arguing, harsh words, and bitter feelings.

Sure, there will be times that we don't agree and discussions may become heated. But we can learn to follow God's guidelines for handling disagreements in our homes.

Pray.

"Is any one of you in trouble? He should pray" (James 5:13a).

Listen.

"My dear brothers, take note of this: Everyone should be quick to listen, slow to speak, and slow to become angry" (James 1:19).

Submit.

"Submit to one another out of reverence for Christ" (Ephesians 5:21).

Settle.

"Do not let the sun go down while you are still angry, and do not give the devil a foothold" (Ephesians 4:26b-27).

Pray, listen, submit, and settle.

If we follow these instructions in God's Word, we can move quickly from disagreements to peace and quiet, and that is better than all the lasagna, garlic bread, and tiramisu in the world.

For further reading: Ephesians 4:26-27, 5:21, James 1:19, 5:13a

DAY 258

"He who covers over an offense promotes love" (Proverbs 17:9a).

Sometimes we can be easily offended, but God calls us to cover over an offense through forgiveness. Often we take offense where none was intended. Maybe we are sensitive in a particular area because of some past hurt.

If we are aware of areas in which we tend to be touchy, we can pray and ask the Holy Spirit to heal our wounds and set us free.

God calls us to promote love, and we do that best by choosing to forgive.

If we are offended by someone, we can ask God to help us think rightly about the situation. We can choose to believe that no offense was intended. We can choose to let the person off the hook and not allow our minds or emotions to be affected by their potentially offensive words or actions.

Think about the options: If we choose to be offended, we will be upset, hurt, and out of peace. We will meditate on what has been done to us and how we think we have been treated. Will any of that lead to peace, love, or joy in our lives?

If we choose to be offended, we may possibly put up a wall between us and someone else so that our relationship is forever strained.

And if we choose to be offended, we give the devil the opportunity to bring strife and unrest in our lives.

But, if we choose to cover over the offense, we are basically saying that even if the other person did intend to offend, we choose to forgive. By doing so, we protect ourselves from harm and promote love toward the other person.

And the Holy Spirit can change our hearts and emotions when we choose to forgive and promote love. So the next time someone says or does something that offends, let the Lord have His way in your heart. Choose not to be offended. Choose love.

For further reading: Matthew 6:14-15, 18:21-22, Mark 11:25, Ephesians 4:26-27, Colossians 3:13

DAY 259

"...but whoever repeats the matter separates close friends"
(Proverbs 17:9b).

We learned yesterday that we can choose to cover over an offense through forgiveness. The real test of that forgiveness is whether or not we feel the need to repeat the matter to someone else. Honestly, it feels good to tell someone else when we've been offended. We have the need to have our pain validated by others. If we can get a friend to agree with us about someone else's bad behavior, somehow we don't feel quite as hurt.

The problem with this way of thinking is that repeating the matter to someone else usually closes the door on the relationship with the offending person. In other words, we haven't really forgiven her. If we still feel the need to be validated, we are holding onto the offense.

God calls us to forgive and let the matter go. That means we don't repeat it to someone else. We don't try to get others on our side. We don't disparage the other person's character in an attempt to get even for what she did to us.

Real love covers over the offense and lets it go, even if the pain is very real. Oftentimes, we will have to renew our commitment to obedience over and over. We may have to get up every day and say, "I choose not to be offended, and I will not repeat what _____ did to me."

You know what happens when we choose this radical obedience? The power of sin and Satan lose their grip on us. The enemy wants us to feel hurt and offended. He wants to create strife and broken relationships, especially in families and in churches.

But we have the Living God inside us to lead, to heal, to correct, and to empower us to walk in His Spirit. Let's renew our commitment to not be easily offended and to not repeat a matter to others. Our friendships are worth our sacrifice.

For further reading: Proverbs 18:19, 19:11, Ecclesiastes 7:21-22, Ephesians 4:2-3, 1 Peter 2:23

DAY 260

*"Starting a quarrel is like breaching a dam; so drop
the matter before a dispute breaks out" (Proverbs 17:14).*

Here in South Carolina, we have endured some major flooding over the last couple of years. When river levels rise, it affects everything downstream, leading to many dams that have been breached. Openings in those dams cause powerful currents of water to flow in areas of both commercial and residential structures, leading to millions of dollars in damage and the lives of thousands of people affected.

Breaching a dam can not only lead to severe damage; it can ultimately lead to death. Starting a quarrel is like breaching a dam: It can lead to untold damage in relationships and even the end of some.

Why do we start quarrels? Usually we want to validate our opinion or prove that we are right. Of course, there are areas of doctrine that we should stand firm on in our defense of the gospel. There may be times that we need to take a stand for what is morally right. We may need to be firm with our children, which could start a quarrel.

But for those times in which we argue just to prove a point, we should let the matter drop. Unless we are standing for something potentially harmful to someone else, our opinion is just that—our opinion. If we are right about something, it will bear truth eventually.

Our pride doesn't want to drop an argument we think we can win, but God tells us to do just that. Being right is highly overrated. In the end, we are left with our victory and little else.

So the next time you sense a useless argument coming on, just swallow your pride and let the matter drop. You have the power to stop a flood of angry words and hurt feelings. And chances are the argument wasn't that important anyway.

For further reading: Galatians 5:19-21, Ephesians 4:29-32, James 4:1-3

DAY 261

"Of what use is money in the hand of a fool,
since he has no desire to get wisdom?" (Proverbs 17:16).

Money is a tool—it is only useful as a source for trade. What we trade our money for will reveal where our hearts lie. Many people have good sources of income but trade their money for what they want while ignoring things they need. They find themselves in a financial bind, even when they have the sources to provide for themselves. God teaches us that we need wisdom to use money rightly. As a tool, money can be used for great good.

The wise use of money teaches us that everything we have belongs to God, and we should give back to Him first through our tithes. Then we should pay our taxes. Next, we should make a budget of our monthly expenses that covers our basic needs—shelter, food, clothing, and transportation. We should also plan for emergencies by saving some each month.

After covering those essentials, whatever money is left should then be designated for those things which we want but don't necessarily need, such as television, internet, and entertainment. Wisdom teaches us to give, to save, to pay for necessities, and only then to spend on those things we want.

Our family has always lived by a budget, even at the ridicule of others. But we have always had our needs met and most of our wants. We seek to be wise in how we spend our resources and share with others who have needs. We pray about how and where to give above our tithes.

If you struggle in the area of finances because you simply don't have enough to meet your basic needs, then seek God and ask Him to help you. But if you struggle because you don't use wisdom in how you spend, then prayerfully seek the guidance of the Holy Spirit as you plan a budget.

Then ask God to give you the wisdom and self-control to stick to your budget, even when your flesh doesn't like it. I promise you will be blessed and grateful in the end.

For further reading: Proverbs 13:11, Malachi 3:10, Matthew 22:21, Romans 13:8, 1 Corinthians 16:2, 2 Corinthians 9:7

DAY 262

"A friend loves at all times, and a brother is born for adversity"
(Proverbs 17:17).

One of the greatest blessings in life is true friendship. A real friend is one who shares your love for Jesus, for apart from the Holy Spirit, we are not capable of true love. Oh sure, we can say we love one another, but when love calls us to sacrifice or speak truth, without the Holy Spirit we will fail.

We all need a friend who will love us even when we are going through difficult circumstances, even when we are falling into sin. A real friend will speak truth even when we don't want to hear it, even when we get angry.

Read friends hold us accountable. They will sit right down in the mire with us and hold our hands, but they won't let us stay there. In times of adversity—whether from the world, the enemy, or that of our own making—a real friend won't leave us.

That's what they were born for—to stick close to us and hold us up.

Real friends are hard to come by. We may have thousands of social media friends, but only one true friend. I used to feel sad that I didn't have friends to shop with or hang out at a coffee shop. But then I realized that I do have friends who will speak truth into my life, and that's more important.

Take some time to evaluate your friendships. If you have friends who are not believers, do you share the love of Jesus with them and pray for them, or do you just enjoy hanging out with them? If the latter is true, then are you a real friend?

If you have friends who are believers, do you only speak what they want to hear, or do you lovingly speak truth into their lives?

You may have only one good friend in this world, but if you do, you are indeed blessed.

For further reading: 1 Samuel 18:1, Proverbs 18:24, Ecclesiastes 4:9-12, Ephesians 4:15

DAY 263

"A cheerful heart is good medicine, but a crushed spirit dries up the bones" (Proverbs 17:22).

My children grew up with their great-grandmother right next door. My daughter was very close to her and loved to nurse her as she got older and had health problems. We were home schooling at the time and the only family members who could care for her, so we did most of our schooling from her house is order to prepare her meals and oversee her medications. I vividly remember a time that she was hospitalized for congestive heart failure.

Because we took her to all of her doctors' appointments, Bethany was very well-acquainted with all of Grandma's doctors and nurses. One day at the hospital, Bethany decided we should put a Scripture on the whiteboard in her hospital room—the one normally used to write patient information on.

So we put this proverb on her board. Every time nurses or doctors came in the room and saw it, they commented that it was so true. They had personally seen how cheerfulness and smiles and laughter had helped patients get better more quickly.

Studies actually show that people who have a good attitude have better recovery rates, but the evidence has been here in Scripture all along.[81] Of course, being cheerful can't cure every disease, but the principle holds true.

While being discouraged and depressed can cause us to actually be sick, a cheerful attitude can help us feel better and respond better to our circumstances. So, how can we be cheerful if we are actually sick or depressed?

We can listen to positive, uplifting music, read Scripture, pray, and spend time with people who will encourage and lift us up. If we are watching, listening to, or being around people or things that are dark, negative, or sad, the opposite is true.

So, let your heart be cheerful today!

For further reading: Psalm 68:3, Proverbs 15:13, 30, James 5:13

DAY 264

"Even a fool is thought wise if he keeps silent,
and discerning if he holds his tongue" (Proverbs 17:28).

You may be wondering why there are so many verses about the tongue, lips, mouth, words, and speech. Well, maybe because God knows that is one of the most difficult areas of sin for us to overcome. I know this: I need to read these verses every day.

Holding the tongue is often one of the hardest things to do, especially if you are a talker like me. Yet we know that when we talk much we often speak words we shouldn't because we aren't mindful and prayerful about our words.

Words have such power, but we wield them as if they are harmless. Some good questions to ask about our conversations are these:

Do our words build up or tear down? Do we always have to share our opinion? Do we listen to what other people are saying, or are we simply thinking about our response? Do we wait on people to finish talking or interrupt with our own words? Do we think prayerfully about our words or say whatever comes to mind? Do we experience times that we keep silent and choose to hold our tongue?

According to this verse, the wise and discerning are those who do keep silent at times, who know there is a time to speak up and a time to be quiet. If you struggle in this area, ask the Holy Spirit to give you wisdom, to slow your words, and to empower you to think before you speak.

Maybe with God's help we might be considered wise.

For further reading: Psalm 19:14, Matthew 12:36-37, Colossians 3:8, James 3:1-12

DAY 265

"One who is slack in his work is brother to one who destroys"
(Proverbs 18:9).

I'm a firm believer that all we do should be done with excellence. Some would call me a perfectionist, but I have learned to be content with less than perfect.

The other end of the spectrum is laziness or mediocrity. There are those who do enough to get by but never really strive to do anything well. When we are slack in our work, we are like those who don't care, who put no effort into anything.

Anything worth having is worth working to achieve. Some things take more effort than others, but God calls us to put forth our best in all that we do. We don't have to be perfect, but He calls us to excellence with grace.

As believers, we should work hard to do things as well as we possibly can, not settling for less than our best.

"So whether you eat or drink or whatever you do, do it all for the glory of God" (1 Corinthians 10:31).

"Whatever you do, work at it with all your heart, as working for the Lord, not for men" (Colossians 3:23).

"Serve wholeheartedly, as if you were serving the Lord, not men" (Ephesians 6:7).

We are encouraged to be diligent and not slack.

"Be diligent in these matters; give yourself wholly to them, so that everyone may see your progress" (1 Timothy 4:15).

Strive to be excellent in your lifestyle, your work ethic, and your service, but don't be controlled by perfectionism. Do your absolute best with all diligence, and then trust His grace to meet your weakness.

For further reading: 1 Corinthians 10:31, Ephesians 6:7, Colossians 3:23, 1 Timothy 4:15

DAY 266

"The name of the LORD is a strong tower;
the righteous run to it and are safe" (Proverbs 18:10).

There are times in life when all we can do is call on the name of the Lord. In times of sickness, grief, or distress, we may not have the words to pray, but we can just cry, "Jesus, help me." Praise God, He hears the cries of His children when we call out to Him.

The name *LORD* is the English rendering of the Hebrew *yhwh* (or what we would say in English because we need vowels: *Yahweh*). *The NIV Exhaustive Bible Concordance* defines *LORD* this way:

"The proper name of the one true God; knowledge and use of the name implies personal or covenant relationship; the name pictures God as one who exists and/or causes existence."[82]

In other words, only those in a personal, covenant relationship with God through His Son Jesus can run to Him for safe keeping. Only those who are righteous through the blood of Jesus find Him to be a strong tower.

Many people abuse the name of the Lord. Some take His name in vain, use it lightly or irreverently, or call on Him without really knowing Him. But for those who belong to Him, His name is a safe place.

"Yet to all who received him, to those who believed in his name, he gave the right to become children of God" (John 1:12).

If you have received Jesus as your Lord and believed in His name as the one true God who desires a personal relationship with you, then you are His child. You can call on His name, and you can run to Him for safe keeping.

For further reading: Exodus 3:15, 20:7, Psalm 9:10, Acts 2:21, 4:12, Romans 10:13

DAY 267

"A gift opens the way for the giver and ushers him into the presence of the great" (Proverbs 18:16).

I love to give gifts. There's nothing like picking out something that you know someone else will love, and then watching his face as he opens that gift and lights up with joy.

My husband is one of those who people who is difficult to buy for. He knows precisely what he wants, but he usually has to pick it out himself. I'm glad that he's happy with what he gets, but I so want to personally pick out something for him that he will LOVE!

For our anniversary this year, I really wanted to get him something he would know nothing about but that he would really be excited to receive. After much thought and prayer, I decided to get him basketball tickets for his favorite team.

I could hardly wait for him to open his card. Like a little child, my heart was about to burst to see his expression when he saw those tickets. And I was not disappointed. He was thrilled to receive something that I chose for him and surprised him with.

Giving gifts is a way that we can express our love for others, and gifts can open doors for us in ministry. For instance, when we go into a particular area of our community to share the gospel, we often serve a meal or give out blankets.

The love shown through those gifts opens the hearts of those we share God's love with. And when we give, we are modeling the greatest Giver of all.

"For God so loved the world that he gave his one and only Son, that whoever believes in him shall not perish but have eternal life" (John 3:16).

God made the greatest sacrifice of all when He gave us His Son. How can you model giving today?

For further reading: Matthew 7:11, Luke 11:13, John 3:16, 14:16, Romans 8:32

DAY 268

"The first to present his case seems right, till another comes forward and questions him" (Proverbs 18:17).

Have you ever watched one of those courtroom dramas on television? The first lawyer will give closing arguments that will convince you his client is innocent. Then the opposing attorney will share his arguments, and suddenly you are filled with doubt.

The lesson to be learned here is that we always need to hear both sides of a situation, whether it involves our spouse, children, church family, or coworkers. When we only hear one side of an argument, we are not being fair to all people concerned.

I've often heard my husband say he tells his students he is tough, but he is fair. He will always listen to both sides.

Oftentimes, we jump to conclusions based on hearsay or only one side of things. How many arguments, divisions, and hurt feelings could be avoided if we would just wait until all sides present their case?

There will always be disagreement if we live among others. We don't always have to agree, but we should always be willing to listen before we make a judgment.

When there are two sides to an issue, a good practice is to have both parties sit down. Beginning with prayer, let one side share their case with the stipulation that the other side cannot reply until the first side is finished. Then the other side presents their case while the first side remains quiet.

Only after both sides have the opportunity to share should a decision be made. When we practice these biblical principles in our families and in the church, we can avoid strife and division.

For further reading: Proverbs 18:13, James 1:19

DAY 269

"The tongue has the power of life and death,
and those who love it will eat its fruit" (Proverbs 18:21).

Our tongue has the power to do great harm if left unchecked. Jesus said that we would give an account for every careless word we have spoken (Matthew 12:36). Wow.

Yet as I go through any given day, I rarely give that much thought to my words. The Bible has much to say about our words, but many of us don't consider what we say as much as we should. Of course, we know we shouldn't lie, slander, gossip, or curse. But how much of our words are negative or complaining?

With the words of His mouth, God spoke the world into being. Now, I'm not God and neither are you, but we do know that He says our tongues have the power of life and death, so how much "death" are we speaking over our lives?

In other words, if we are negative all day long, we will have a bad attitude which will spill over into the lives of those around us. If we complain all the time, we are creating an atmosphere in which we may not be able to even recognize our blessings.

You've heard the expression we will eat our words. Proverbs tells us this is true.

"From the fruit of his mouth a man's stomach is filled; with the harvest from his lips he is satisfied" (Proverbs 18:20).

We declare into the space around us what we will take in with our senses. When we speak, we hear and take in the words we have spoken, as well as those in our midst. Think about that. Our very being—our mind, will, and emotions—is so tied to what we say.

Let's be those who guard our tongues, who think before we speak, knowing that the words that leave our mouths are those with which we will be fed.

For further reading: Psalm 34:1, 2 Corinthians 8:7, 1 Timothy 4:12

DAY 270

"It is not good to have zeal without knowledge,
nor to be hasty and miss the way" (Proverbs 19:2).

Oh, don't I know this one to be true? I'm one of those people who acts now and thinks about it later. I would rather make a bad decision than to be indecisive. My husband, on the other hand, thinks things through (sometimes forever) before making a decision.

Though he drives me crazy, it looks like he's right. All my zeal and hastiness without seeking God first just leads to sin.

Yep, that phrase "miss the way" is a common Hebrew expression for sin.[83] So, my zeal and passion to get things done is a waste of time if I don't slow down and seek knowledge first. At the least, I'm missing out on something better. At the worst, I'm actually choosing the wrong way.

Zeal is great if we back it up with knowledge. In other words, we need to know what we are doing. For instance, I get emails all the time about publishing opportunities, software I need for my business, conferences and webinars I should register for.

When I first started out, if it looked interesting, I subscribed or bought in to whatever was being offered—and many times wasted money that could have been better spent elsewhere. I have hastily edited or pushed through a project in my "zeal" to get it done, only to find I had huge mistakes that cost me much to fix.

So, I'm learning to slow down and consider the choices before I run into the next thing. I'm taking the time to learn and consider all the options and outcomes as I pursue ministry and business.

What about you? In what areas of life do you need to slow down and consider all the options? Zeal is great—when tempered with understanding.

For further reading: Proverbs 21:5, 29:20, Ecclesiastes 5:2, 1 Timothy 5:22

DAY 271

"A man's own folly ruins his life, yet his heart rages against the LORD" (Proverbs 19:3).

I know people who used to walk with the Lord, attend church regularly, and serve the Lord. Then life didn't turn out the way they planned, and they turned away from God. In their hearts, they blamed Him because of a false belief: If I choose to serve God, then He owes me something. The problem with this line of thinking is that God has promised us much, but He owes us nothing. We are the ones with a debt of sin that we could never repay. God paid the price for us out of His great love.

Our surrender and sacrifice to God should come from a heart that loves and fears the Lord. If we serve God because we expect Him to make our lives perfect in return, we have the wrong motivation.

We live in a fallen world with a heart that is prone to sin. Sometimes bad stuff just happens, and more often than not, our own choices catch up with us. We want fire insurance, but we don't want to live by God's standards.

The Bible clearly teaches that we will reap what we sow.

"Do not be deceived: God cannot be mocked. A man reaps what he sows. The one who sows to please his sinful nature, from that nature will reap destruction; the one who sows to please the Spirit, from the Spirit will reap eternal life" (Galatians 6:7-8).

When our own foolish choices lead to ruin, we shouldn't blame God but repent and surrender to Him. We all make poor choices at times, but raging against the Lord when we suffer the consequences only leads to further pain and suffering.

If you are suffering as a result of poor choices you have made, turn your heart back to God and let Him guide you into His perfect will. There may be suffering in His will, but you can trust that He will work it all together for your good (Romans 8:28).

For further reading: Isaiah 59:2, Romans 8:28, Galatians 6:7-8, Hebrews 12:11

DAY 272

*"Discipline your son, for in that there is hope;
do not be a willing party to his death" (Proverbs 19:18).*

The word *discipline* in the Hebrew means "to correct, instruct, or train."[84] Parents are to instruct their children and train them up in the right way to go. We should teach our children what is right and wrong according to God's Word.

We should teach our children a biblical worldview. They are going to have to live in a culture that is increasingly counter to their beliefs. We need to give them the tools to judge right from wrong and to hold everything up to the standard of God's Word.

Part of that training includes correcting our kids when they go astray. They will never learn to do what is right if there are no consequences for what is wrong.

I'm certainly no expert when it comes to discipline or parenting, but the Word of God is. In Deuteronomy we can read how Hebrew parents were to teach their children the Word of God (Deuteronomy 6:4-9).

With so much abuse and neglect toward children in today's society, discipline can be a touchy subject; however, if we will use the Word of God and common sense, we can do our best to raise our kids in an atmosphere that is tempered with both truth and grace.

If we allow our kids to go undisciplined when they make poor choices, it may seem easier at the time, but we are being "a willing party to their death" as the Scripture says. Left unchecked, sin leads to death (Romans 3:23).

The most important thing we can do for our children is lead them to a saving relationship with Jesus Christ. As we live by example, our kids will learn to follow Jesus, and that is the best discipline we can give.

For further reading: Deuteronomy 6:4-9, Romans 3:23, Ephesians 6:4, Hebrews 12:11

DAY 273

"Wine is a mocker and beer is a brawler; whoever is led astray by them is not wise" (Proverbs 20:1).

The drinking of alcohol among Christians is another disputed and touchy subject. The Bible does not say that drinking alcohol is a sin, so many Christians do drink. The Bible does have much to say about drunkenness, however, which is listed as a sin (Romans 13:13, Galatians 5:21, 1 Timothy 3:3, 1 Peter 4:3).

"Do not get drunk on wine, which leads to debauchery. Instead, be filled with the Spirit" (Ephesians 5:18). This verse is in the context of living with wisdom and not foolishness.

My father was an alcoholic, which eventually led to his death. I can honestly say that I have never seen alcohol lead to something good. If I have the choice of either being filled with wine or filled with the Spirit, I'm going to choose the Spirit every time.

There are many warnings in the Bible about alcohol, which is an addictive substance that affects our bodies in many ways. The American Addiction Centers report that alcohol has significant impact on our cognitive abilities:

"Occasional and moderate drinkers: memory impairment, blackout, recklessness, impaired decision-making; Heavy and/or chronic drinkers: diminished gray matter in the brain, inability to think abstractly, loss of visuospatial abilities, Wernicke-Korsakoff syndrome, memory loss, loss of attention span."[85]

Because alcohol affects our cognitive abilities, we can't always effectively stop before we have gone from drinking to drunkenness, and therein lies the problem for a Christian. Proverbs tells us it is not wise to be led astray by wine and beer.

Whatever your conviction is, just use wisdom.

For further reading: Romans 13:13, Galatians 5:21, Ephesians 5:18, 1 Timothy 3:3, 1 Peter 4:3

DAY 274

*"The purposes of a man's heart are deep waters, but a
man of understanding draws them out" (Proverbs 20:5).*

The purposes of the heart are the motives behind what we say and do. And let's be honest. Most of the time we don't even understand what is really in our hearts. We often react out of past hurts and insecurities that result from them. When we see someone else reacting with anger or harsh words, it's hard for us to know the purpose of her heart. We usually feel defensive and turn inward to protect ourselves, but what if we prayed for understanding instead? What if we paused our reaction and asked the Holy Spirit to give us discernment?

Anger is an emotion that results when we feel fearful, anxious, threatened, insecure, or powerless. Oftentimes there are years of pain that have been pushed down deeper and deeper into those waters, and anger is the only emotion many people know how to express.

We can be the person who responds with more anger, criticism, harsh words, and retribution; or we can be the one with understanding who helps draw out the motives behind their reactions. We may not have a psychology degree, but we do have the Holy Spirit. The Holy Spirit is our Counselor, and He can lead us to counsel someone else. Let's be the friend who encourages others to think about the purposes of their hearts.

And while we're at it, let's slow down and think about why we often respond the way we do. When others are critical of us, do we react out of past insecurities? Are we easily offended because of the way we have processed prior offenses? Jesus died to set us free from all that. But we have to acknowledge it.

Let's be people of understanding who seek to draw out the purposes of our own hearts and help others do the same. We will save both them and ourselves much heartache.

For further reading: 1 Chronicles 28:9, John 14:16, 26, 15:26, Philippians 1:17-18

DAY 275

*"Many a man claims to have unfailing love,
but a faithful man who can find?" (Proverbs 20:6).*

Love that doesn't fail is not something we can manufacture on our own, but something the world surely needs. How many past hurts in your life resulted from love that failed—human, selfish, fleshly attempts at love that couldn't hold up to the ideals that we hold?

We all long to be loved unconditionally, right? We want to be measured by the intent of our hearts and not always by our mistakes and failures. We want to be faithful, but we fall short of perfect love. Love is tempered by our human nature, fear, and selfishness. A faithful person who can find?

Praise God that perfect love casts out fear, and God is perfect love!

All those things that keep us from loving as we should are overcome by the cross. God sent His Son because of His unrelenting love for us. When we surrender our lives to Him, that love comes to live in our hearts.

God calls us to walk in His Spirit, and the fruit of His Spirit starts with love. So we should do a love-check daily. How is my love walk? Am I demonstrating love to those around me by allowing God to love others through me?

What fears and insecurities do I allow that keep me from being faithful in love?

As we search our hearts daily and study Scriptures on love, God will grow and mature our hearts to become more like His. Maybe we can never love perfectly this side of eternity, but we can certainly grow in our love toward others.

We must be intentional about how we love. We must choose to forgive those who hurt us, to overlook offenses, and to walk in love even when it isn't reciprocated. Not easy. But possible.

God is love. Apart from Him, we can do nothing. So if we want to have unfailing, faithful love in our lives, we need more of the life of Jesus living in and through us. Let Him love through you today.

For further reading: Romans 5:8, 1 Corinthians 13:1-13, 1 John 4:7-21

DAY 276

"Who can say, 'I have kept my heart pure;
I am clean and without sin'?" (Proverbs 20:9).

We like to think we're perfect, but we're not. It's much easier to point out the mistakes and shortcomings of others than to see our own, but God's Word tells us we are all sinners.

"...There is no difference, for all have sinned and fall short of the glory of God" (Romans 3:23).

When I compare myself to someone else, I may be able to convince myself that I'm pretty good, but when compared to God, I fall far short.

I want a pure heart, though.

It's funny how apart from Christ, I am the worst of sinners (1 Timothy 1:15), yet in Christ I become the righteousness of God (2 Corinthians 5:21).

We can't keep our hearts pure on our own. But as we abide in Christ daily, we can certainly seek a pure heart and clean hands. We do that by coming to God, searching our hearts, and repenting of our sins. It's a daily process.

One prayer I like to pray is Psalm 139:23-24:

"Search me, O God, and know my heart; test me and know my anxious thoughts. See if there is any offensive way in me, and lead me in the way everlasting."

Praying a blanket prayer of "Please forgive all my sins" keeps us from really identifying and dealing with the sin in our lives. We need to ask God to show us and convict us of sin so we can truly repent—which means to turn away from it.

Who can say his heart is pure and without sin? Only Jesus. But if Jesus lives in you, that's a good start.

For further reading: Psalm 139:23-24, Romans 3:23, 2 Corinthians 5:21, 1 Timothy 1:15

DAY 277

"Even a child is known by his actions, by whether his conduct is pure and right" (Proverbs 20:11).

I'll bet you know some kids who are little terrors. They might even live in your house. Seriously, after twenty-two years in education, I can testify that kids are known by their actions. Those who were rebellious and causing trouble were well-known throughout the school. Then those kids who were kind and well-behaved were also known.

If children are known by their actions, how much more are we?

Our reputations are important. Are we seen as those whose conduct is right or as busybodies, gossips, or complainers? We are generally known, not by our slip-ups, but by our character over time.

Sometimes I feel that I have been misunderstood or unfairly characterized by a particular failure, but when I really assess the situation, it has become part of my conduct. And yes, we will be known by our actions.

So, my job is to think about how I am viewed by others—not in a self-condemning way but an honest assessment of my conduct and whether others would view it as right.

No matter who we are, if we call ourselves Christians, we have a certain responsibility to live in a manner worthy of His name. Not perfect—but not careless either.

"Whatever happens, conduct yourselves in a manner worthy of the gospel of Christ" (Philippians 1:27).

Do you want to be known as one whose conduct is pure and right? Take time to think about how you think, talk, and act. And conduct yourself in a manner that is above reproach. When you mess up, just admit your shortcomings with humility and honesty. That's a character others will trust.

For further reading: Ephesians 4:1, Philippians 1:27, Colossians 1:10

DAY 278

"Do not say, 'I'll pay you back for this wrong!'
Wait for the LORD, and he will deliver you" (Proverbs 20:22).

Has anyone ever hurt you so badly you just wanted to get her back? You want the other person to suffer as you have suffered. It only seems fair.

The problem is that when we take vengeance in our own hands, we usually do so out of anger, frustration, and pain. It may seem like justice, but it's coming out of a sinful attitude.

It's our way of dealing with the offense to feel better about the harm that was done to us. And it's taking matters into our own hands.

The best way to deal with wrong that is done to us is to trust God with it. I'm not saying that's the easiest way, it's just the right way. We have to let go of the offense and trust that God will deal with it. As long as we hold on to it and seek retribution, we are enabling our own pain.

God is just. We can trust Him to deliver us from the pain and abuse caused by others, but to do so, we have to wait on His timing. And that can be hard.

Do you trust God to deliver you from the pain caused by others? Are you willing to let go of the offense and let God deal with the other person's sin?

If you are struggling with the desire for payback, I encourage you to remember that God's grace is sufficient for whatever we face. Ask Him to give you the peace and the faith to trust Him. Let go of the offense and let God be just.

Not only will you be set free, but God will vindicate your cause and bring justice to your situation. The favor of God is better payback that we could ever get ourselves.

For further reading: Romans 12:17-19, 2 Corinthians 12:9, 1 Peter 3:9

DAY 279

"The lamp of the LORD searches the spirit of a man;
it searches out his inmost being" (Proverbs 20:27).

Have you ever felt completely laid bare before the Lord, all of your thoughts, sins, and motives exposed? That's what happens when we spend time in His Word, His lamp.

"Your word is a lamp to my feet and a light for my path" (Psalm 119:105).

While it may be uncomfortable and even painful, God's conviction and exposure do two things: they give us awareness of the truth about ourselves, and they give us the opportunity to repent and change our hearts and minds.

"For the word of God is living and active. Sharper than any double-edged sword, it penetrates even to dividing soul and spirit, joints and marrow; it judges the thoughts and attitudes of the heart. Nothing in all creation is hidden from God's sight. Everything is uncovered and laid bare before the eyes of him to whom we must give account" (Hebrews 4:12-13).

When we don't allow the Word of God to do spiritual surgery in our lives, the disease of sin spreads like a malignancy, bringing destruction and death to our spiritual lives. We must be intentional about allowing the Holy Spirit to judge our thoughts and attitudes—the secret place of who we really are when no one else is around.

We can pretend to be something we're not around others and on social media, but the truth of God's Word penetrates to the very depth of our being.

Don't be afraid to let it cut. Just as a surgeon can remove a tumor and stop the spread of harmful cells, God's Word can expose the harmful sins we hide and protect, allowing us to turn from them and seek His healing.

Let God search out your inmost being today. Shine the lamp of His Word into your life and expose anything that is not of Him.

For further reading: Psalm 119:105, Mark 4:22, Luke 12:2-3, Hebrews 4:12-13

DAY 280

"The glory of young men is their strength, gray hair the splendor of the old" (Proverbs 20:29).

We live in a society that highly values youth and vitality, yet we live in bodies that are growing older by the minute. Millions are spent each year to stay in shape, reverse aging, or cover those gray hairs, yet as we fight to maintain youth, there is value in growing older. Young people may have strength on their side, but God says we should value knowing Him above all things.

"This is what the LORD says: 'Let not the wise man boast of his wisdom or the strong man boast of his strength or the rich man boast of his riches, but let him who boasts boast about this: that he understands and knows me, that I am the LORD, who exercises kindness, justice and righteousness on earth, for in these I delight,' declares the LORD" (Jeremiah 9:23-24).

There's no point in trying to reverse the aging process. It can't be done. Sure, we should take care of the bodies God has given us by exercising, eating healthy, and drinking water. But spending more time and money on maintaining our looks than we do on our relationship with God is wasteful. And idolatrous.

When the Bible refers to gray hair, it is usually in the context of wisdom that comes from knowing God.

"Gray hair is a crown of splendor; it is attained by a righteous life" (Proverbs 16:31).

In other words, those who have spent their lives serving God and living for Him should be respected rather than looked down on because of their loss of youthful appearance and beauty. As women, we often work hard to maintain our beauty, and nothing is wrong with that. Let's just work even harder to serve God and bring Him glory.

"Charm is deceptive, and beauty is fleeting; but a woman who fears the LORD is to be praised" (Proverbs 31:30).

For further reading: Proverbs 16:31, 31:30, Jeremiah 9:23-24, 1 Timothy 4:8

DAY 281

*"The plans of the diligent lead to profit as
surely as haste leads to poverty" (Proverbs 21:5).*

This is a verse God has to remind me of often. I'm always in a hurry to get something done. But often in my haste I cause more problems, wasting time and money.

On my last book project, I rushed into the formatting process, trying to get the book published on my own self-imposed timeline. In my haste, I accidentally sent the wrong dimensions to the formatter, so they didn't match up with what I sent the cover designer.

Because of my error, the book couldn't be printed. I had to pay the formatter to change the settings, costing me more time and money to get the project finished.

I've asked myself why I'm always in such a hurry to get something done. I think much of the reason is that I'm ready to move on to the next big thing, always hungry for something more to occupy my time and attention.

The Holy Spirit is teaching me the value of going slowly, taking my time to do things right, and savoring the moment. I'm learning to be present where I am, to ask God if there is more He has for me right here instead of always living in the FOMO (Fear Of Missing Out).

I don't want to be lagging behind what God has called me to do, but I also don't want to always be running ahead, doing my own thing because I don't have the patience to wait on Him.

Do you struggle with hastiness that leads to missing out on God's best? Let's ask God to slow us down and teach us how to wait on Him.

His way and His timing are always best.

For further reading: Psalm 27:14, 130:5, 40:1, Acts 1:4, Romans 8:23, Titus 2:13

DAY 282

"If a man shuts his ears to the cry of the poor, he too will cry out and not be answered" (Proverbs 21:13).

All throughout Scripture we are told to care for the poor. We obviously can't help everyone, but we should help those we can. If we can shut our ears to the cry of the poor, we show that we are in the flesh and not in the Spirit.

God has compassion for them. He loves them and wants us to love them and help them. That is the heart of God.

There are many ways we can help the poor around us. We can share food with them, give clothes and household items, and send financial support to organizations that help the poor.

We can participate in ministries that reach out through soup kitchens, clothes closets, and helping build homes for the homeless.

Another great outreach is to help the poor become self-sufficient by teaching them skills that can help with employment.

There are many ways we can respond to God's instruction to help the poor, but the most important thing we can do is share the gospel with them. Whatever God leads you to do in support of those who are in need, remember their greatest need is Him.

When we do any type of ministry to the poor, we are always sure to include Bibles, Bible tracts, or messages that show them how to be saved.

Being lost and without Jesus is worse than being poor and without money. But whatever you do, don't shut your ears to the cry of the poor. Jesus hears their cries, and He expects you to answer the call.

For further reading: Luke 14:13, Acts 9:36, 10:4, 24:17, Galatians 2:10

DAY 283

*"He who pursues righteousness and love finds
life, prosperity, and honor" (Proverbs 21:21).*

What are you pursuing in life? What are you most passionate about?

The world tells us to pursue riches, fame, and relationships. What our culture values and what God values are often at odds with one another.

How many young people do you know today who are seeking righteousness above all else? Yet God tells us that is the secret to life, prosperity, and honor.

We tend to think of prosperity and honor as wealth and fame, but God is referring to prospering in our faith and having the respect of others. These come as we pursue Him.

Jesus said if we hunger and thirst for righteousness, we would be filled (Matthew 5:6). That's the message we should be teaching our children and the young people in our lives. As we lay aside our own wants and needs and pursue God and His righteousness, loving others as He does, we will find the secret to a fulfilling and satisfied life.

So, what are you pursuing? What do you spend most of your time, energy, and money on? Are you pursuing worldly gain or are you pursuing the things of God? Only one will lead to the blessed life we are all searching for.

Trouble and heartache will come either way because we live in a fallen world. But how much better to face trouble with the peace of God in our lives than to seek after vain pleasure and superficial pursuits?

Don't be deceived by the pull of our culture. Only God's Word has withstood the test of time. Pursue the things that matter and teach your children to do the same. Neither of you will regret it.

For further reading: Matthew 5:6, 1 Timothy 6:11, 2 Timothy 2:22, 1 Peter 3:11

DAY 284

"A wise man attacks the city of the mighty and pulls down the stronghold in which they trust" (Proverbs 21:22).

If we are wise, we will do battle in the spirit realm. We have an enemy, and he will take whatever measures necessary to wreak havoc and cause divisions in families, churches, and communities. As children of God, we are called to use spiritual weapons to pull down the strongholds of the enemy.

"For though we live in the world, we do not wage war as the world does. The weapons we fight with are not the weapons of the world. On the contrary, they have divine power to demolish strongholds. We demolish arguments and every pretension that sets itself up against the knowledge of God, and we take captive every thought to make it obedient to Christ" (2 Corinthians 10:3-5).

We would be foolish to just let the devil run all through our homes and churches, causing division, strife, apathy, and confusion. The enemy will cause misunderstandings and hurt feelings. He will lead people into sinful, tempting situations.

We need to use prayer, the Word, fasting, worship, and obedience to fight our battles. When the enemy wages war against us, we fight back in the Spirit.

Strongholds will be broken as we pray in the Spirit and confess the truth of God's Word. Fasting can break the power of sin in our lives. Worship confuses the enemy and tears down walls. And when we continue to obey God even in the face of opposition, we overcome.

What are you battling in the spirit right now? Put on your spiritual armor and go to war in Jesus' name. Trust in God to empower you as you fight with spiritual weapons and pull down the strongholds of the enemy in your life, your family, and in your church.

For further reading: 2 Chronicles 20, Mark 9:29, 2 Corinthians 10:3-5, James 4:7

DAY 285

*"There is no wisdom, no insight, no plan that
can succeed against the LORD" (Proverbs 21:30).*

When the early church got filled with the Holy Spirit and began to pray with power and preach with persuasion, God "added to their number daily those who were being saved" (Acts 2:47). The religious leaders were stirred to jealousy as they felt their authority and power being threatened. They arrested the apostles and threw them into jail, but during the night an angel released them.

The apostles continued to do the work of the Lord, preaching and teaching the people. They had been warned not to teach in the name of Jesus, but Peter and the other apostles feared God more than men. When they were brought before the Sanhedrin, they testified that the very leaders they faced had put the Messiah to death. Their testimony made the religious leaders furious. Finally, one of the Pharisees took their side with these words:

"Leave these men alone! Let them go! For if their purpose or activity is or human origin, it will fail. But if it is from God, you will not be able to stop these men; you will only find yourselves fighting against God" (Acts 5:38b-39).

You see, he understood the truth of this proverb. If we are following the leading of the Holy Spirit, even if we face opposition, we will prevail. Ultimately those who oppose us are really opposed to Him, and no plan can succeed against the Lord.

The key is that we must be certain to follow His lead. If we get in the flesh and start seeking to fulfill our own plans and purposes, we can be sure to fail. But if we give ourselves fully to God, He will guide us into the plans and purposes He has for us. And no weapon formed against us will prevail (Isaiah 54:17).

As you are serving the Lord, some will be stirred to jealousy and may try to discourage your progress. Don't worry, my friend. Fear God more than people, and continue to do what He has called you to do. Neither their wisdom nor their insights nor their plans can succeed against your God.

For further reading: Isaiah 54:17, Acts 2, 5, Romans 8:1-17, Galatians 5:16-26

DAY 286

"A good name is more desirable than great riches;
to be esteemed is better than silver or gold" (Proverbs 22:1).

The more I watch (and love) Fixer Upper, the more I want to incorporate those farmhouse elements into my home—especially since I live on a farm! I'm a very visual person who loves colors and textures, so I have to really choose to stop obsessing on decorating my home (which equals spending more money) and focus my heart on the things of God.

We all know there are more important things in life than money and riches, yet we are surrounded by the temptation to focus on material things. No, there is nothing wrong with having material possessions—I believe God blesses and provides for us to have what we have. But we all know when we become out of balance. When more of our time, energy, and thoughts are geared toward stuff than towards God, we are out of balance.

The enemy loves to use anything he can to get our attention away from God, and he will use wealth and materialism to do it. That's why there are more than 2300 verses in the Bible on wealth, possessions, and money.[86] We need to remember that money is just a tool.

What matters is not that we have riches but that they don't have us. The rich young ruler is a perfect example. Jesus saw his heart and knew that he was not willing to part with his stuff in order to follow Jesus. And the young man walked away sad. What about us? Are we willing to part with some material possessions if God asked us to? Will we sacrifice our "gold and silver" to serve Him better?

Our name is a reflection of our character. If we ever have to sacrifice godly character for worldly gain, then we have sinned. Our desire to do what is right, to love others, and to share the gospel should outweigh our desire for more stuff. Let your name represent one who is esteemed, valued, and blessed—not because of what you have but because of who you are.

For further reading: Matthew 19:16-26, Luke 12:15, 1 Timothy 6:17-19, Hebrews 13:5

DAY 287

"Train a child in the way he should go, and when he is old he will not turn from it" (Proverbs 22:6).

The statistics for young adults in Christian homes who turn away from church are staggering. Research shows that about 70% of young adults who attended church in high school later drop out. But the truth is that almost two thirds of them return.[87]

This wisdom from Proverbs is not a promise—it's a principle. And the principle holds true. There are many factors that contribute to young adults who are raised in Christian homes later deciding not to pursue church attendance.

Some have to experience life apart from God in order to realize their need for Him. Some of them were entertained in church but not discipled. And some of them never had a strong faith to start with.

But here's the truth in this proverb: When we train up our children in the Word, in worship, and in a demonstration of authentic relationship with God in our own lives, they are much more likely to serve God for themselves.

Will there be some children who choose their own way and rebel against God despite their parents' guidance? Yes, because God has given each of us free will, and that includes our children. But when that happens, our job is to continue to trust God, pray for our children, and set an example for them.

Young people need to experience God for themselves. So we can and should train them in the ways of God through family worship, church, and godly values in our homes. But at the end of the day, each child has to seek his own relationship with the Lord.

So, if your child goes through a period of doubt, disbelief, or even rebellion, just hold on. Place your child in God's hands, and let the Holy Spirit lead her back to Him. Like the father of the prodigal son, He is waiting, willing, and eager to receive your child back home.

For further reading: Deuteronomy 6:4-7, Luke 15:11-32, 2 Timothy 3:14-15

DAY 288

"Pay attention and listen to the sayings of the wise; apply your heart to what I teach, for it is pleasing when you keep them in your heart and have all of them ready on your lips" (Proverbs 22:17-18).

I used to memorize Scripture. It was a lot of hard work, but I loved being able to call on God's Word when I needed it. Often during Bible studies or Sunday school, I would have the opportunity to quote a verse, whether during teaching or just sharing an encouragement with someone.

But I noticed that later people would make comments such as, "Well, I may not be able to quote it chapter and verse, but I know what it means, and that's what really matters." I started to feel condemned for memorizing and quoting verses, as if that somehow made me a Pharisee. I started to sense that others thought I was boasting about what I knew, even though that was the furthest thing from my mind. So I stopped. I quit memorizing and quoting Scriptures around other people. I assumed that studying the Word and knowing what it meant was truly more important than memorizing it.

Soon I really missed the time that I had spent committing a verse to memory one word at a time, one phrase at a time, copying it over and over until I could repeat it. God calls us to not just listen to His Word and apply it to our hearts, but He is pleased when we hide the Word in our hearts and have it *ready on our lips*—ready to quote, to share, to encourage.

And I learned a great lesson. It matters not what others think about us. God certainly knows our hearts. If He puts a verse on our lips to share with someone, then we need to trust Him enough to share it, regardless of what anyone else thinks. Scripture memorization requires time and commitment, but it's so worth it when we have God's Word in our hearts and on our lips.

Memorizing Scripture doesn't make you a Pharisee unless you become prideful about it. Instead, it allows you to have the word of God ready when you need it to fight your battles or when a friend needs to hear it. What verse could you begin learning today?

For further reading: Deuteronomy 11:18, Joshua 1:8, Psalm 119:11, 2 Timothy 3:16

DAY 289

"Do not make friends with a hot-tempered man, do not associate with one easily angered, or you may learn his ways and get yourself ensnared" (Proverbs 22:24-25).

Have you ever noticed how easy it is to pick up the habits of those you hang around? I used to spend a lot of time with a friend who talks with a very Southern accent, dragging out her vowels with more than one syllable. Even Siri couldn't understand her. But I realized that after spending time with her, I would start talking the same way.

We become like those we associate with whether we realize it or not. That's why the Bible warns us against making friends with those who have bad habits, such as a hot temper. If we are easily angered, we will spend much time in conflict with others, always dealing with hurt feelings and broken relationships. The Holy Spirit in us should bear the fruit of "love, joy, peace, patience, kindness, goodness, faithfulness, gentleness, and self-control" (Galatians 2:20). Those are qualities that inspire good relationships and build trust.

But spending time around those who are walking in the flesh will keep our minds on those fleshly attitudes. We need to keep our minds on the things of God so we can walk in the Spirit and not in the flesh (Romans 8:5).

Remember, these proverbs are principles. Build relationships with unbelievers so that by your witness you can share the love of Jesus with them. But when it comes to your close friends that you do life with, choose those who will help you be a better child of God.

Choose friends who will tell you the truth in love and with whom you can share honestly as well. Those are the relationships God can use to develop in each of us the character of Christ.

For further reading: John 15:5, Romans 8:5, Galatians 2:20, Ephesians 4:31-32, Colossians 3:8

DAY 290

*"Apply your heart to instruction and your
ears to words of knowledge" (Proverbs 23:12).*

How much time do you spend studying the Word of God? I'm not talking about reading a devotional like this one or sitting in a pew. I mean, are you committed to regular, intentional study of God's Word in a Bible study, small group, or Sunday school?

We can go to church all our lives and never really dig deep into God's Word and let it saturate our souls. Oftentimes what many of us are missing in our lives is the hunger and thirst for the Word of God that satisfies. We may struggle with pain, relationships, and problems in our lives, but when we know the truth of God's Word, we have a secure foundation on which to build our trust in Him.

We live in a culture that is increasingly searching for truth, but many have decided that truth is relative, depending upon our circumstances or our own opinion. Not so. We need to "apply our heart to instruction" so that we can form a biblical worldview and teach that worldview to our children. If we don't, we can be assured that society will impress its worldview on our children and even our own understanding. We can easily be swept away by the ungodly tide of humanistic thinking so prevalent in our culture.

Sacrifice and dedication are required to become serious students of God's Word, but we will never regret the time we spend getting to know our God. He is worthy of our worship, and His Word is worth our effort. Be encouraged to study the Word of God, to apply your mind to understanding.

Use the inductive method to study: observation (What does it say?), interpretation (What does it mean?), and application (How should I respond?).

Don't let other priorities crowd out time you can spend in God's Word. You will never regret it.

For further reading: Psalm 119:103, 105, 130, Isaiah 55:11, 2 Timothy 2:15, Hebrews 4:12

DAY 291

"Do not withhold discipline from a child; if you punish your child with the rod, he will not die. Punish him with the rod and save his soul from death" (Proverbs 23:13-14).

We live in a very undisciplined culture. As parents, we have a responsibility to teach our children right from wrong. If we allow bad behavior to go unchecked, it becomes normal behavior. Many parents today shy away from this Scripture, however, because so many children have been abused. When we first read these verses, it seems the Bible is teaching us to hurt our children.

When we look closer at the Hebrew word for *rod*, it gives us a different meaning. The Hebrew word is *sebet*, meaning "rod, staff, a stick used to assist in walking, discipline, and guidance."[88] The rod was used by shepherds to fight off the wolves and those that would harm the sheep. It was used to guide them onto safe passage and away from danger. The rod wasn't used to beat the sheep but to keep them safe.

Similarly, this poetic form of writing is using the rod as a symbol for discipline used to correct, teach, and protect our children from harm. If we withhold discipline from our children, we are allowing them to continue in destructive behavior. Kids need discipline. They need to know what the boundaries are, and they need consistency in our maintaining those boundaries. That consistency helps them feel safe and secure.

Punishment should always be with love and grace, not anger and yelling. Whether we agree with spanking or not, we can find a form of discipline that will encourage our children not to repeat bad behavior. If we teach them in this way with firmness but love, they will learn to walk in the discipline and self-control that characterizes a follower of Christ. The Great Commission begins in our homes. So, don't be afraid to discipline your children; you may save them from destruction.

For further reading: Proverbs 1:8, 13:24, 29:17, Matthew 28:20, Revelation 3:19

DAY 292

"Do not let your heart envy sinners, but always be zealous for the fear of the LORD" (Proverbs 23:17).

Do you ever look around at people who are not following God but seem to have it all together? They just look so happy and content on the outside (or on social media), but you are struggling to make it, grappling with sin, while they are just living it up?

That's easy to do and then become discouraged. We may wonder why we can't get away with the slightest sin without God convicting us, while others can break every commandment in the Book and seem to be getting along just fine.

My friend, don't be fooled by their outward behavior. Those who don't follow Jesus may appear to be just fine in their sinful ways, but they are miserable on the inside. They don't have the peace of knowing Jesus, the security of their salvation, the hope of eternity, or the unconditional love of a heavenly Father.

They are living on borrowed time, enjoying the pleasures of sin, but never knowing when their time is up, and they will have to face the Judge of all the earth.

We may struggle with sin, but the truth is that we have been set free. The more time we spend with God, the less we will be tempted by the lifestyles of others. We are free to worship, to pray, to trust, to bless, to give, and to enjoy the abundant, full life that Jesus died to give us.

So, don't envy sinners. Instead, remember their helpless state before God and pray for them. Be zealous for the Lord in your life and share His truth with them every opportunity you get.

You just may turn a sinner from death to life.

For further reading: Psalm 73, 1 Corinthians 10:13, Galatians 6:1-2, Hebrews 12:1-4, James 5:20

DAY 293

"By wisdom a house is built, and through understanding it is established; through knowledge its rooms are filled with rare and beautiful treasures" (Proverbs 24:3-4).

Although the house here is symbolic of our lives, which we should build on the understanding of God's Word, I believe we can also apply these principles to our homes. Much of our lives are surrounded by home and family, so as we build our lives on the Rock, we are establishing our homes too.

So, how are we building? Are we focused on building a home filled with the latest fashions, jewelry, and technology? Are our rooms filled with the sounds of television, video games, or arguing? Do we focus on our careers, sports, and hobbies, while leaving little time to focus on the things of God? It's so easy to do in our culture where we are bombarded daily through social media and television. It's so much easier to go with the flow and tell ourselves it's not so bad.

But how much better would our homes and families be if we prioritized worship and the Word in our homes? What if we made dinner at the table the rule rather than the exception? What if we turned off the television and video games and played board games with our kids and made them put down their phones for an hour. How about if we devoted our family to putting God first by having family worship and devotions? What if we gave up some extra-curricular activities in order to serve God together as a family? Or what if we spent less on entertainment and eating out and used the funds to support a child in a third-world country?

Those are the things our children will remember when they are grown. They won't care about the television shows or how many likes and comments they had or who won their X-box tournament. The rare and beautiful treasures that will fill each room of our homes will be the fragrance of Christ. That, my friends, is what will permeate their hearts for years to come.

For further reading: Deuteronomy 11:19, Matthew 7:24-27, Luke 6:46-49

DAY 294

"A wise man has great power, and a man of knowledge increases strength" (Proverbs 24:5).

When we think of power and strength, we tend to think of physical aptitude or authority. True wisdom and knowledge, however, lead to *spiritual* power and authority. We live in a fallen world where Satan reigns as the prince of the power of the air. We must walk in the wisdom and knowledge of God in order to have spiritual victory. How do we walk in God's wisdom?

Of course, we need to spend time with God daily and study the Word of God. We also need to learn to walk in the Spirit. Romans tells us that we must have our minds set on what the Spirit desires and not what the sinful natures desires.

That's easier said than done.

But we have a Helper, the Holy Spirit, who will lead and guide us just as He did the early church. When they received the Spirit, they became powerful!

"But you will receive power when the Holy Spirit comes on you; and you will be my witnesses in Jerusalem, and in all Judea and Samaria, and to the ends of the earth" (Acts 1:8).

Through the Holy Spirit, we have been given spiritual power to overcome sin, to follow Jesus, and to witness to those around us.

"His divine power has given us everything we need for life and godliness through our knowledge of him who called us by his own glory and goodness" (2 Peter 1:3).

We have all that we need to live a powerful life in the Lord. So, if you struggle with feeling weak and powerless over your situation, remember that God is all-powerful. In Him, you can walk in spiritual wisdom and strength, as you surrender to His ways and His leading.

For further reading: Acts 1:8, Romans 8:5-7, Ephesians 3:20-21, Colossians 1:10-14, 2 Peter 1:3

DAY 295

"Do not exalt yourself in the king's presence, and do not claim a place among great men; it is better for him to say to you, 'Come up here,' than for him to humiliate you before a nobleman' (Proverbs 25:6-7).

Have you ever dined with a king? That's pretty amazing if you have, but I haven't. The principle here applies to any situation in which we could be tempted to think more highly of ourselves than we ought.

When we enter a room, are we thinking about how we are being received, or are we focused on the people around us?

This verse is about humbling ourselves before others rather than having the attitude that we should be honored. We may have done great things, but who gave us the ability to do them? Only God.

Humility is about letting God get the glory for all the great things He has done in our lives. If we try to promote ourselves, chances are, others will see us as foolish. We may even be humiliated, such as taking a prominent seat and being asked to move. Ouch.

If God wants us to be honored, He will be the One to do it. We don't have to put ourselves out there and pretend we're something we're not.

"Humble yourselves, therefore, under God's mighty hand, that he may lift you up in due time" (1 Peter 5:6).

"Humble yourselves before the Lord, and he will lift you up" (James 4:10).

Who does the lifting? God does.

May we be women who walk in humble gratitude for all God has done and give Him glory when He lifts us up.

For further reading: Philippians 2:3, Colossians 3:12, James 4:10, 1 Peter 5:5-6

DAY 296

"A word aptly spoken is like apples of gold in settings of silver"
(Proverbs 25:11).

Fruit was often used symbolically in the Bible to represent good works of the Spirit. In Hebrew culture, bringing a golden apple to someone was a sign of goodwill. Placing those apples in beautiful, filigree silver baskets gave everyone the opportunity to enjoy their beauty. When we speak the right words, at the right time, and in the right way, we can bring that kind of good work, good will, and beautiful spirit to the lives of those around us.

Ecclesiastes 3:1-8 tells us there is a time for everything. Just because we speak truth doesn't always mean we speak it at the right time or under the right circumstances. For instance, we may need to correct someone, but we should do it when her heart is ready to receive it.

The only way to know when to share the right word is by the leading of the Holy Spirit. When we allow Him to guide our words, we can be sure they will be aptly spoken. Not only do our words need to be spoken at the right time, but they also need to come out in the right way. We all know that truth spoken with a bad attitude, the wrong expression, or with anger doesn't get received well. If our words aren't received, we are wasting our time.

The Hebrew language used to describe a word as "aptly spoken" literally means "a word spoken on its wheels."[89] This description calls to mind what rolls smoothly and easily off the tongue and finds its place as it should.

The right word at the right time, spoken in the right way, can actually save us from death and trouble.

"Remember this: Whoever turns a sinner from the error of his way will save him from death and cover over a multitude of sins" (James 5:20).

Speak words of truth that people need to hear, but be sure to allow the Holy Spirit to give you the right words, at the right time, and in the right way.

For further reading: Ecclesiastes 3:1-8, Ephesians 4:14-16, James 5:20

DAY 297

"Like one who takes away a garment on a cold day, or like vinegar poured on soda, is one who sings songs to a heavy heart" (Proverbs 25:20).

I can recall a time right after my father died when I was at our local grocery store. As I was shopping in the produce section, some friends came in who were laughing and talking and having a great day. My first response in my heart was anger. Honestly, I was thinking, "Don't you know my daddy is gone? How can you be acting as if nothing happened?" Then I realized it hadn't happened to them. The rest of the world wasn't suffering with me.

Because Israel had been taken captive and deported to an enemy land, they struggled to sing the "songs of Zion" (Psalm 137:3). We, too, may struggle to sing a victorious song when we are going through a trial that seems to be defeating us. And having someone else celebrate when we are suffering can be crushing to our spirits. We need to remember when others are suffering that their hearts are so tender. Their pain is raw, and they can be easily wounded.

"Rejoice with those who rejoice; mourn with those who mourn" (Romans 12:15).

The best response to those around us who are suffering is to suffer right along with them. We may want to cheer them up and offer an encouraging word, but they may need us to just validate their pain. It's okay for us to just hold a hand or give a hug and say nothing. Honestly, I had a friend bring me a candle when my father died, when everyone else was bringing food. It was a sign of great comfort to me. I don't remember a single dish that came to our house, but I remember that candle.

We worry about how to respond to those who are suffering, but rather than trying to respond with words or songs, let's just sit and cry with them. There will come a time when words and songs are just the right thing; until then let the Holy Spirit be their comfort.

For further reading: Psalm 119:76, 137:3, Romans 12:15, 2 Corinthians 1:3-4, 1 Peter 5:7

DAY 298

"If your enemy is hungry, give him food to eat; if he is thirsty, give him water to drink. In doing this, you will heap burning coals on his head, and the LORD will reward you" (Proverbs 25:21-22).

When someone hurts us, our first response is usually revenge. We may not voice it, but in our hearts we are thinking of ways to get back at him—it's just human nature. But it's our sinful nature. God calls us to do good to our enemy, instead. This principle is teaching us to think of our enemy in a different light.

Jesus continued this teaching when He told us to love our enemies, pray for them, and do good to them (Matthew 5:44, Luke 6:27-36). I have found that it's hard to stay mad at someone you are praying for. Through our prayers, God will change our hearts and give us love for those who hurt us.

Paul also expanded on this concept in Romans:

"Do not take revenge, my friends, but leave room for God's wrath, for it is written, 'It is mine to avenge; I will repay,' says the Lord" (12:19). He then goes on to quote Jesus in the above passages.

What God is teaching us through His Word is that if someone has hurt us, we need to trust Him to take care of it. If not, we will allow unforgiveness and bitterness to build up in our hearts.

When we do good to our enemy, many times God will use that to bring conviction to her. And God rewards our trust in Him.

Don't forget that ultimately, people are not our enemy anyway—Satan is (Ephesians 6:12). So, put on the armor of God, pray for the person the devil is using, and look for ways to do good to him.

God will bless you with peace.

For further reading: Matthew 5:44, Luke 6:27-36, Romans 12:19, Ephesians 6:12

DAY 299

*"Like a city whose walls are broken down is a
man who lacks self-control" (Proverbs 25:28).*

Self-control is like discipline. It's the ability to make yourself do what you should. Self-control is a fruit of the Spirit (Galatians 5:23). Those who belong to God should walk in self-control, but we can only do so in the power of the Holy Spirit. What does it look like to not walk in self-control? Proverbs tells us a person without self-control is like a city whose walls are broken down.

First, he is vulnerable. The walls of a city are there to protect the citizens from invasion. When we allow our own will and wants to dictate our decisions, rather than controlling our appetites by the Spirit of God, we become vulnerable to the enemy.

We are allowing the enemy to come in and have his way in us. We open a door to spiritual attack and oppression. We are called to stand guard against the enemy, but we can't do that if we are vulnerable and let the walls be broken down. The guards would position themselves on the walls of the city in order to see the enemy approaching. If the walls are broken, the city has no warning that the enemy is already upon them.

Second, the person who lacks self-control is defenseless. When the enemy would attack a walled city, the soldiers would attack from the top of the walls because they were in a position to see from a higher perspective.

When we lack self-control, we are no longer in a position to fight. We are allowing our sinful nature to guide our decisions, which God certainly gives us the right to do. The problem is that when we ignore the Spirit's urgings to do right, He lets us have our way. And we can't fight the enemy on our own.

So, if we want to have victory in our lives, we need to keep our defenses up and be prepared for spiritual warfare. We can only do that as we walk in the self-control given to us through the Holy Spirit.

For further reading: 1 Corinthians 10:13, Galatians 5:23, Ephesians 6, 2 Peter 1:5-7

DAY 300

"Without wood a fire goes out; without gossip a quarrel dies down"
(Proverbs 26:20).

Somebody said something recently that I didn't like. He wasn't necessarily wrong, but because I didn't agree, and his words had the power to change something I felt strongly about, I rebelled a little in my spirit. It could have ended there, but later I shared with a couple other people my thoughts about the situation. I wasn't angry or upset; I just didn't agree and felt there was a better solution. So I discussed the problem and talked about why the other person was wrong.

I honestly thought that was the end of it. Until a week later I overheard the situation being discussed by some others who now had "heard" about it. They *were* upset about it. I thought back over the situation and the fact that had I dropped it to start with, the whole argument could have died down. The real problem at the heart of my "discussion" (read: gossip) is that I didn't trust God enough to handle the situation without my opinion in the middle.

I had the opportunity to encourage the people I was with initially to trust God and let Him work it out. But in my desire to fight for my opinion and get my way, I gossiped, which only stirred the pot.

Our words have the power to change circumstances and to stop quarrels. Of course, there are times that we need to speak up for truth and be a voice of change, but we must be careful to seek the right motive.

When we are willing to trust God and let go of our right to be right, God can use us to have great influence and bring peace. Only with peace and unity will our efforts be blessed.

When we are tempted to gossip, let's ask God to remind us to trust Him and keep our mouths shut. Let's stop throwing wood on the fire and watch God put out some fires.

For further reading: Ephesians 4:29, 2 Corinthians 12:20, 1 Timothy 5:13, Titus 3:1-2

DAY 301

"A lying tongue hates those it hurts, and a flattering mouth works ruin" (Proverbs 26:28).

Why do we tell little white lies? Why do we flatter and exaggerate?

We tend to tell those lies that will keep us out of trouble or make us look better in someone else's eyes. But God's Word says those lies are harmful.

Take, for instance, the lies we tell on social media. You know, the way we use filters to make ourselves look better in those selfies or the pictures we post of our perfect family who were arguing five minutes before that shot was snapped.

How are those lies harmful?

Well, they perpetuate the belief that our lives are perfect when they're not. They communicate to others that their appearance and their families are not good enough. We flatter ourselves but work ruin in others.

Those lies show that we hate those we hurt. If we truly love the other women who see our posts, we will be real with them. We'll stop spreading the fake lifestyles so others will know that it's okay to not be perfect.

Social media is not a place to air all our dirty laundry, so we don't have to be so real that we tell it all! But we can be truthful about who we are and welcome others to be themselves, too.

God calls us to walk in truth. Let's let all we say and do be honest, so others will know they can be real as well. Because after all, this is who we are—not always picture perfect, but the "worst of sinners" growing in knowledge and grace.

For further reading: Psalm 145:18, John 8:31-32, Ephesians 6:14, 1 Timothy 1:15, 2 Peter 3:18, 1 John 3:18

DAY 302

*"Let another praise you, and not your own mouth;
someone else, and not your own lips" (Proverbs 27:2).*

Sometimes we are so excited over something we have accomplished, that we can't wait to tell others. But then when we do, it comes across as pride. Nobody likes a braggart, someone who's always tooting her own horn.

The truth is that we can do nothing apart from Christ.

"I am the vine; you are the branches. If a man remains in me and I in him, he will bear much fruit; apart from me you can do nothing" (John 15:5).

So, God should get the glory for anything we have done. When we keep our focus on Him, we will realize that we don't need or deserve the praise.

We want others to acknowledge our hard work and effort, but the beauty of trusting God is that when we humble ourselves, He lifts us up. He will cause others to notice and honor our work for Him when we keep our hearts in the right place.

Whatever we do, we should do it unto Him and for His glory. Therefore, all praise for our achievements and success belongs to Him.

Trust God with your accomplishments and give Him all the glory. Keep a humble attitude and remember that you could do nothing without Him.

He will lift you up in due time, and then another mouth will praise you and not your own.

For further reading: Psalm 115:1, Matthew 5:16, 1 Corinthians 10:31, Colossians 1:27

DAY 303

"As iron sharpens iron, so one man sharpens another"
(Proverbs 27:17).

I have a cousin who brings his knife sharpener every time he comes to my house. He loves to cook, and we have had some fun in my kitchen. But he hates my knives, because they are always dull.

Kyle's sharpener gets them right back in shape, though. A few swipes and my knives will slice through an apple like soft butter.

Because iron sharpens iron.

And we sharpen one another. When our lives grow dull, wearisome, and heavy, a sister can come along and share just the encouragement or rebuke that we need.

That's why fellowship was so important in the first century church and is so important to us now. We need each other.

We have a common enemy, you and me. His name is Satan and he came to steal, kill, and destroy. You and I have the ability to fight with our spiritual weapons, including the sword of the Spirit, which is the Word of God.

But if we grow dull, if we slack off in our time with God and in His Word, or if we go through a trial that sets us back, we need our brothers and sisters in Christ to come alongside us and remind us of His faithfulness. We need our swords sharpened.

Do you need to be sharpened today? Call a friend in Christ who can be iron to your iron and give you the sharpness you need.

And don't forget to turn back and strengthen your sisters when they are growing dull and weary. Your iron doesn't have to be perfect to be helpful. You just need to be available. A little swipe goes a long way.

For further reading: Ecclesiastes 4:9-12, 1 Thessalonians 5:11, Hebrews 10:23-25, 1 Peter 4:8-10

DAY 304

"The crucible for silver and the furnace for gold,
but man is tested by the praise he receives" (Proverbs 27:21).

Silver and gold both have impurities when they are discovered. They must go through the refiner's fire in order to remove those impurities and come through pure. Then their beauty can shine, and they can be useful.

We, too, are full of impurities because we have a sinful nature. God wants to use us to build His kingdom on earth, but we will often face trials and tests before God can use us. He needs to prove our faith and work out the impurities so we can grow to be the leader He is calling us to be. Many times when we are in the fire, we can't see the purpose for it. We may struggle with the test, trying to understand or make sense of what we are going through.

I'm sure Joseph felt the same way. Sold as a slave by his brothers, thrown into prison for something he didn't do, Joseph could easily have given up and just settled with getting by and doing the best he could to make it. But God had called him to more.

The testing and trials he went through were a refiner's fire, testing Joseph's humility and faith. A young man who boasted to his brothers about his dreams of their submitting to him, one day grew into a man who led a nation with a humility that gave God all the glory.

When we receive praise for something we have done, we are being tested to see if our hearts are truly humble before God. How do we react? Do we take pride in what we have done and enjoy the flattery, or do we give all the glory to the Lord who empowered us in the first place?

Don't be sucked in by the praise or flattery of others. All that we do is by God's provision and for His glory. Let's allow God's refining fire to burn off the pride in us that we may come forth as pure gold.

For further reading: Genesis 37-50, Romans 12:2, 2 Corinthians 13:5, James 1:3

DAY 305

"Evil men do not understand justice, but those who seek the LORD understand it fully" (Proverbs 28:5).

I once heard a woman talking about her favorite television show. She said it was all about people who had been wronged, but they sought revenge and got it. She loved the show because she enjoyed seeing people paid back for the wrongs they had done. I get it. A little. We all long for justice, especially when we see tragedy that could have been avoided or evil that destroys someone's life.

The problem with revenge is that it doesn't leave room for God's wrath. Revenge shows that we don't understand the justice of God. We feel the need to take matters into our own hands. But God is just.

Those who love and seek the Lord understand that when wrong has been done, they can trust Him to make it right. Wrongdoers will face judgment at the hands of God. Those who have been wronged will one day experience His justice and peace.

You see, we really deserve God's wrath for all the wrong we have done. It's funny how we want revenge for others who sin against us, but we want mercy for our own sin.

God is faithful and just to forgive us and to cleanse us from all unrighteousness when we come to Him in faith. He is also faithful and just toward those who do not repent. They will receive the justice that is due them.

Only those whose sins are forgiven through the price that Jesus paid on the cross will escape the divine wrath of God. So we can let go of grudges and vengeance and trust God to be God.

Those who seek the Lord understand His justice. They leave evildoers in His hands.

For further reading: Isaiah 30:18, Matthew 7:12, Romans 12:19, Hebrews 10:30

DAY 306

"He who conceals his sins does not prosper, but whoever confesses and renounces them finds mercy (Proverbs 28:13).

I got spanked by the principal in the first grade. Yes, I'm old enough to have lived through corporal punishment. I was singing loudly in the bathroom, and the principle heard me in his office. I'm not sure why that was a capital offense, but straight to the office I was called.

I clearly remember being tough and defiant about it. I was determined that I would not cry, but I also was determined not to tell my parents.

When I got home, my mom asked me how school went that day. I told her great, just fine, no problems whatsoever. She then proceeded to tell me about her conversation with the principle who told a different story.

I was horrified. Needless to say, the second spanking I received from her did make me cry.

When we try to hide our sins, whether from God or others, we only bring harm to ourselves. We will not prosper from lying and covering up our wrongdoing. In fact, it usually makes things worse.

Had I gone home that day and humbly confessed to my parents what had happened at school, I probably would have found mercy and forgiveness. But instead I faced disappointment and pain.

God knows all our sin and He offers us mercy and forgiveness, but we must be willing to come clean with Him, to confess our sins, and to renounce or turn away from them. His heart for us is like that of a Father who longs to show love and compassion to His child.

Jesus paid a great price for our forgiveness. Let's not spurn His sacrifice by hiding our sin. Come clean before God and receive His mercy today.

For further reading: Psalm 32:5, Acts 2:38, 10:43, Romans 6:23, 1 John 1:8-9

DAY 307

"Blessed is the man who always fears the LORD, but he who hardens his heart falls into trouble" (Proverbs 28:14).

What does it mean to fear the Lord? We have already looked at the fear of the Lord as the beginning of wisdom, but what does it really mean?

We sometimes downplay the fear of the Lord by quoting New Testament verses that tell us God is love and that perfect love casts out fear. But we can sometimes become too flippant about the truth that God is to be feared.

God is holy, sovereign, and completely in control of our destinies. He hates sin and will one day judge all sin. For those who choose not to follow Jesus, only hell awaits.

In this verse we see the man who fears the Lord in contrast with the one who hardens his heart. So, when we fear the Lord, we open our hearts to Him and His truth. It means that we follow Jesus and seek to please Him in all that we do because the alternative is trouble.

So, yes, God is love and His love is perfect. When we follow Him and walk in His love, we do not fear death, sickness, pain, or suffering because we know we are in His hands. We trust His perfect will for us.

But if we harden our hearts and rebel against God's gift of salvation in His Son, then we don't fear the consequences of our sin. When we don't fear the Lord, we are proving that we don't believe that the God of the Bible—who is both love and judgment—really exists.

God is love to those who fear Him, but to those who reject that love, only trouble and judgment await.

For further reading: Matthew 10:28, 25:46, 1 John 4:7-21, Revelation 20:15, 21:8

DAY 308

"Where there is no revelation, the people cast off restraint;
but blessed is he who keeps the law" (Proverbs 29:18).

The Hebrew word for *revelation* in this verse is *hazon*, meaning "vision, revelation, a message from God."[90]

In the Old Testament, God spoke through the prophets. The prophets would share the message with God's people, but many times they didn't listen. There were also times, such as the 400 years prior to Christ's birth, in which God just didn't speak.

This proverb tells us that when we don't have God's Word to guide us, we will do what is right in our own eyes. When the people didn't listen or God wasn't speaking, the people "cast off restraint" that would have protected them, and they fell prey to their enemies.

Today, God speaks to us through His written Word. As we spend time in God's Word, He will lead and guide us by His Spirit. But like the Israelites, sometimes we too want to throw off restraint. Following God may seem burdensome, too hard, too binding.

We are naturally self-centered creatures who like to do things our own way. So, we ignore His Word and try to make our own way in the world.

But God's Word is there to guide us into His will, His purposes for us, and His protection. When we throw off restraint, we expose ourselves to the enemy. But if we listen to and abide in His Word, we will be blessed.

Don't ignore the revelation of God in His Word. His Words are life and truth, and in keeping them is great reward.

For further reading: Judges 17:6, Psalm 19:11, John 15, Romans 1:5

DAY 309

"Every word of God is flawless; he is a shield to those who take refuge in him" (Proverbs 30:5).

Our God is perfect; His Word is flawless. But how do we know that the Bible we read can be trusted to be the flawless Word of God? We know, for instance, that the Bible is comprised of 66 books written over a period of 1500 years by 40 authors and has been copied numerous times. We don't have any of the original documents. Surely, there have been errors in the copying of manuscripts over the centuries?

Here's the thing: The Bible is the divine, living Word of God (Hebrews 4:12). We can be sure that if God intended us to have the Scriptures, then He is big enough to make sure we have what He intended. The Bible is made up of many different genres—history, prophecy, poetry, and letters. Where the Bible is historical in nature, it is astoundingly accurate. Other historical documents testify to that truth. The Word of God is inerrant in all that it teaches. But that doesn't mean it is always interpreted accurately. The error is not with God but with man. Our job as students of the Bible is to first, trust that it is flawless and inspired by God (2 Timothy 3:16-17).

Second, we must be careful that we study the Word in solid translations that have been under careful counsel and done with accuracy in mind. Paraphrases (rewordings of the Scripture) are intended for devotional reading but not serious study.

Third, always consider the context of a Scripture, meaning the passage, chapter, book, and the whole counsel of the Word of God. Looking at the cultural and historical background, the genre, and the intended audience and message, helps us to understand and interpret accurately.

So, is "every word of God" truly flawless? Yes, it is, because it says it is. The Word we have in our hands today is the inspired, inerrant, holy Word of God. From Genesis to the Revelation, the Word of God reveals to us the Savior of the World, and "he is a shield to those who take refuge in him."

For further reading: Psalm 12:6, 18:30, Isaiah 40:8, 2 Timothy 3:16-17, Hebrews 4:12

DAY 310

"Keep falsehood and lies far from me; give me neither poverty nor riches, but give me only my daily bread" (Proverbs 30:8).

What we all really need is truth—not material wealth, not social status, not fame or success—just truth.

Society will tell us that we can't really know the truth. When we take away any standard for truth, we are left with chaos in which everyone does whatever best suits and secures herself.

But we can know truth.

"Jesus answered, 'I am the way and the truth and the life. No one comes to the Father except through me'" (John 14:6).

Many times in Scriptures Jesus states "I tell you the truth."

Now, we can either believe that He is truth or that He is a liar. If Jesus is a liar, then we can't trust any of the Scriptures. If the Bible is not true, then we have no hope, no identity, and no future.

A truthless society is sought by many because with truth comes responsibility. If we know the truth, we are held accountable to that truth. It calls us to a higher standard. Many reject that standard because it requires sacrifice and obedience.

But to reject truth is to also reject God and His Word. If my truth based on God and His Word is wrong, then I lose nothing; but if those who reject God are wrong, they lose everything.

Thank God, we do have a source of truth. In a culture that is confused about so many things, we have the Word of God to give us truth.

We don't want poverty to cause us to covet, nor riches to make us proud; we simply need our daily bread. For that, we can give thanks.

For further reading: Matthew 6:11, John 8:31-32, 14:6, 17:17, 1 John 3:18

DAY 311

"A wife of noble character who can find?
She is worth far more than rubies" (Proverbs 31:10).

I used to be jealous of the "Proverbs 31 woman." Honestly, I just thought there is no way anyone can meet this standard, yet the verses are so beautiful and deep, and I so wanted to be just like her. When I began to break down the verses and think about the context of Proverbs, I realized that she is an ideal to strive for, not a person to be jealous of. Proverbs is a wonderfully rich collection of principles for life, and this section is no different. When we read of this amazing woman, what we find is God Himself giving us a description of what it means to be a wife of noble character.

The Hebrew word translated *noble character* has several meanings: "strength, capability, skill, valor, wealth, army, troop, warrior."[91] Interestingly, most of these definitions don't seem very feminine, yet they are descriptions, not of the woman herself, but of her character.

So, what does it mean to be "a wife of noble character?" Character has to do with who we are when nobody is watching—the outward manifestation of the inward person. Here we find a woman who is strong in her faith, not easily swayed, capable of making decisions, skilled in the Word, brave in her walk, a prayer warrior.

She is wealthy because she is rich in faith. She is an army because she fights for what is right. Because of her values and moral integrity, her husband trusts her. He doesn't worry that she is gathering with her friends to ridicule and devalue him because that's not who she is (Proverbs 31:11). Trust me, she's not perfect. But she strives to be all God created her to be. Her heart is for God and for her family. She seeks to protect her husband's reputation and be a helper and a blessing to him (Proverbs 31:12).

We don't have to be intimidated or jealous of the "Proverbs 31 woman." Instead, we can ask God to give us a heart and mind to walk in these principles and be wives of noble character too.

For further reading: Genesis 2:18, Philippians 4:13, Colossians 3:18, Titus 2:3-5, Hebrews 11:6

DAY 312

"She gets up while it is still dark; she provides food for her family and portions for her servant girls" (Proverbs 31:15).

Okay, so this may be the verse most of us hate—nobody wants to get up before dark to cook, right? But what we see here is simply the principle of being a doer. She is a mama who takes care of her family, even if sometimes it means getting up before everyone else. You know why I think she gets up early? To spend time with God before she has to start preparing breakfast and getting everyone ready for school.

I know what you're thinking: If you had servant girls, you could handle all that too, right? Remember, these words were written to a culture in which having servants was normal. Each household had to grow food, make clothing, and possibly raise animals. So much work was required just for survival, so oftentimes poor families would give their children as indentured servants to a wealthier family. The servants would work for a particular amount of time in exchange for housing and food that their own family couldn't provide for them.

The woman of noble character is one that not only gets up early to seek the Lord, but she is a caretaker who works hard to meet the needs of her entire household. She treats her servant girls with love and grace. She purchases the material that is needed and works hard to provide clothing for her family (Proverbs 31:13). She goes to the market to purchase whatever food they can't grow (31:14). She can make decisions about purchases, plant, grow, and earn her own money. She's a hard worker who is savvy, smart, and profitable, willing to stay up late to finish her work if necessary (31:17-18).

Since this passage describes principles and not a particular person, I believe God is telling us that it's okay to be any of those things. If we are stay-at-home moms, we should work hard at that. If God calls us to work outside the home, we should give that our all. No matter what the arena, we are called to be women who are industrious and give our best effort.

For further reading: Proverbs 16:3, 1 Corinthians 10:31, Colossians 3:23, 1 Thessalonians 4:11

DAY 313

*"She opens her arms to the poor and extends
her hands to the needy" (Proverbs 31:20).*

A noble woman is one who is generous and kind to others. She is marked by compassion for the poor and needy, willing to not just wish them well, but actually put her faith into practice by helping them. We can follow her example in so many ways.

When she opens her arms to the poor, I picture her taking in orphans and raising them herself, providing for their needs. When she extends her hands to the needy, I see her working in a soup kitchen, serving food to the homeless.

She makes clothing and linens of the very best quality for her household because she wants to show them they deserve the very best (Proverbs 31:21-22). But she also works hard to make and sell items in order to be able to provide for her family (24).

Sometimes we want to have the best, but we're not willing to work for it. Or we may know people who have lots of material goods, but they aren't willing to share them. A noble woman is neither of those things.

Out of her compassion and generosity, she will do what it takes to help others, even if it means late nights at the staff (19). She is willing to work hard but also to share what she has with others. What can we learn from her example?

We can adopt or foster children, sponsor a child in a third-world country, support programs that provide for needs, volunteer at local shelters or soup kitchens—the opportunities are many.

Let's not be so busy trying to have the best of everything that we take short-cuts to do so. And let's not be greedy with what God has blessed us with. Let's ask for a heart like this woman of noble character and find some way to serve the poor and needy that God puts in our path or on our hearts.

For further reading: Isaiah 58:6-7, Proverbs 14:31, 19:17, Luke 14:12-14, James 2:14-17

DAY 314

*"She is clothed with strength and dignity;
she can laugh at the days to come" (Proverbs 31:25).*

Our matronly model is more concerned with her inward life than her outward one. Oh yes, she makes sure her family is clothed well, but she clothes herself with the things that matter—strength and dignity. A strong woman is one who fights for her family. Satan hates families, marriages, and homes where Jesus reigns. He will do everything in his power to sow discord, strife, and rebellion in our homes.

And you had better believe that if we do nothing, he will have his way. Ladies, we need to gear up and stand our ground on behalf of our families. What does that look like?

It means praying over every room in your home as you vacuum. It means creating space in the day for dinner at the table to talk, connect, and pray. It means setting boundaries with our children and remaining firm in those principles. It means making time for our spouses and putting their needs ahead of our children's. A strong woman knows how to fight in the spirit realm with the weapons of her warfare—on her knees, in her prayer closet, where no one sees or hears but her and God.

But she also can carry herself with class and dignity. She doesn't grovel, beg, and plead for her children's attention or affection. She lovingly demands their respect. She doesn't nag her husband when she doesn't get her way. She inspires his devotion by her gentle spirit.

You know why she can laugh at the days to come? Because she knows that as long as she stays in the Spirit and abides in the Vine, Satan just won't win. Oh, she doesn't let her guard down—she's strong. But she doesn't walk in fear and defeat either—she's dignified. May we all be women of strength and dignity who can laugh at the days to come.

For further reading: Deuteronomy 28:7, 2 Corinthians 10:3-5, Ephesians 6:10-18, James 4:7

DAY 315

"She speaks with wisdom, and faithful instruction is on her tongue"
(Proverbs 31:26).

Boy, our tongues sure can get us in trouble. James said they are a "world of evil." One of the qualities that make a Spirit-filled woman of God so influential is her ability to speak with wisdom. We all know that "taming the tongue" is one of the most difficult things we can do, but it's not impossible. It's something we grow in as we mature in Christ.

I have found that the more I try to guard my tongue, the worse it gets. I will find myself in situations where my emotions move faster than my brain, and my tongue is quick to follow.

As we grow in our understanding of God's Word, I think we will find that what He wants is for us to draw closer to Him. The more time we spend with the Lord, the more we become like Him. As we fill our minds with His truth from the Word of God and spend more time in fellowship with Him through prayer and worship, our hearts will become more in line with His.

That sanctification process only happens as we surrender to Him and abide in His presence. He begins to live His life through us. It doesn't mean we become perfect, but as we allow ourselves to "be perfected" in Him, one of the natural products of that is we speak more slowly and more thoughtfully.

Eventually we will find that not only do we have more wholesome speech, but we will desire to use our lips for good. When our hearts are aligned with His will, we will speak with "wisdom" and "faithful instruction" that build others up. We will offer wise counsel to our family and friends and offer encouragement to them. Our mouths can be used for great harm or tremendous good. It may not be easy to bring our lips in line with the Word of God, but that's not an excuse for poor speech. Rather than trying in our own power to overcome this area, let's spend more time with Jesus.

Let's allow His Words to live in our hearts and minds, and eventually they will be on our tongues as well.

For further reading: Psalm 19:14, 141:3, 2 Corinthians 8:7, James 3:1-12

DAY 316

"She watches over the affairs of her household and does not eat the bread of idleness" (Proverbs 31:27).

Most of us probably would not consider ourselves to be lazy. We work hard to take care of our homes and families, serve our church and community, and earn a living. I love that Mrs. 31 is busy, but sometimes I feel guilty for taking a break. When I have a day off and just lounge around in pajamas and drink coffee and read a book, I often feel that I'm being idle and wasteful of my time.

But God has created us so that we need times of rest and Sabbath built into our schedules. Not only do our physical bodies need rest, but our minds and emotions need down times as well.

What we should guard against is neglecting the work that needs to be done and allowing ourselves too much idle time. If we become slack in keeping our homes, we introduce disorder and chaos that will always cost us something.

Once we become slack in keeping our homes, we will get lazy about our relationships as well. Marriages need intention and care. Our children need consistency in discipline. We have to guard against allowing our spirits to become lazy in how we serve the needs of others. When we become careless about maintaining our relationships, they will suffer, which will lead us to look for others with whom we can compare ourselves and come out on top. Whether in church or on social media, our idleness will then lead us to become busybodies. God's Word warns us against that spirit:

"We hear that some among you are idle. They are not busy; they are busybodies. Such people we command and urge in the Lord Jesus Christ to settle down and earn the bread they eat" (2 Thessalonians 3:11-12).

So, when your body and soul need a rest, take it. Allow the Lord to recharge you, but then get back up and back to work. Don't let the devil lure you into being a busybody. And don't let him make you feel guilty for taking a break. God gave us Sabbath for a reason.

For further reading: Exodus 20:8-11, Matthew 11:28-30, 2 Thessalonians 3:11-12, 1 Timothy 5:13

DAY 317

"Her children arise and call her blessed;
her husband also, and he praises her" (Proverbs 31:28).

I can't think of too many goals more worthy than to live a life that causes our family to praise us. No one knows us better (except God, of course!)

Sure, we can fake it to an extent with the outside world. What our co-workers, church family, and social media friends see is one thing. But what our family witnesses in us is a whole different matter. Yet who we are behind closed doors is who we really are. We can't fool the people who see us at our worst and know us best—the good, the bad, and the ugly.

When my kids were still at home, I would read this verse and think they would never bless or praise me. I had done far too much for them to think that highly of me. Often when we are still in the parenting years of discipline and instruction, we feel we are failing.

But one thing I always tried to do with my children is to just be real. I tried to be the same person at home that I was in public. When I messed up with them, I always tried to admit it and ask their forgiveness. Now that they are grown, they often praise me. I realize it has little to do with who I am and mostly to do with the faithful God I serve. My family blesses me because they did me see fail often. They saw the good, the bad, and the ugly, but they saw me seek a God of restoration and forgiveness.

My number one goal in life is to live a life that blesses the Lord, but if my family who knows me best can also say I lived a life worthy of praise, then I will be satisfied with that, far above riches and fame.

If we want a family that will one day arise and call us blessed, who will praise us for our faithfulness to God, we must live an authentic Christian life before them—one that exemplifies transparency, truth, and lots of forgiveness.

Don't try to be something you're not. Your family will see through your façade. Just be real.

For further reading: Romans 12:9, Hebrews 10:22, 1 Peter 1:22

DAY 318

"Charm is deceptive, and beauty is fleeting; but a woman who fears the LORD is to be praised. Give her the reward she has earned, and let her works bring her praise at the city gate" (Proverbs 31:30-31).

Beauty brings a lot of praise in our world today. From the film and music industry to modeling and social media, physical appearance is the key to success. Not only that, but relationships are often built on physical attraction alone. But there is an ugly side to this obsession with beauty—bullying, self-hatred, and sexual exploitation.

When we don't like what we see in the mirror, we rarely consider the deception of thinking that beauty is everything. We spend billions in efforts to look younger and more beautiful, knowing full well that even natural beauty fades. It's all a demonic deception that keeps us either insecure or prideful. What if instead of running after the latest skincare or fashion or laser treatment, we ran after the Lord? What if our hunger was for holiness instead of getting more likes and comments on our latest selfie post?

One hundred years from now, your earthly beauty will not matter. But your fear of the Lord will. Those things that last for eternity—the impact we made on those around us, the people we led to the Lord—those are the things that really matter today. But we are too blinded by the charm of others and the deception of beauty. Yes, everything God made is beautiful. But God's definition of beauty is slightly different from ours.

"Your beauty should not come from outward adornment, such as braided hair and the wearing of gold jewelry and fine clothes. Instead, it should be that of your inner self, the unfading beauty of a gentle and quiet spirit, which is of great worth in God's sight" (1 Peter 3:3-4).

When we focus our hearts on Him, He produces in us the fruit of His Spirit, which comes forth as unfading beauty. So, go ahead. Get dressed, fix your hair, and look your best. But remember that real beauty is who you are on the inside. That's a beauty that never grows old or fades.

For further reading: Psalm 139:14, John 15:16, 2 Corinthians 4:18, Hebrews 12:1-3, 1 Peter 3:3-4

DAY 319

"'Meaningless! Meaningless!' says the teacher. 'Utterly meaningless! Everything is meaningless!'" (Ecclesiastes 1:2).

We have all had that moment when we became aware that our existence was something to be pondered—when we began to question life, death, and purpose. For many of us, the questions become endless and futile. As we grow and mature in life, we become aware that much of life is unfair. Good people often suffer. Hard work can go unnoticed. People starve to death while others have abundance. Evil can appear to win.

Much like the Teacher in Ecclesiastes, we can grow cynical as we realize that all our efforts to find happiness and satisfaction in life appear "meaningless." The Hebrew word *hebel* can mean "vanity, meaningless, futility" or literally "vapor, breath, or wisp of air."[92] Compared to eternity, our lives are just a vapor, but we all want to find some meaning to life. Why are we here, and what difference does it make? Will our lives mean anything, or is it all just vanity? The truth is that apart from God, life *is* meaningless.

The fact that we ponder life and its vanity shows that God has placed in us a desire for meaning but also the knowledge that we are limited in what we can control. Death, sickness, poverty, and disaster are often things beyond our grasp to contain.

What these elements do is point us to a hope that can only be found in Christ. They show us our need for the One who is in control. What looks haphazard and unfair to us may be part of God's plan. Sometimes in the pain we learn most about who we are and who God is to us.

We long for satisfaction, and as the Teacher explores through the book of Ecclesiastes, most of what we seek doesn't fill us. Only a personal relationship with Jesus Christ can make sense of the pain and futility that sometimes characterize life as we know it. Through life in Christ, we can enjoy the many blessings God has bestowed on us—even if only for a brief time—knowing that in Him all things will be made new in His time.

For further reading: John 15:5, 1 Corinthians 1:18-31, 3:18-20, Ephesians 4:17-24

DAY 320

"I denied myself nothing my eyes desired; I refused my heart no pleasure. My heart took delight in all my work, and this was the reward for all my labor. Yet when I surveyed all that my hands had done and what I had toiled to achieve, everything was meaningless, a chasing after the wind; nothing was gained under the sun"
(Ecclesiastes 2:10-11).

We can spend our entire lives living for our own pleasure, gain, and satisfaction, denying ourselves nothing that we desire. We may really take delight in all that we do and suffer nothing for it in this life. I know people who live by their own desires and seem to be happy and successful. But I have also seen people who seem to have it all take their own lives. All of the success, money, and pleasure the world has to offer can never bring us true peace and fulfillment. We will always be lacking apart from God, whether we admit it or not.

And as author John Ortberg noted in his book, *When the Game Is Over, It All Goes Back in the Box*, no matter what game we are playing, when we leave the table, we take nothing with us.[93] Sometimes it may seem that as followers of Christ, we sacrifice our desires and pleasures for nothing. It may seem better at times to just follow the crowd and do what we want. After all, others seem to get away with it. But we can't fall for that lie. Just like a good monopoly game, we can acquire houses, businesses, and property, but at the end of our days on this earth, they are left behind for someone else to claim. The pleasures we indulge in will always cost us something—poor health, broken relationships, or financial lack.

The Teacher in our passage today had it all. Yet to him, it was meaningless, "a chasing after the wind." What are you chasing after today? Unless our pursuit is for God, we will be left disappointed eventually. Put your hope in Him, and run after Him with all your heart.

For further reading: Psalm 16:11, Proverbs 21:17, Galatians 5:19-21, 2 Timothy 2:22

DAY 321

"He has made everything beautiful in its time. He has also set eternity in the hearts of men; yet they cannot fathom what God has done from beginning to end" (Ecclesiastes 3:11).

Songs have been sung and recorded about this chapter in Ecclesiastes where the Teacher tells us that there is a time for everything. His message, however, is not that we are to justify the times that we choose to, for instance, kill, tear down, or hate, but that we are subject to the different seasons of life with little control. We do go through seasons of war, uprooting, mourning, and brokenness. There is little you and I can do to control sickness, death, or changes that come to us with no known cause or reason. Like the Teacher, we may wonder at the futility of it all.

But the good news in this passage is that the teacher also realized that God will one day make everything beautiful in His time. The reason our hearts rebel against pain and suffering is that God has set eternity in our hearts. We long for a world where right is right and wrong is wrong; where pain doesn't exist and husbands don't leave; where children don't die and cancer can't grow; where love and joy and peace are the only thing we will know.

This world is not our home, and we will never be fully satisfied here. Only in a living, growing relationship with Jesus can we know peace and comfort in our pain. But one day—praise God!—we will live forever in the place our hearts only hope for. Yes, there is a time for everything. We can enjoy the gifts and pleasures the Lord provides for us today: the sunrise after a storm, the healing of an ill family member, the reconciliation of a broken marriage, the prodigal child who comes back into our arms.

But we need not grieve as those who have no hope when the answers don't come. For we have waiting for us just on the other side a hope eternal. And there will be all the time in the world to enjoy that season.

For further reading: 1 Corinthians 15:35-58, 1 Thessalonians 4:13, 2 Peter 3:13, Revelation 21:3-5

DAY 322

"Two are better than one, because they have a good return for their work: If one falls down, his friend can help him up. But pity the man who falls and has no one to help him up!" (Ecclesiastes 4:9-10).

I think we sometimes underestimate the value of a friend, whether it's our spouse, our long-time bestie, or a sister in Christ. I have gone through periods of time in which I felt I had no friends—no one to shop with or get a coffee. Oh sure, I have plenty of "friends" on social media, acquaintances at church and in the community, but it's not the same as having someone you can do life with. A true friend is one who can listen without judgment but will speak truth when we need it. A real friend is there when you need to put a paintbrush or a moving box in her hands. Friendship is so much more than coffee and shopping bags and road trips. Quality friendship is about working side by side for the Kingdom. It's about helping each other up when we fall into sin.

A real friend can encourage us in a way that no one else can because she truly knows us. But in order for that level of intimacy to occur, we have to be willing to open ourselves up to the risk of being hurt. Vulnerability is a requirement for genuine relationships to occur. As women, we often get burned with a friend we thought we could trust. Then the walls go up, and we aren't willing to let anyone else in. We should be cautious and wise in how we choose friends. For those true sisterhood commitments, we should look for the following:

Someone who walks with Jesus and will only give us advice based on His Word. Someone who is not afraid to tell us the truth even if it makes us mad. Someone who is willing to sacrifice her own time and energy when we have a need. You know how to find this kind of friend? The same way your mama always taught you: If you want to have a friend, you have to be a friend. Sometimes the best relationships come from the places we least expect them. Instead of mourning that you don't have a good friend, go be a friend to someone who needs one. Open your heart up and be willing to be hurt. After all, that's what real love is all about.

For further reading: Proverbs 17:17, 27:5-6, John 15:13, Philippians 2:4, Ephesians 4:15

DAY 323

"Do not be quick with your mouth, do not be hasty in your heart to utter anything before God. God is in heaven and you are on earth, so let your words be few" (Ecclesiastes 5:2).

As I started to write this devotion for today, I was reminded of the song "Let My Words Be Few" by Phillips, Craig, and Dean. So I pulled up a video of the live version of the song. I'm here to tell you that I just had five minutes of worship here at my kitchen counter where I'm writing. I didn't even sing along. I couldn't. And I think that's what the Teacher was getting at. There is a moment where we realize the majesty and glory of a God who created all things, who holds all of eternity in His hands, who reigns over the entire universe, and still cares for you and me. And we just have to be silent.

I am so in love with a God who loves me that much. I just want to love and worship Him for who He is. Every day I sit before the Lord to seek Him in the solitude of the morning hours, but I do most of the talking. Sure, I read His Word, study, and pray, but I don't take enough time to just be quiet before Him.

I think the Teacher wanted us to remember when we come before Him to tell Him how we think He should do things, we need to just be quiet. Before we start our grocery list of what we want from Him, we need to remember who He is. He's not our genie in a lamp we can rub the right way to get what we want. He's not granting three wishes and then we're out of luck. God is not a fairy godmother granting our requests because He feels sorry for us.

He is King of kings and Lord of lords! He is in heaven and we are on earth. We live to do His bidding, not the other way around. And we approach Him on His terms. Oh, that we would take more time each day to just stand in awe of who He is. We would start to see the world in a whole different light. Our momentary troubles would fade away in light of the One we serve who reigns over it all. Get before Him today and let your words be few. Just know He is God.

For further reading: Exodus 14:14, Psalm 23:2, 37:7, 46:10, Hebrews 12:28

DAY 324

"A good name is better than fine perfume, and the day of death better than the day of birth" (Ecclesiastes 7:1).

We typically celebrate the day of one's birth but mourn the day of one's passing. Birth is the beginning of new life, a precious soul that God has created and placed on this earth. We have reason to celebrate that day and every day that one lives on this celestial ball. I'm sure you've heard it said that what matters is not the beginning and ending date on a tombstone, but what we did with the dash—the time in between. We don't all get the same amount of time for that dash, but we should live our lives in such a way that the day of our death is cause for great celebration of a life well-lived and well-loved. The day of our death can be a better day than that of our birth if we live with eternity in mind.

We're good at going to church and making promises, but we're not always so great at the follow-through. Paul said, "I have fought the good fight, I have finished the race, I have kept the faith" (2 Timothy 4:7). The funny thing about Paul's life is that he started out as a man who was outwardly religious, but he didn't really know God. Instead, he fought against God by persecuting Christians (Acts 9). But once he came to know Jesus, he set his life's focus on serving God well. He didn't have a great start, but he had a great finish.

You, too, may not have experienced a great beginning. Maybe you have been in church but not serious about walking with Jesus. Maybe you have only recently been saved and mourn the years you have wasted. Know that you can start living a life of faith and service to Jesus right now. It doesn't matter what yesterday looked like, today can be your beginning of a life well-lived for Christ.

What matters is how you finish. Let's be determined to fight the good fight and finish well.

For further reading: Ecclesiastes 7:8, Acts 9, 2 Corinthians 6:1-2, 2 Timothy 4:7

DAY 325

*"It is good to grasp the one and not let go of the other.
The man who fears God will avoid all extremes" (Ecclesiastes 7:18).*

Our culture is so polarized into extremes today. We tend to love the ditches more than the road. It's a me-against-them mentality: right or left, with no in-between.

Even in our personal lives, we struggle with eating right and exercising or making poor health choices; staying on a budget or spending lavishly; being productive or enjoying too much free time. Any of these in extreme can be harmful.

Balance is hard to maintain.

We see this not only in the world but also in the church. There are those who are legalistic and follow rules for the sake of rules. Then there are those who take their freedom in Christ for granted and live a sinful lifestyle, while trusting God's grace to save them.

We can tend to fall on either side of desiring a God of love or a God of justice. The truth is that He is both. The concept of having two opposite characteristics at once seems impossible, until we understand that God's judgment *is* love.

It is possible to be sinners saved by grace and seeking holiness at the same time.

We can acknowledge sin and still love people.

We serve a God of order and balance, and He calls us to the same. When we get out of balance, we open the door for sin, whether through failing to sympathize with others or through becoming rigid and legalistic.

Balance only comes as we call on God daily for help. He alone can empower us to avoid extremes and stay in the middle of the road.

For further reading: Romans 3, 7:7-25, 11:22, Colossians 2:20-23

DAY 326

"Do not pay attention to every word people say, or you may hear your servant cursing you—for you know in your heart that many times you yourself have cursed others" (Ecclesiastes 7:21-22).

Guess what?

Everybody doesn't like you.

I know, it's hard to believe, because what's not to like, right?

I used to get so upset when people didn't act friendly toward me or said something negative about me, but then I realized that I don't always treat others the way I want to be treated either.

There will always be people who don't like our personality, our words, our products, or our services. We will never have 100% fans. But the good news is that we don't have to. As long as we are seeking God and following Him to the best of our ability, it doesn't matter if we have a few haters.

Paul said if he had been trying to please people, he wouldn't have been able to please God (Galatians 1:10). When we get caught up in people-pleasing, we will never be happy because we can never please all the people all the time.

When negative reviews, harsh critics, or biting gossip threaten our peace of mind, we need to remember who we are in Christ. Our aim is to please Him in all we say and do. When that becomes our focus, we can be relieved of the pressure to perform for others.

Are you striving to please God or meet the approval of people? Ask God to give you a heart that seeks His approval. And if a few people aren't happy with that, choose not to be offended. Strive to be above reproach and not give people a reason to accuse you of wrongdoing, but find your significance in your relationship with God alone.

For further reading: Psalm 118:6-9, John 14:23, Galatians 1:10, Colossians 3:23-24, 1 Thessalonians 2:4

DAY 327

"So I commend the enjoyment of life, because nothing is better for a man under the sun than to eat and drink and be glad. Then joy will accompany him in his work all the days of the life God has given him under the sun" (Ecclesiastes 8:15).

God has given us life in Him to be enjoyed. Sometimes we get so caught up in working and serving that we forget that it's okay to enjoy life. In fact, the joy of life will overflow into our work if we have the right attitude. Jesus said that He came so that we could have life to the full (John 10:10). Every day won't be sunshine and rainbows. The truth is that we will have much trouble in this world (John 16:33). But there will be days that we can enjoy the sunshine and not feel guilty about it. We can eat a meal and fellowship with friends and be glad. We should enjoy our families and spending time with them.

In fact, if we never take the time to enjoy life, we will grow frustrated and even cynical. How can we walk in the light of life if we never take the time to enjoy the little things?

The Teacher has concluded, after a life of having much wealth, wisdom, and pleasure, that it all is vanity. Why? Because at the end we all die and none of us can take any of it with us. So, while we are here on earth, we should be grateful for all God has given us and take pleasure in our lives in Him. If we have food, shelter, and clothing, we are blessed. If we encounter a new bud in spring, the warmth of a summer day, or the crunch of fall leaves beneath our feet, we can enjoy them. If God has provided pancakes and coffee on a cold winter morning, we can be thankful.

If the Lord has blessed us with family, friends, and work that is fulfilling, we can enjoy them and give thanks. In all that God has given us to do under the sun, He also is gracious to allow us many pleasures at His hand. Be grateful and enjoy them. Rest on the Sabbath. Go on vacation. Dance with your daughter. It's okay to enjoy this life. You'll be getting good practice for the one to come.

For further reading: Psalm 16:11, Proverbs 17:22, John 10:10, 16:24, 33

DAY 328

"Now all has been heard; here is the conclusion of the matter: Fear God and keep his commandments, for this is the whole duty of man" (Ecclesiastes 12:13).

If we are looking for purpose in life, the Teacher has summed it up here: Our purpose is to worship and obey God. That's why we were created. You and I were made to bring Him glory. Our lives are meant to be lived in right understanding of who God is. Yes, we revere and honor Him because of His holiness and glory. But we also should fear His judgment. He is God, and we will all one day give an account to Him for the life we are leading now.

True worship is to fear God. When Isaiah encountered the Lord in the temple, his first reaction was "Woe to me!...I am ruined!" (Isaiah 6:5). Our God is a consuming fire (Hebrews 12:29). He will not be mocked (Galatians 6:7), and He will not be second (Exodus 20:3).

When we truly fear the Lord, we will be in the best possible place because we will realize our own sinfulness as Isaiah did. That's when we are able to come humbly before Him and surrender to His Lordship in our lives. His holiness calls us to holiness, and we can't measure up to that no matter how hard we try. We are called to keep commandments we can't keep, and that's why Jesus came. He lived out the perfect life of obedience and then went to the cross to pay the price for our sin.

If you are in Christ, you are covered with His righteousness (2 Corinthians 5:21). We love and obey Him because He loved us first (1 John 4:19). And we are empowered by His Holy Spirit to live the life we can't on our own. The Teacher was right in every way. Life is utterly meaningless apart from God. But in Him, we have purpose and significance. We have a great call on our lives to follow Jesus, and He will lead us to some interesting places. As we fear God and follow Him, He will take us on an amazing journey to share His love with others. That's a life worth living.

For further reading: Exodus 20:3, Isaiah 6:5, 2 Corinthians 5:21, Galatians 6:7, Hebrews 12:29, 1 John 4:19

DAY 329

"Pleasing is the fragrance of your perfumes; your name is like perfume poured out" (Song of Songs 1:3).

Song of Songs is a lyrical poem celebrating the beauty of romantic love. Over the years, scholars have debated the interpretation of the poem, but no doubt exists about its description of love and romance. The Song describes the love and sexual attraction between Solomon and his beloved, Shulammith, which literally means "Mrs. Solomon."[94] Throughout the Song, we see the attraction, intimacy, and beauty of romance and marriage as God intended.

Because of the world's perversion of sex, we often shy away from the Song of Songs because it seems explicit, but the beauty of the poem is that sexual attraction and intimacy were created by God and intended to be enjoyed in a marriage relationship.

These eight chapters actually have much to teach us about the nature of true love. Solomon's beloved began the discourse by declaring her love for him, but contrary to the world's idea of romance, her ideal man was one of integrity.

In the time and culture in which this was written, one's name was associated with his reputation. When she described his name as "perfume poured out," Shulammith was declaring that he was a man of character, whose reputation was a pleasing fragrance to those around him.[95] True love isn't based just on physical or emotional attraction. Real love for another should be founded on the character and integrity of the person.

As followers of Jesus, we should seek a mate who also loves Jesus. To be unequally yoked with an unbeliever is to invite much trouble and pain into one's life (2 Corinthians 6:14-15). Marriage requires that a couple agree about their worldview, especially if they intend to have a family.

God is love (1 John 4:16). True love comes from Him and can only be enjoyed when a man and woman seek Him together as one. Physical attraction is an exciting and essential component of love and romance, but integrity and character are what make us truly attractive.

For further reading: Genesis 2:18, 2 Corinthians 6:14-15, 1 John 4:8, 16

DAY 330

"Do not stare at me because I am dark, because I am darkened by the sun. My mother's sons were angry with me and made me take care of the vineyards; my own vineyard I have neglected"
(Song of Songs 1:6).

I have always hated my cankles. My daughter despises her nose (which is adorable to me!). We all have something about ourselves that makes us self-conscious, but true love overlooks our flaws. Solomon's beloved was self-conscious about her skin. She was a working girl who cared for the vineyards, naturally bronzed in the blazing sun. She had tended the vines but neglected the care of her own skin, causing her to feel embarrassed about it. Compared to the other young ladies around her who didn't have to work outside, she felt she didn't measure up. And in the eyes of Solomon, she longed to feel beautiful and admired.

When we begin to compare ourselves to others, we will always find some area in which we feel we don't measure up. The enemy will keep our eyes focused on ourselves, self-conscious and critical. But Solomon had eyes only for her. He was portrayed as a shepherd who also would have worked out in the sun. He appealed to her on the basis of their common ground. They both knew what it was like to work, to be darkened in the sun, and that made her all the more beautiful to him. He described her as "the most beautiful of women" (Song of Songs 1:8). What woman doesn't want her man to feel that no matter what her flaws are, he finds her the most beautiful of all?

True love finds our best qualities to highlight, while overlooking those flaws that make us self-conscious. When our heart and attention are focused on one another instead of on ourselves, we find the love and maturity to build one another up with words and encouragement. Genuine love and affection are rooted in our love for God, who is the most beautiful of all. As we grow in our relationship with Him, we will find the freedom to see the best in others and overlook their flaws. Let us love one another as Jesus has so deeply loved us.

For further reading: 1 Corinthians 13:4-13, Ephesians 5:25, 1 Thessalonians 5:11, 1 John 4:18

DAY 331

"We will make you earrings of gold, studded with silver"
(Song of Songs 1:11).

What's the sweetest gift you've ever been given?

Sometimes gift-giving gets a bad rap because we don't want to focus on material possessions. Rather than giving gifts, we will opt for spending time together or encouraging one another.

While those are important ways to show love, gift-giving is also important. When we give to one another we are reflecting the love of God, who gave us His very best when He gave His Son.

Solomon, in assuring Shulammith of her beauty, was inspired to make her earrings that would enhance her lovely dark skin. His desire to make the earrings for her showed that he wanted to give not just any gift, but one he created just for her.

Gifts don't have to be expensive to be meaningful. Oftentimes those simple items we make ourselves have more meaning to our beloved than expensive jewels or perfumes.

Gifts that reflect the desire of another's heart show that we pay attention to their wants and needs. Nothing touches our hearts more than for our mates to give us something we really wanted because he was paying attention.

Gifts have the ability to open another's heart, to show that our thoughts were on him, and that we wanted to please him.

As Solomon prepared to give to his beloved, he demonstrated to us that true love gives. Real love seeks the best for the other person. It's not selfish, but generous.

Part of romance and love is the ability to know our lover's heart and give him the desire of his heart. And that makes us more like God.

For further reading: Proverbs 18:16, John 3:16, Romans 5:8, 2 Corinthians 9:15

DAY 332

"My lover is to me a cluster of henna blossoms
from the vineyards of En Gedi" (Songs of Songs 1:14).

Relationships have the ability to bring us great joy.

While we probably wouldn't describe our beloved as a cluster of flowers, Shulammith's description of Solomon here shows us that she found great joy in their relationship and time spent together.

As Solomon and Shulammith enjoyed dinner, the fragrance of her perfume filled the room (1:12). As she inhaled the sweet aroma, she was reminded of the blossoms that grew in En Gedi.

En Gedi was "an oasis watered by a spring." The flowers could be found in the midst of a wilderness, much like his love, blossoming in the dry places of her heart.[96]

She also compared Solomon to the fragrance of myrrh, which was in her perfume, too. Myrrh was used in many instances, such as to anoint a king and to perfume wedding gowns.[97]

As she compared Solomon to these fragrances, Shulammith was saying that he was to her like a spring in the desert, refreshing and satisfying. She bestowed a blessing on him as both a king and a future husband to her.

When we are in the right relationship, we will experience joy and fulfillment. No person can completely satisfy us because only Jesus can fill us completely. But true love enjoys spending time together. There is a mutual fondness and commonality that allows us to be ourselves and be at peace with one another.

Solomon and Shulammith show us that love brings joy.

For further reading: 1 Corinthians 13:4-7, Galatians 5:22, 1 Peter 1:18, 1 John 4:7

DAY 333

"How beautiful you are, my darling! Oh, how beautiful!
Your eyes are doves" (Song of Solomon 1:15).

Have you ever watched couples in a restaurant? You can usually spot the ones who have been married a long time. They often eat without looking at each other or speaking to each other. But you can spot young love, as they will gaze into each other's eyes, hold hands, and talk continuously.

Solomon and his beloved began to speak to each other rather than about each other as their relationship progressed. He told her she was beautiful. She replied that he was handsome. As their conversation developed, they saw more and more qualities to be admired in one another. And they shared them.

Over the years, we tend to take our mates for granted. We think they already know how we feel about them, so we no longer need to tell them. But, just the opposite is true. To keep a relationship alive and growing, couples must communicate. Part of that dialogue should always include words of affirmation, appreciation, and admiration. We need to build our spouses up with words of encouragement, reminding them and ourselves daily of the reasons we love them.

Sometimes it's easier to voice the complaints and criticisms. We can easily get caught up in looking only at what's wrong with our mate instead of what we love. True love will focus on the beauty we find in one another. And true love will speak the words our beloved needs to hear: You are beautiful. I love you. I want you. You make me happy.

Solomon made his beloved feel that she was the only woman in the world:

"Like a lily among thorns in my darling among the maidens" (Song of Songs 2:2).

Find those things that attracted you to your spouse in the first place and share them with him today.

For further reading: Ecclesiastes 4:9-10, Ephesians 4:29, Philippians 2:3, 1 Thessalonians 5:11

DAY 334

"Do not arouse or awaken love until it so desires" (2:7b).

While the world encourages sexual freedom, God's Word teaches that sex belongs within the boundaries of the marriage covenant. Sex outside marriage causes pain and confusion, and it destroys the beauty of monogamous love and affection.

As Solomon and Shulammith grew in intimate conversation and attraction, their sexual anticipation grew, too. They both began to dream of the moment when their love would be consummated. They longed to be with each other and were "faint with love" (Song of Songs 2:5).

But they also knew where to draw the line. They knew that although they wanted to be together, keeping their relationship pure would be worth the wait. They would not arouse their love until the right time when they were under the marriage covenant.

In a culture in which sexual promiscuity is almost the norm, we have to be very intentional about protecting purity. We must teach our children that sex is not bad. God created man and woman and gave them physical desire for one another. He said what He created was good.

The world has perverted sex through pornography, homosexuality, and sex outside marriage. But we can't allow the perversion of sex to keep us from enjoying the gift of God within His parameters. So our children should be taught the truth about sex within the boundaries God created.

While physical attraction and the desire for sex are normal, we must exercise self-control. In a culture that seeks self-fulfillment and immediate gratification, maintaining purity requires discipline and prayer.

Because Solomon and his beloved were willing to wait, their passion and promise gave them hope, security, and the anticipation of a new life together.

That's the beauty of purity and true love, which only desires God's best.

For further reading: Genesis 1:28, 31, 1 Corinthians 6:18, 1 Thessalonians 4:3-5, Hebrews 13:4

DAY 335

"My lover spoke and said to me, 'Arise, my darling, my beautiful one, and come with me'" (Song of Songs 2:10).

When two people know that God has chosen them for one another and their passions are exclusively for one another, God will lead the two together as one in the covenant of marriage. In Genesis, God defines marriage as a covenant between one man and one woman (Genesis 2:24). Solomon and his beloved were filled with love and passion for one another. The joy of their mutual love and attraction propelled them towards marriage.

The words "Arise, my darling, my beautiful one, and come with me" are considered to be Solomon's proposal to Shulammith.[98] The winter was past, and as spring neared, they set the time of their marriage celebration when "flowers appear on the earth; the season of singing has come, the cooing of doves is heard in our land" (Song of Songs 2:12). The celebration of their love for one another and the promise of their new life together brought such joy! He longed to see her face, perhaps from behind her wedding veil; he delighted in hearing only her voice (Song of Songs 2:14).

God created us for monogamy and exclusivity in marriage. When we look for love outside the marriage covenant, we break the bond of mutual exceptionalism. We are drawn to one particular person because he shines brighter to us than all the rest. That's how it should be. And that attraction is meant to last throughout our earthly lives. When two people enter into marriage, it should not be with the idea that if it doesn't work out, we will find someone else. We enter marriage with our hearts committed to one other person for life. No one else on earth should take the place of the one God created us for.

When temptation comes to seek comfort elsewhere, we should be reminded that we committed to God and to our spouse to love and cherish him forever, exclusively. Solomon's beloved declared her intentions to marry him: "My lover is mine and I am his" (Song of Songs 2:16).

For further reading: Genesis 2:24, Proverbs 18:22, Matthew 19:2-9, Mark 10:5-9, Ephesians 5:33

DAY 336

"Catch for us the foxes, the little foxes that ruin the vineyards, our vineyards that are in bloom" (Song of Songs 2:15).

Satan hates marriage because it is a reflection of God's love for His people. He will do whatever he can to drive a wedge between two people who are committed to each other. Where he can get a foothold, he can take a stronghold and eventually tear down. Often, it's the little things that start driving that wedge—he doesn't help me around the house; she doesn't listen to me. But just as little foxes can ruin a vineyard, those little irritations can grow into big problems if they are not dealt with.

Solomon knew they would have to do whatever it took to protect their marriage. Communication is the key to catching the foxes, the irritations and disagreements that can lead to division. Many outside factors can affect a marriage: money, children, and sex are the biggest issues that cause problems. When a couple is willing to communicate their thoughts and feelings without being critical and demeaning of the other, the issues can be resolved before they grow into something larger.

Two practices can help catch the foxes.

Never go to bed angry. We made a commitment early in our marriage that we would obey the words of Paul in Ephesians 4:26-27. When we don't resolve issues by talking about them, they fester and become worse. The devil will put all kinds of thoughts in our minds that aren't even true. But if we walk in spiritual maturity, we will come together and discuss the issue humbly and calmly.

Pray together every day. It's hard to pray with your spouse and still be angry with him. If there are "little foxes" trying to ruin the vineyard, most of the time they disappear when we pray. And the bigger foxes we can give to the Lord and entrust to Him.

Solomon knew that there would be challenges, but he and Shulammith were determined to face them together and keep their vineyard in bloom.

For further reading: Ephesians 4:26-27, 5:33, Colossians 3:18-19, 1 Peter 3:7

DAY 337

*"All night long on my bed I looked for the one my heart loves;
I looked for him but did not find him" (Song of Songs 3:1).*

True love involves risk. To truly give our hearts away completely to another person makes us vulnerable to pain and loss. Sometimes fear of loss can keep us from enjoying the life Jesus died to give us.

As Shulammith considered that she was giving herself away completely to Solomon she began to fear losing him, as seen in a dream. She awakened and went searching for him, so afraid that something would happen to him before their wedding day.

When she found him she "held him and would not let him go" (Song of Songs 3:4b). But since their day had not arrived, she again reminded herself not to arouse her love until the desired time.

The truth is that we do make ourselves vulnerable to pain and loss when we commit to one person for life. When our love is so deep and so real, sometimes we are afraid that we will lose all that we have given ourselves to.

The answer is to give ourselves completely to Jesus first.

If our hearts are held in His hand, then even earthly loss cannot destroy us. Though pain, sickness, and even death may come, when we are first committed to the Lord, He will be with us and carry us through it.

Married love is a beautiful gift of God, but without Jesus at the center, we can be left devastated if our marriage ends in death, divorce, or desertion.

The fear of loss can cause some people to never give themselves fully to another. But the only way to experience true love is run the risk of pain. Only a heart that has truly loved and been loved can appreciate that the risk is worth it.

For further reading: 1 Corinthians 13, Colossians 3:14, 1 Peter 4:8, 1 John 3

DAY 338

"Come out, you daughters of Zion, and look at
King Solomon wearing the crown, the crown with which
his mother crowned him on the day of his wedding,
the day his heart rejoiced" (Song of Songs 3:11).

One of the greatest days of my life has been the wedding of my son and his bride. When Kenneth and I got married, we had a beautiful Christmas wedding with family and friends. It was a sweet day that I will never forget, but we intentionally kept it small and intimate.

When Josiah and Moriah married, we rented a retreat center in the mountains. They were married in the woods at an amphitheater, surrounded by family, friends, and the beauty of God's creation. It was a glorious day, made all the more beautiful by the Spirit-filled young woman God brought into his life after our prayers for him since he was born.

Weddings are some of the most joyful events we celebrate on earth. When a man and woman come together, declaring their love for God and for one another, I think all heaven rejoices.

The wedding celebration in Old Testament times was a feast that lasted seven days! There was food and dancing and great joy over the new life that couple would enter into, and we have similar celebrations today.

Song of Songs tells us that Solomon's "heart rejoiced" on the day of his wedding. He arrived in a royal carriage he made himself with wood from Lebanon, gold and silver posts, and upholstered with purple fabric.

On his head was a crown or wedding wreath made by his mother. I can imagine how she must have felt. What a day to rejoice and celebrate the beauty and majesty of love and passion!

True love is celebrated when God brings together a man and woman who pledge their love for one another. What joy!

For further reading: Genesis 2:18, 24, Proverbs 18:22, Isaiah 62:5, Mark 10:6-9

DAY 339

"All beautiful you are, my darling; there is no flaw in you"
(Song of Songs 4:7).

All the passion and love and physical attraction were finally released in sexual pleasure as Solomon and Shulammith consummated their marriage on their wedding night. The anticipation and joy of finally being completely one with each other were realized. The wait was worth it.

Solomon couldn't contain his admiration for her beauty when he finally saw her completely and intimately. She was beautiful and completely satisfying to him. Their virginity and purity made their union all the more special and perfect. Solomon declared that she had stolen his heart.

When sex is enjoyed as God intended—within the boundaries of marriage between one man and one woman—it is a beautiful demonstration of the unity and purity of two becoming one flesh. There's no guilt and no shame. Since God created the physical union as the means of both pleasure and procreation, we should respect the boundaries He has set. When we do, love is so much more delightful and satisfying.

Maybe you didn't wait and you feel a sense of shame over your past. God wants you to know that in Him you can find forgiveness and peace. He is bigger than our mistakes. There may still be consequences, but there is grace. God can renew you and restore you as you trust in Him. So many have allowed sex outside of marriage to lead to further sin, such as promiscuity, abortion, and adultery. All of these choices have consequences that bring further pain and suffering.

If your past sexual sin has caused pain and suffering in your life, ask God to forgive and cleanse you and commit to Him now that you will respect the gift of sex within the boundaries He has set. Sex was never intended to be a stumbling block to you. Let God redeem what the enemy has stolen. You are cherished and beautiful to the Lord. You have stolen His heart. Let His love fill the emptiness you have tried to fill in relationships. God is true love.

For further reading: Matthew 5:28, 1 Corinthians 6:18, 10:13, 1 Thessalonians 4:3-5, Hebrews 13:4, James 2:13

DAY 340

"I have taken off my robe—must I put it on again? I have washed my feet—must I soil them again?" (Song of Songs 5:3).

Marriage is difficult and requires commitment and intentionality. I once had a very wise woman tell me that marriage attracts opposites because as we rub each other the wrong way, we learn to be polished and refined by one another. Marriage helps us grow out of selfishness because we have to learn to sacrifice our own desires and put each other's needs ahead of our own.

When Solomon came to Shulammith for affection, she wasn't in the mood. Before she thought about her love and attraction to him, she responded out of frustration and selfishness. It just seemed a bother to her to give herself to him in that moment.

We often get comfortable in our relationships and neglect to meet the needs of each other. But if we will take the time to remember our love for each other and all the good qualities we find in one another, we will be less apt to respond with selfishness and frustration.

After Shulammith came to her senses and realized her abruptness with Solomon, she went to find him, but he was gone. Perhaps he went for a walk to cool off, but his absence made her realize even more how much she loved and wanted him. Once she found him, they made up quickly because she didn't lose sight of her love and passion for him. Once again, she recited to him all the things she found perfect in him and her heart remembered her great love and desire for Solomon.

We, too, can get caught up in our own selfish needs and forget that our spouse has needs too. While we can't meet all our spouse's needs—only Christ can—we are in marriage to submit to one another in love (Ephesians 5:21). We should take time to be reminded daily of what we love and admire about one another. As we focus less on the little frustrations and our own selfish desires, we will see more clearly all that makes him beautiful to us. We can keep our love passionate and strong when we strive to serve one another rather than to be served.

For further reading: Genesis 1:27-28, 1 Corinthians 7:1-7, Ephesians 5:21

DAY 341

"How beautiful you are and how pleasing,
O Love, with your delights!" (Song of Songs 7:6).

God created sex that we might find pleasure and fulfillment within the confines of the marriage relationship. The world will tell us that we need many partners, pornography, or casual sex in order to be satisfied. God's Word tells us that a man and woman in a marriage relationship can find pleasure in one another.

Because we are so bombarded with the sexual immorality in our world today, we have to protect ourselves from those negative influences. Movies, romance novels, and magazines can pull our hearts away from the blessings God has given us and draw us into a fantasy world of pleasure. At least it seems that way in our minds. But the truth is that all sin comes with a price.

If we don't capture those thoughts and turn away from them, we can allow the enemy to draw our hearts away from God and our spouse. Soon we will no longer feel fulfilled in our marriage and start seeking satisfaction somewhere else.

It's a dangerous, slippery slope to allow such thoughts to stay. God tells us to take captive every thought that is not of Him (2 Corinthians 10:5). We have to make our minds subject to the will and mind of God (Philippians 4:8).

Satan's deception is that there is something better outside our marriage relationship, and if we are not careful, we will start to believe His lies. But it's all a carefully designed plot to destroy marriage. Satan is the father of lies (John 8:44). But Jesus is the truth (John 14:6).

Trust the Word of God with your marriage. Protect your eyes and your heart from those things that would lead you astray. Guard your mind from fantasies and illusions.

God wants you to delight in the spouse He gave you.

For further reading: John 8:44, 14:6, 2 Corinthians 10:5, Philippians 4:8

DAY 342

"Place me like a seal over your heart, like a seal on your arm; for love is as strong as death, its jealousy unyielding as the grave. It burns like blazing fire, like a mighty flame. Many waters cannot quench love; rivers cannot wash it away" (Song of Song 8:6-7a).

Love and marriage must be nurtured, cherished, and valued. Often we grow accustomed to our spouse and begin to take him for granted. We may reach a point in which we just want him to meet all our needs and satisfy us. But marriage is meant to cause us to grow out of our selfishness as we sacrifice our wants for the sake of each other. True love cherishes and values the relationship. Real love doesn't look like the world's idea of love. If we want to know what real love is, God gave us that pattern in 1 Corinthians 13:4-7:

"Love is patient, love is kind. It does not envy, it does not boast, it is not proud. It is not rude, it is not self-seeking, it is not easily angered, it keeps no record of wrongs. Love does not delight in evil but rejoices with the truth. It always protects, always trusts, always hopes, always perseveres."

It may seem that this is too difficult to accomplish. That's true. Real love is not something we can manufacture on our own. It is the fruit of walking in the Spirit, because apart from God, we can't do it (John 15:5). That's why the fake love we see in our culture is not really desirable at all. Oh, the enemy is good at making it look like what we think we want, but God's love is so much deeper than that. It's a love that wants the best for one another, even at the risk of our own satisfaction.

When we truly cherish another person, we will love him not just with our heart, minds, and even our bodies. We will love him with our spirit, because real love is deeply spiritual. God is love. Apart from Him we can't even know love. So to truly love someone, we must know God. When our marriage relationship becomes more about our relationship with God than with each other, we will enjoy the love that even rivers cannot wash away.

For further reading: John 15:1-17, 1 Corinthians 13:4-7, 1 John 3

DAY 343

"If she is a wall, we will build towers of silver on her. If she is a door, we will enclose her with panels of cedar" (Song of Songs 8:9).

This beautiful love story in Song of Songs started with Shulammith's brothers making her work in the vineyard; but at the end the story returns to the time when she was young and immature. Her brothers recalled how they had desired to protect her purity and innocence.

As parents, we sometimes wish we could build a wall around our kids or keep them locked behind a door to protect them from premarital sex. Of course, these metaphors were used to describe the brothers' desire to protect their sister from unwanted advances. In their culture, brothers took responsibility for their sisters' betrothals.[99]

We, too, can protect our children by teaching them the truth about sex. Sex is a beautiful expression of love between a man and a woman that God created and blessed. The world has perverted it, but that doesn't change what God made sex to be. Our children need to understand the sexual feelings and temptations they will encounter as they grow are normal. We should place boundaries on what they see, especially concerning television and internet. We can guard our children from images that are inappropriate as they learn to deal with their feelings.

We also need to teach our children the consequences of sin. Sex outside marriage is wrong and will bring pain and confusion in our lives. But when sex is guarded and protected as a gift intended for the one and only person we marry, it is a beautiful expression of physical, mental, emotional, and spiritual love for another person. Only in that context can we experience the pleasure and freedom which God intended us to enjoy in an intimate marriage relationship.

We can't lock them up in a tower, but we can teach our children God's truth about intimacy so they can make good decisions and enjoy married love as God intended.

For further reading: Matthew 5:28, 1 Corinthians 6:18-20, Galatians 5:19, Ephesians 5:3, 1 Thessalonians 4:1-8

DAY 344

"He has taken me to the banquet hall, and
his banner over me is love" (Song of Songs 2:4).

I would not be true to myself if I did not share that I believe the Song is also an allegory of God's love for us. For Jews and the early church, this understanding was paramount. The Jews believed that the books of Solomon represented the temple: Proverbs represented the Outer Court, Ecclesiastes the Inner Court, and Song of Songs the Holy of Holies, where God's presence dwelled.[100] Throughout the Bible, our relationship with God is often compared to a marriage relationship.

"For your Maker is your husband—the LORD Almighty is his name—the Holy One of Israel is your Redeemer" (Isaiah 54:5).

"As a bridegroom rejoices over his bride, so will your God rejoice over you" (Isaiah 62:5b).

In the New Testament, we also see this comparison:

"'For this reason a man will leave his father and mother and be united to his wife, and the two will become one flesh.' This is a profound mystery—but I am talking about Christ and the church" (Ephesians 5:31-32).

"I am jealous for you with a godly jealousy. I promised you to one husband, to Christ, so that I might present you as a pure virgin to him" (2 Corinthians 11:2).

God is jealous for us because He will not be second to our other loves. He calls us into intimate fellowship with Him, to the secret place, the Holy of Holies, where we worship and seek His face. We are the Bride of Christ (Revelation 19:7).

One day, our betrothal will be complete and we will be joined together with Christ, the Bridegroom, for all eternity. The intimacy we have experienced here on earth will be nothing compared to seeing Him face to face. He will take us into His banquet hall and we will rest under the banner of His love.

For further reading: Isaiah 54:5, 62:5b, 2 Corinthians 11:2, Ephesians 5:31-32, Revelation 19:7

DAY 345

"In the land of Uz there lived a man whose name was Job. This man was blameless and upright; he feared God and shunned evil"
(Job 1:1).

Blameless and upright. Oh, don't you wish God could say that about us? Truth be told, the Bible tells us there is no one righteous in God's sight (Romans 3:10), so how could Job have been? The Hebrew word translated as *blameless* is used in Genesis to describe one who walks closely with the Lord. The word for *upright* actually means "straight (not crooked or twisted).[101] These words imply that Job lived by God's standards in his life and character.

"This sterling description of Job does not necessarily imply sinlessness, but certainly it presents him as a man of extraordinarily high moral character."[102] In other words, Job was a man of integrity. He walked with God every day and sought to live his life in a way that pleased God.

Do you think that level of character is out of reach for you? I sometimes do. When I'm struggling with sin or temptation, I often think less of myself, wishing I could be more like someone else who seems to have it all together. The truth is that in Jesus, we have been made righteous.

"God made him who had no sin to be sin for us, so that in him we might become the righteousness of God" (2 Corinthians 5:21).

I know. That's pretty hard to wrap your head around, huh? So here's the deal. When we surrender our lives to God, we are accepting Jesus' payment for our sins. His righteousness becomes ours. The point is that's the only way we can be in right standing and have a relationship with a holy God.

But that's not where it ends. We also are called to live a life of righteousness by faith in Christ's work for us on the cross. So, rather than just "wishing" to be like someone else, God calls us to walk by faith in His righteousness by pursuing it. "Flee the evil desires of youth, and pursue righteousness, faith, love, and peace, along with those who call on the Lord out of a pure heart" (2 Timothy 2:22). Fear God and walk with Him by faith. That's what it means to be blameless.

For further reading: Genesis 17, Romans 3:10, 2 Corinthians 5:21, 2 Timothy 2:22, 1 Peter 2:24

DAY 346

"Early in the morning he would sacrifice a burnt offering for each of them, thinking, 'Perhaps my children have sinned and cursed God in their hearts.' This was Job's regular custom" (Job 1:5).

The stench of burning flesh rose in the air as Job once again brought an offering before the Lord for his children. In those days, only a sacrifice of blood and flesh could appease the wrath of God towards sin. So, Job would slaughter an animal and sacrifice it before God to cover the sins of his children. Job lived before the sacrificial system was put in place by Moses, so each father functioned as the priest for his family.[103] His job as a righteous parent was to intercede for the lives of his children.

We can't cover the sins of our children, as much as we may want to. Sin brings pain, and we would do anything to protect our children from the destruction and suffering of sin, just as Job wanted to protect his children. The good news is that Jesus has already been offered as the perfect sacrifice to appease the wrath of God towards sin. Our job is to intercede for them. We have a responsibility for our children's salvation in three ways.

First, we pray for them. We should daily pray for our children, that God would move in their hearts and draw them to himself. We intercede for the Lord to save them until they come to Him in faith. Then we pray for them daily that they would cooperate with His work in their lives.

Second, we share the gospel with them. Our children are our disciples, and we have a responsibility to share God's Word with them and teach them His truth.

Third, we model a godly life for them. Sometimes we are afraid for them to see our shortcomings, but it's our honesty that will impact them the most. We need to confess and ask forgiveness when we fall short. They need to see us spending time with the Father and living for Him every day, We can't save our children, and sacrifices are no longer necessary. But we can intercede for them with the Father, lead them to saving faith, and disciple them in the ways of God. Let that be our regular custom.

For further reading: Deuteronomy 6:4-9, 1 Samuel 1:27, Matthew 28:19-20, Romans 12:12, 1 Corinthians 11:1

DAY 347

"The LORD said to Satan, 'Where have you come from?'
Satan answered the LORD, 'From roaming through
the earth and going back and forth in it'" (Job 1:7).

God is omniscient, meaning He knows all things. God wasn't unaware of where Satan had been. He was asking Satan to give an account of himself, which shows us that Satan is subject to God.

The name Satan means "accuser." After Satan fell from heaven along with one third of the angels, apparently he began looking for people on earth to find fault in so that he could bring accusations against them to God.

Evil hearts are always looking for others to accuse. But don't lose sight of the bigger picture here: Satan is subject to God. He's not God's equal. He's not God's opposite. He is a created being who fell from grace.

With that in mind, we must remember that he does have great power; if you belong to Jesus, he is certainly your enemy and seeks to bring you down. God tells us to be alert to his strategies (1 Peter 5:8-9).

The Word says he prowls around, just as he did in Job's day, roaming around looking for someone to accuse before God. But notice he is "like" a roaring lion. He loves to imitate God and offer cheap substitutes. But Jesus *is* the Lion of Judah. Satan is a poor counterfeit. The devil is powerful, but he is still under the control of God (1 John 4:4).

We serve the Greater One. So, we need not fear the enemy, only be aware of his tactics and resist him (James 4:7). As we dive into Job's story, don't be intimidated by what appears to be Satan's attack on Job. Nothing touched Job that God didn't allow, and He allowed it for a reason.

All that God does is out of His love for our good and for His glory. You can be sure you are in His hands as well.

For further reading: Isaiah 14:12, Luke 10:18, James 4:7, 1 Peter 5:8-9, 1 John 4:4

DAY 348

"Then the LORD said to Satan, 'Have you considered my servant Job?'" (Job 1:8a).

I don't know of any words that can cause us to shudder quite like those. God Himself initiated this conversation that led to Job's extreme testing and loss. While it may be difficult for us to wrap our minds around why God would allow such pain in the life of someone who was so devoted to Him, it teaches us a great lesson about pain and suffering.

God initiated this test because He knew Job's heart. No one knew Job like God did—not his wife, not his children, not his friends, and most certainly, not Satan. God absolutely knew that Job would pass this test. Often when we are going through a dark time of intense suffering, we may feel that God has abandoned us, because we tend to think that if we serve God, then we shouldn't have to suffer pain. But God never promised that in His Word.

In fact, He promised quite the opposite. Because we often fall for the "Granny Gospel" (as my friend Michelle calls it), we get caught up in believing what our granny told us, rather than what the Bible actually teaches. For instance, you've probably heard it said that God won't put on us more than we can handle, but that's not true. That belief is a twisting of this verse:

"No temptation has seized you except what is common to man. And God is faithful; he will not let you be tempted beyond what you can bear. But when you are tempted, he will provide a way out so that you can stand up under it" (1 Corinthians 10:13).

First of all, this verse is about temptation, not testing. God does not tempt us, but He does sometimes test us in order for us to grow in our faith. Secondly, the point here is that God does sometimes allow more on us than we can handle so we will learn to depend on Him and not ourselves (2 Corinthians 1:8).

We don't know why God brought Job to Satan's attention or why God allowed such intense suffering in his life. But we do know that God never promised that we wouldn't experience suffering in this world, only that He would be with us.

For further reading: Deuteronomy 8:2-3, John 16:33, 1 Corinthians 10:13, James 1:13-15

DAY 349

"'Does Job fear God for nothing?' Satan replied. 'Have you not put a hedge around him and his household and everything he has?'" (Job 1:9).

Do we fear God for nothing, or do we serve Him for the promise of benefits? Sure, we are drawn to God because He is love, truth, grace, mercy, peace, and light. Most of us would rather live in the house of the Lord than dwell in the tents of the wicked (Psalm 84). Proverbs especially affirms that principle of righteousness that leads to blessings, so do we serve God because of His blessings?

Honestly, that's a dangerous place to be. I believe that's why many fall away when times get hard. They came to God on the promise of His many blessings and didn't expect to face suffering. We do people a disservice when we lead them to Christ with only half the gospel.

Jesus said to count the cost before we decide to follow Him (Luke 14:25-35). The whole gospel shows us the suffering of Jesus, and He is the One we are called to follow. Job is a type of Christ, because He shows us an example of one who is righteous, but suffers at the hands of evil. Jesus was sinless, yet the Father allowed Him to suffer greatly (1 Peter 2:21).

When we look to this life as all there is, suffering can seem pointless and horrendous. But when we remember that this world is not our home, we can take comfort in the fact that Jesus has overcome. In the midst of our suffering, God is with us. His promise is not that we will live our best life now, but that our best life is still to come.

So why do we serve a God who doesn't promise us a perfect life on earth? We serve Him because we love Him, and we love Him because He first loved us. God made a way for us to know Him through Jesus. His promise to us is that we can live this life with His presence in us and with us, and that we will spend eternity with Him. That's the promise for following Him. If we came to Him for any other reason, we need to surrender to the truth of His Word.

For further reading: Psalm 84, Luke 14:25-35, James 5:7-11, 1 Peter 2:21, 1 John 4:19

DAY 350

"The LORD said to Satan, 'Very well, then, everything he has is in your hands, but on the man himself do not lay a finger'" (Job 1:12).

The accuser had been given power to cause tremendous suffering in Job's life, but only as God allowed it. Satan may have great power, but he has no authority outside of God's jurisdiction. Remember, God knew Job's heart, and this contest was a match in which God would win. Job may not have known that, but God did. And so do we.

When we face trouble and hardships in life, we can take comfort in the fact that God knows the end from the beginning. He knows all things, and He knows how He will see us through it, even when we don't. Satan has power to wreak havoc in our lives, but he is on a leash that God controls. The one who knows us best and loves us completely is the one in ultimate control.

"Since the children have flesh and blood, he too shared in their humanity so that by his death he might destroy him who holds the power of death—that is, the devil—and free those who all their lives were held in slavery by their fear of death" (Hebrews 2:14-15). Jesus came to destroy the power of Satan over us (1 John 3:8).

"And having disarmed the powers and authorities, he made a public spectacle of them, triumphing over them by the cross" (Colossians 2:15).

Jesus has defeated Satan and the power of death over us. The enemy can destroy our physical bodies, but he cannot touch our souls.

"Do not be afraid of those who kill the body but cannot kill the soul. Rather, be afraid of the One who can destroy both soul and body in hell" (Matthew 10:28).

Satan can accuse us, he can afflict us, and he can cause suffering in our lives, but he can't do anything our Heavenly Father doesn't allow. So, we need not fear him nor the suffering that may come our way. Satan came to kill, but Jesus came to bring us life (John 10:10). If you are in Christ, you are in the hands of the Almighty. There's no greater place that you can be.

For further reading: Matthew 10:28, John 10:10, 19:11, Colossians 2:15, Hebrews 2:14-15, 1 John 3:8

DAY 351

*"At this, Job got up and tore his robe and shaved his head.
Then he fell to the ground in worship and said: 'Naked I came
from my mother's womb, and naked I will depart. The LORD
gave and the LORD has taken away; may the name of
the LORD be praised'" (Job 1:20-21).*

I can't imagine anything worse than to lose a child. The loss of Job's wealth was tough, but the cattle could be replaced. Losing his servants was probably heart-breaking, but more servants could be found. When Job heard that news that all ten of his children had been killed, however, he began to grieve. Job tore his robe and shaved his head, the signs of mourning in his culture. The fear of every parent's heart had come to him. These were the kids he prayed and sacrificed for every day because of his great love for them. How does one deal with such loss?

"This posture of humble reverence and devotion to God demonstrates that his faith has not been subverted by his suffering."[104]

Only Job's relationship with God allowed Him to go through such horrific loss with faith and worship. In essence, Job declared that God was good and worthy of praise no matter what. Job didn't have the Word of God as we do. The fact that he "feared God and shunned evil" reveals to us a relationship between Job and God. Job's understanding of God would have come simply through the revelation of God Himself.

Out of that revelation, God had shown Himself to be worthy of praise. Job had learned to acknowledge God in his blessings. He would also praise Him in his losses. When we face crushing loss that wounds us deeply and leaves us gasping for breath, the only thing we can do is to fall on our knees before God and worship Him. Everything we have in this life is a gift from Him.

May God give us wisdom and grace to face the suffering of this life and bring Him glory, even when it hurts.

For further reading: Psalm 30:5, John 16:33, Romans 8:18, Revelation 21:4

DAY 352

"In all this, Job did not sin by charging the LORD with wrongdoing"
(Job 1:22).

One of the hardest things about recognizing the sovereignty of God is knowing that He has the power to do absolutely anything, yet He sometimes chooses not to. We often wonder what we have done to cause suffering in our lives, especially if God answers a prayer for healing for someone else but not for our loved one. We know He has the power and we have the faith, so what is the problem? Why does God sometimes heal and sometimes not? Why does He answer some prayers and not others?

It's okay to question God. The Word is full of questions, and our God is big enough to handle them. When we seek the Lord with questions, we acknowledge that He is the One with the answers.

"Ask and it will be given to you; seek and you will find; knock and the door will be opened to you. For everyone who asks receives; he who seeks finds; and to him who knocks, the door will be opened" (Matthew 7:7-8).

In times of intense suffering, we should look to God for comfort and answers. But, we must realize that the answers don't always come this side of eternity. Our questions must always derive from a place of deep humility and surrender. Otherwise, we can grow bitter toward the Lord because we don't understand His ways.

Job grieved. He mourned deeply over the loss of his ten children. I'm sure he had plenty of questions in that moment, although we don't hear them until later. But he didn't charge God with wrongdoing. Job trusted the wisdom of God even in the midst of his pain.

God is all-powerful. There is nothing He can't do. But there are some things He chooses not to do. We may not understand, but we can walk in faith, knowing that He is good and He is love. If He allows it in our lives, He will redeem it for our good and for His glory.

For further reading: Jeremiah 32:17, Matthew 7:7-8, John 1:3, Romans 8:28

DAY 353

"'Skin for skin!' Satan replied. 'A man will give all he has for his own life. But stretch out your hand and strike his flesh and bones, and he will surely curse you to your face'" (Job 2:4-5).

Here we get a glimpse at Satan's motive. He wanted to prove to God that Job didn't serve God for nothing. The accuser believed that if he was allowed to strike Job with physical pain and suffering, Job would curse God to His face. Isn't that what Satan always wants? He hates God and the people who love Him. Sure, he wants to cause us intense pain and suffering, but he also wants to see us turn our backs on God. He wants his own sin and rebellion to be vindicated. He wants to prove God wrong.

According to God, Job had maintained his integrity (Job 2:3) even throughout the loss of his wealth, his servants, and all of his children. So the accuser looked for another angle to come against Job. He charged him with selfishness. Selfishness is at the root of most sin. When we are preoccupied with self, it's impossible to be fully surrendered to God. God wants us to love Him with all our hearts, souls, minds, and strength (Mark 12:30). The enemy wants to attack where we are most vulnerable and cause us to sin.

God allowed Satan to afflict Job's body, but he was not allowed to take his life. Again we see that Satan only has the authority that God gives him. And God knew Job's heart. He knew that even in this cosmic battle for Job's faith and integrity, God would give Job grace to overcome. I know people who endure intense physical suffering every day. Yet they love God. They don't blame God for the pain they are in; they trust God to help them through it. How do they endure?

Only through the grace that God extends.

We may never understand the reason for our suffering, but we can trust in God's grace to carry us through.

For further reading: Mark 12:30, 1 Corinthians 10:24, 2 Corinthians 12:7-9

DAY 354

*"His wife said to him, 'Are you still holding on
to your integrity? Curse God and die!'" (Job 2:9).*

Have you ever been through a time of deep suffering, only to have someone come along and say something that made it even worse? Before we judge Job's wife, though, let's remember that this mom just lost all ten of the children she carried in her womb, fed at her breast, rocked to sleep at night, taught to walk, and nursed when sick. Can you even imagine the level of pain and grief in her heart?

They lost all their wealth, which supported her as well. And then for her husband who always walked with integrity to be suffering such physical pain was just more than she could bear. We don't know the exact nature of Job's sickness, except that he had painful sores, nightmares, scabs, disfigurement, bad breath, excessive thinness, fever, and pain day and night.[105]

Job was sick to the point of death, so her command to "curse God and die" seemed to be all that was left for him to do. Satan tempted her to cause Job to sin just as Eve tempted Adam in the Garden. For Job's wife, it may have seemed like the only way for him to be relieved of his suffering. But for Job, he would rather die than to curse His God.

"He replied, 'You are talking like a foolish woman. Shall we accept good from God, and not trouble?' In all this, Job did not sin in what he said" (Job 2:10).

Sometimes in our pain, others will not understand. They may think we should just get over it. Or they may not understand our faith, and like Job's wife, encourage us to blame God. Rather than responding to their foolishness, we have to keep our focus on the Source of our help. Because we live in a fallen world marred by sin, we often will suffer the consequences of that sin, even if it's not our own. If others tempt us further in our suffering, we can look to God for help (Psalm 121:1-2).

Job had to lift his eyes from his circumstances and the naysayers around him, and turn his eyes to the only true source of help—the Lord.

For further reading: Genesis 3:1-7, Psalm 118:7, 121:1-2, Matthew 4:1-11

DAY 355

"When Job's three friends, Eliphaz the Temanite, Bildad the Shuhite, and Zophar the Naamathite, heard about all the troubles that had come upon him, they set out from their homes and met together by agreement to go and sympathize with him and comfort him" (Job 2:11).

I once had a close friend who lost her father. I, too, had lost my father a few years back, and I wanted so badly to comfort her. I shared some of my experience, hoping to encourage her; but in that moment, it wasn't what she needed to hear. I chose the verse above because I wanted to emphasize the fact that Job's three friends really did have good intentions. Their motivation was to sympathize with Job and bring him comfort.

Sometimes we really intend to help someone, but because we want to be the one to share just the right word with her, we make it about ourselves instead of our friend. Often what someone needs in a time of sorrow is just our presence. They may just need a hand to hold, arms to comfort, a warm body beside them.

Job's three friends wept when they saw him. They tore their robes and grieved right along with him. "Then they sat on the ground with him for seven days and seven nights. No one said a word to him, because they saw how great his suffering was" (Job 2:13).

When we experience a friend go through intense suffering, the best response may be silence. Platitudes don't mean a lot when you've lost a loved one. And as powerful as the Word of God is to heal and strengthen and comfort, when someone is in the stages of grieving, she may need time before she is ready to hear that. If we want to really bring peace and comfort when a friend is grieving, we should pray. Ask God to comfort and strengthen her. Wait on the Holy Spirit to guide you when you do speak. But most of all, just be there and offer a hand to hold. Weep with your friend and validate her pain.

For further reading: Psalm 23:4, 34:18, 119:50, 2 Corinthians 1:3-4, Revelation 21:4

DAY 356

"'What I feared has come upon me; what
I dreaded has happened to me'" (Job 3:25).

Do you allow fear and dread to keep you awake at night? When we dwell on things that could happen, we allow the enemy to get a foothold in our thoughts. I used to stay awake at night, worrying about my children—much like Job. When they were young, I was afraid they would be kidnapped. When they started driving, I feared they would be in an accident. As they got older, I worried about their relationships.

The more we allow fearful thoughts to take hold, the more we act on those fears in choices we make, sometimes to the point of being obsessive—and definitely to the point of insomnia. One thing I learned early on is that we can choose what we think about. So when the enemy started filling my head with fearful thoughts at night, I would quote Bible verses in my head. I would speak the Word over my children.

This practice worked better than prayer, because sometimes prayer can just become desperate pleadings that keep us focused on the fear. The Word of God changes our focus from us and our problem to God and His provision. Job was a godly man, but he hadn't surrendered his fears to God.

God tells us in His Word what to think about: "Finally, brothers, whatever is true, whatever is noble, whatever right, whatever is pure, whatever is lovely, whatever is admirable—if anything is excellent or praiseworthy—think about such things" (Philippians 4:8).

He also tells us not to fear: "'So do not fear, for I am with you; do not be dismayed, for I am your God. I will strengthen you and help you; I will uphold you with my righteous right hand'" (Isaiah 41:10).

If you struggle with dread and fear, find some Scriptures that will encourage your heart and commit them to memory. The next time fear keeps you tossing and turning, let the Word bring you peace and rest.

For further reading: Isaiah 41:10, Philippians 4:8, 2 Timothy 1:7, 1 John 4:18

DAY 357

"'But if you will look to God and plead with the Almighty, if you are pure and upright, even now he will rouse himself on your behalf and restore you to your rightful place'" (Job 8:5-6).

After Job's friends sat by his side and mourned with him, Job began to pour out his heart. He couldn't understand why God allowed him to even be born if He were going to bring such pain in his life. We all want to make sense of our suffering, so his friends began to share with Job why they believed this tragedy had occurred and what Job could do to make things better.

Eliphaz believed in the doctrine of retribution, that the righteous are blessed and the wicked suffer. While this is a general principle that we see in other wisdom literature, such as Proverbs, it doesn't mean that everyone who suffers is being punished.

Bildad also encouraged his friend to repent because he believed that Job was experiencing punishment because God is just. While God certainly is just, that doesn't equate that all suffering is punishment or that all gain is the result of righteousness. Zophar went so far as to suggest that Job had not even suffered all that he deserved! It's true that we don't get all that we deserve, but that hardly seems to be the case for Job.

As we can see, all three of his friends spoke *some* truth, but just as Satan twists the truth and perverts God's Word, Job's three friends distorted the truth and only compounded Job's suffering and anguish. This understanding of suffering being the result of sin was still in the hearts and minds of God's people centuries later (John 9:2-3)

Job continued to stand in faith and defend himself to his friends. He didn't know the whole story—that God was proving his faith to Satan. But he did know God. And out of that relationship Job was able to continue to seek God for understanding.

For further reading: Genesis 3, Luke 13:1-5, John 9:2-3, Romans 5:12

DAY 358

"'But I desire to speak to the Almighty and
to argue my case with God'" (Job 13:3).

What Job needed was a mediator. He acknowledged that he could have sinned and not been aware of it, but because he sought to walk with God in integrity and uprightness, he wanted an appeal. He wanted a chance, not to argue with God, but to state his case and plea for an answer to his suffering.[106]

Job had a relationship with God that had been marred by what he perceived as a misunderstanding. Surely, if he could just appeal to the Almighty, God could help him sort out the problem. Job wanted to have his relationship with God restored. He wanted justice.

The cry of Job's heart was answered in the person of Jesus. Just as Job needed a mediator, so do we. As sinful creatures, we cannot come before a holy God. We have broken His law. Like Job, even our own righteousness is as dirty rags (Isaiah 64:6). All we deserve is death (Romans 6:23).

"For this reason Christ is the mediator of a new covenant, that those who are called may receive the promised eternal inheritance—now that he has died as a ransom to set them free from the sins committed under the first covenant" (Hebrews 9:15).

Under the covenant of the law we are guilty. No one can keep it. But under the covenant of blood through Jesus' death on the cross, we are restored and made right with God. What Job longed for, we have in Jesus. "For there is one God and one mediator between God and men, the man Christ Jesus" (1 Timothy 2:5).

When we feel wronged and justice seems distant, we can remember that we do have a Mediator. The Lord Jesus will go to the Father and appeal on our behalf. Just because we don't see justice doesn't mean that God is not just. Some things are eternal. We can go to God with faith in Jesus and trust that He will make all things right in His time.

For further reading: Isaiah 64:6, Romans 6:23, 1 Timothy 2:5, Hebrews 9:15

DAY 359

"'Though he slay me, yet will I hope in him'" (Job 13:15).

I find it ironic that this verse is often quoted, yet scholars are almost certain that the original Hebrew reads "He will surely slay me; I have no hope—yet I will surely defend my ways to his face."[107]

Here's the deal: Job trusted God. He believed that even if his circumstance ended in death, he would still have the opportunity to seek God's justice face to face. In a time in which there was no written word and no understanding of the resurrection, we see in Job tremendous faith.

Job had no hope that he would experience healing and restoration in this life, but he still had hope for the one to come. That's what salvation is all about.

If we live only for this life, we are sure to be left disappointed; and, at times, we may even lose hope—not hope in God, but like Job, hope for this life. But God calls us to live with our eyes on eternity, and therein we always have hope.

When we are surrounded by pain and confusion, we can turn our eyes to our God.

"So we fix our eyes not on what is seen, but on what is unseen. For what is seen is temporary, but what is unseen is eternal" (2 Corinthians 4:18).

You may sometimes feel that hope is elusive, but know it all depends on what (or rather whom) our hope is in.

Put your hope in God and not a particular outcome. Trust Him with this life and the next. Only then can you declare that even if you don't see your victory in this life, you will see it in the one to come.

"Let us hold unswervingly to the hope we profess, for he who promised is faithful" (Hebrews 10:23).

He is, indeed.

For further reading: Romans 15:13, 2 Corinthians 4:18, Hebrews 10:23, 11:1, 1 Peter 1:3

DAY 360

*"'My days have passed, my plans are shattered,
and so are the desires of my heart'" (Job 17:11).*

Broken. Desperate. Shattered.

We are surrounded by those who feel that way—lost, lonely, confused, and broken by the curse of sin. Whether they suffer the consequences of their own mistakes or the sins of others, many people feel hopeless.

That's why so many suffer from depression, anxiety, and stress. Millions are spent each year in counseling, drugs, and therapy to help people cope with the losses in their lives. We are not mentally, emotionally, or physically created to endure trauma and heartbreak.

The natural response to pain is to look for comfort. Unfortunately, most people look in the wrong place. Alcohol, drugs, relationships, sex, food, shopping—all of these can be attempts to find some comfort in the midst of our pain.

All sin—whether ours or the sins of the world around us—brings pain. But how we respond to that pain will determine our recovery. We can comfort ourselves with unhealthy responses, or we can seek comfort in the arms of God.

"The eternal God is your refuge, and underneath are the everlasting arms" (Deuteronomy 33:27).

Let's keep our eyes open to those who are suffering around us. Without judgment, let's share the love of God with them and lead them to the everlasting arms. How they respond to the gospel is up to them, but whether or not they hear it is up to us. There is comfort to be had, even in the midst of horrible suffering. May our lives point to the One who is the Comforter.

"Praise be to the God and Father of our Lord Jesus Christ, the Father of compassion and the God of all comfort" (2 Corinthians 1:3).

For further reading: Deuteronomy 33:27, Acts 1:8, Romans 10:14, 2 Corinthians 1:3

DAY 361

"'I know that my Redeemer lives, and that in the end he will stand upon the earth'" (Job 19:25).

When all hell breaks loose in this life, let me tell you what you can know. Your Redeemer lives. What does it mean to be redeemed?

From our perspective after the cross, it means that Jesus has paid the price to rescue us from the penalty of sin and bring us back to a new way of life. But from Job's perspective, to be redeemed meant to be delivered, avenged, and justified.

Job's declaration was a statement of faith. He believed that even if he never got an audience with God or an advocate that would plead on his behalf, that one day he would have God Himself. As followers of Christ, we have both. We have a Savior right now, One who will forgive, redeem, restore and cleanse. We have a Defender, an Advocate, who will go before the Father on our behalf and plead our case.

And we have the Holy Spirit of the Redeemer living in us. We have God Himself—His very presence—to carry us through whatever we face in life. And one day He will stand upon the earth and every foe will be vanquished, every pain will be healed. Because He reigns in victory over death, hell, and sin, we can be assured that we will overcome whatever pain, fear, grief, sin, or trial we are in right now. Jesus has already fought the battle and we win!

My friend, I don't know what you are struggling with today, but just know deep in your heart that your Redeemer lives. And He wants you to know that your Redeemer loves, because that's what keeps appearing on my screen every time I try to type "your Redeemer lives."

He lives and He loves, and at the end of the day, that is all you need. This world is not your home and its pain is not your final destination. Suffering doesn't get the last word. Your Redeemer does.

For further reading: Psalm 19:14, Romans 8:7, Ephesians 1:7, Hebrews 11:6, 1 John 5:4

DAY 362

"Then the LORD answered Job out of the storm" (Job 38:1).

Throughout all of the discourses between Job and his friends, God has been referred to with the designation *Elohim,* the name that emphasizes that He is the One True God, the Creator, with all power and authority. But it is the LORD, *Yahweh,* the God of the covenant, who responds to Job. Elohim is the oldest designation for God and would have been the name known to Job and his friends. But the narrator of this account recognizes the God of Israel who keeps His promises.

After all that time, Job finally got what he desired: an answer from the Lord. And God proved to Job that he had an audience with Him all along. God had never left him, and God had heard every word of his heart. "He said: 'Who is this that darkens my counsel with words without knowledge?'" (Job 38:1b-2). I love this question, because when we are upset and struggling, how often do we come to God with our complaints, often to find out later we didn't know the whole story. God is saying to Job, "Son, just be quiet. You don't know the whole story." Job was unaware of how proud God was of him, that God initiated the entire drama with Satan because he knew Job's heart, or that God was the One who was for him and with Him all along.

Job just didn't know. But God began to question Job to prove to him how limited his understanding actually was. What a beautiful gift we receive when God shows us how much we just don't know! It relieves our striving to understand. We can rest in our lack of understanding and trust the One who knows it all (Isaiah 55:8-9). We humans want to understand, when sometimes God is calling us to just believe. I think of Martha when Jesus allowed Lazarus to die, even though He could have come in time to save him. When Jesus came to the tomb where Lazarus lay, Martha questioned what Jesus was doing (John 11:39).

"Then Jesus said, 'Did I not tell you that if you believed, you would see the glory of God?'" (John 11:40). This is the God who revealed Himself to Moses as Yahweh, the God of the covenant, who keeps His promises even to an unbelieving, covenant-breaking people.

For further reading: Proverbs 3:5-6, Isaiah 55:8-9, John 11:39-40

DAY 363

"Then Job replied to the LORD: 'I know that you can do all things; no plan of yours can be thwarted. You asked, "Who is this that obscures my counsel without knowledge?" Surely I spoke of things I did not understand, things too wonderful for me to know'" (Job 42:1-3).

Have you ever stood at the edge of the sea and marveled at a Creator who designed tides controlled by the moon? Perhaps you have gazed at a star-swept sky and wondered how their patterns of movement have been consistent over thousands of years. Maybe you have held a newborn baby in your arms and felt the magnitude of One who designed fingernails, DNA, and senses too wonderful for us to have ever imagined on our own.

We serve a God who is beyond our wisdom and understanding. His plans cannot be thwarted. He does as He wills, and He does it all with our best in mind, sinful as we are. Job came to a moment of revelation. "Where were you, Job? What could you possibly understand about my ways when you can't explain how you got here?"

With all the advancements in technology and science today, nobody can understand the ways of God. If He could be understood, He wouldn't be God. If we could bring Him down to our level, He wouldn't be worthy of our worship. We not only serve a God beyond our understanding, but we serve a God who lowered Himself to become one of us, whose love and compassion are also beyond comprehension, yet who desires to make Himself known.

All that He is would be more than we can handle, but all we need is available for the asking. The Lord has revealed Himself to us as His Son, and He has come to dwell in us as His Spirit. The God that Job couldn't comprehend now lives in you and me! Life is hard. Pain is inevitable. But the God of all creation is in you to comfort, guide, help, and teach. Let your questions lead you to the Source of all the answers, even if His answer is just, "Here I am."

For further reading: Romans 11:33, 1 Corinthians 6:19, 13:12, Ephesians 1:13, Philippians 2:5-11

DAY 364

*"'My ears had heard of you but now my eyes have seen you.
Therefore I despise myself and repent in dust and ashes'"
(Job 42:5-6).*

Growing up, I knew very little about God. I visited church a few times and had been to vacation Bible school, but I really understood nothing about having a relationship with Jesus. Even when I prayed a prayer of confession and made a profession of faith, I really didn't understand what that meant.

But there came a day of revelation when I understood that Jesus really loves me and wanted to be in my life—not just to save me from hell, but to be in relationship with me and to live in me. It was like I had heard of Him, but then I really had my eyes opened to see the truth.

Job had heard of God. He had walked with God. He was a man of character and integrity. But until He heard God's voice for Himself, he hadn't really experienced God. Although his trial and suffering were so intense and painful, his cry to the Lord allowed him to truly experience God in a new and fresh way. And it brought him to his knees in repentance.

We can go to church all our lives, understand the plan of salvation, and be on our way to heaven, but unless we have an experience with God, we will never really have our eyes opened to who He is. Sometimes pain is the event that makes us desperate enough to seek Him in that way.

We may never understand why children suffer or Christians are persecuted or wicked people seem to prosper. But what we can know is that God is good, He is just, He is love, and He is eternal. What we experience here is not all there is, therefore we must trust that there's more to the story. Our only response should be to bow our knees before a holy God and repent of our own need to know it all. He is God and we are not. "Now faith is being sure of what we hope for and certain of what we do not see" (Hebrews 11:1). Even as God opens our eyes to the truth in His Word and in His presence, we still do not see it all. So we walk by faith, knowing one day, we will see Him face to face (1 Corinthians 13:12a).

For further reading: 1 Corinthians 2:14, 13:12a, 1 Timothy 6:16, Hebrews 11:1, 6

DAY 365

"The LORD blessed the latter part of Job's life more than the first"
(Job 42:12).

This devotional began with Psalm 1—a comparison of two paths in life: the righteous who are blessed and the wicked who are cursed. Now we end with Job, whose story seems to fly in the face of Day 1. Unless, as Paul Harvey said, you know the rest of the story. If we live this life with only us and our world in mind, all would seem meaningless, as the Teacher in Ecclesiastes declared. But there's more to the story, just as there was much more to Job's story.

Every word of God is true, and He does keep His promises. We just have a limited view. A life surrendered to God and His ways will be blessed for all eternity. God does, indeed, reward righteousness. And a life lived for self and the world will suffer for all eternity. We just need an eternal perspective.

As we surrender our lives and loves to the One who has overcome, we may not always receive answers, but we will always have His presence. The God of restoration will make all things beautiful in His time. God has opened my eyes to the beauty of Job's story, and now it's becoming a favorite. You see, we read Job all the wrong way. We see his story as a tale of pain and suffering and "the patience of Job."

But it's not about Job at all. It's the story of God—a God who keeps His covenant promises, who fulfills His plans for us, who is beyond our understanding, and who loves us in spite of ourselves, who speaks to us and makes Himself known, and who redeems all things in His time. And it's a timeless story that points to an endless hope found in Jesus alone. For the persecuted Christian, the abandoned wife, the mother who lost her child, the lonely widower, the cancer patient, the sick, slandered, abused, disgraced, and mistreated, the one who has given up hope, He is the Restorer of all things (1 Peter 5:10-11).

You can make it, I promise. In the whole scheme of eternity, it will be just a little while, and He will make all things new. And that's the *truth*.

For further reading: John 16:33, Romans 5:3-5, 1 Peter 5:10-11, Revelation 21:4

How to Have New Life

We were each created by God to know and worship Him. God loves you and desires a personal relationship with you.

The Bible teaches us that we are all sinners. Romans 3:23 says, "for all have sinned and fall short of the glory of God." God is holy and righteous and good. But we are all born with a sinful nature because He made us with a free will—the opportunity to choose whether or not we will follow Him. Left to ourselves, we will fall short of His glory and righteousness. This sin separates us from God and leads only to death. Romans 6:23 says, "For the wages of sin is death."

Because God loves us so much, He made a way for us to know Him through His Son. "But God demonstrates his own love for us in this: while we were still sinners, Christ died for us" (Romans 5:8). God sent His only Son, Jesus, who lived a perfect life, to die on the cross for us as payment for our sin. He took the punishment on Himself so that we could be free from sin's penalty. The rest of Romans 6:23 (above) says this: "but the gift of God is eternal life in Christ Jesus." We are sinners, and yet through Jesus and the gift of God, we can have eternal life. The truth is that we really can have a personal relationship with God through His Son, Jesus.

Romans 10:9-10 tells us "That if you confess with your mouth, 'Jesus is Lord,' and believe in your heart that God raised him from the dead, you will be saved. For it is with your heart that you believe and are justified, and it is with your mouth that you confess and are saved."

If God is speaking to your heart right now and you want to be saved, pray a prayer like this one:

> Lord God,
>
> I believe that You are God and that You created me to know You. I believe that You sent your Son to die on the cross for my sins and that He rose again and lives forever. I know that I am a sinner and I confess my sins to You now. I ask You to forgive me and cleanse me and come to live inside my heart and be the Lord of my life. I choose to follow You and live for You from this day forward.
>
> In Jesus' name,
>
> Amen

Get Grounded and Keep Growing

You want to study the Bible and grow your faith. I know you do. And I know you want to start each day with a habit of spending time with Jesus. I also know that even when your heart is right, life can often get in the way.

Groceries must be shopped, laundry folded, homework checked, meals prepared, work done, relationships built, ministry carried out. And even when we have the best of intentions, it's really hard to stay consistent with in-depth Bible study.

But when we don't stay in the Word, we don't grow. Relationships are harder, work suffers, real ministry is impossible, and our hearts grow discontent. That's because apart from HIM we can do nothing. And His Word is the truth we need to walk in day by day.

The good news is that it doesn't have to be that way. You don't have to just settle for the crumbs from the Master's table. That's a lie from the enemy. Instead, you can sit down and feast on His Word. Even if you are super busy.

Grounded and Growing is a ministry dedicated to encouraging your spiritual growth through practical strategies and helpful resources for serious Bible study that transforms lives. Just scan the code below for more resources.

- Books and Bible studies

- Anatomy of the Bible course

- The FOCUSED 15 Challenge

- Private Facebook group, *Growing Your Faith*

- Devotional Blog

- Quiet Time Guide

- Speaking Events

Acknowledgments

My heart's desire for this devotional is that it would spark in many women a desire for truth—not as the world defines it but as the Word defines it.

I am so thankful for the many spiritual leaders and mentors in my life who have encouraged me to search for truth.

Kenneth, I am so blessed to be doing life with you. I'm so thankful we held on during the hard years. These days are sweeter than ever.

Josiah and Moriah, you make my heart sing! Thank you for being such a godly example of grace and truth.

Bethany, my baby girl, I'm so grateful for your light-heartedness that lifts me up. You bring such joy into my life.

Mema, thank you for being a mother and a friend, for editing every week, feeding me lunch every day, and traveling with me when I speak. You are the biggest support behind this ministry.

To my Bible Study group, I wouldn't want to do life without you. Your laughter, tears, prayers, and presence in my life are one of the many blessings God has granted (not to mention, your agreeing to help with last-minute edits!).

And to Jesus, the reason I write, thank you for being the Truth.

About the Author

Jennifer Hayes Yates is a wife, mama, writer, and speaker with an empty nest and a Southern accent. Having taught in Christian education for twenty-two years, she has a passion for communicating God's truth and inspiring busy women to grow their faith one quiet moment with Jesus at a time.

Jennifer is now a blogger, best-selling author, and passionate speaker. Lover of all things Jesus, books, and coffee, she can be found in quiet corners or busy spaces, sipping lattes, studying commentaries, and chatting up strangers.

But she's still just a small-town girl hoping to glorify God in all she writes and make a few disciples along the way.

You can follow Jennifer on Facebook, Instagram, Amazon, and at Jenniferhyates.com.

Note from the Author

Thank you for reading this book!

I am so humbled and thankful that you chose this devotional for your quiet time with Jesus.

I would love to hear your thoughts. Your feedback means so much to me and will help me in preparing future books.

Please leave a helpful review on Amazon, letting me know what you thought of the book.

Thanks so much!

Jennifer

End Notes

[1] John R. Kohlenberger, Ed., *NIV Exhaustive Bible Concordance*, Third Edition (Grand Rapids: Zondervan, 1990, 1999, 2015), 1473.

[2] Kenneth Barker, *The NIV Study Bible,* (Grand Rapids: Zondervan, 1973, 1978, 1984), 808.

[3] Kohlenberger, 1369.

[4] Patrick Franklin, Touch Bible KJV + Concordance, (Apple App Store: 2011).

[5] Barker, 832.

[6] https://www.thattheworldmayknow.com/ (accessed February 28, 2019).

[7] https://www.merriam-webster.com/dictionary/dread (accessed February 28, 2019).

[8] https://www.merriam-webster.com/dictionary/overwhelm (accessed February 28, 2019).

[9] Barker, 853.

[10] Franklin.

[11] Kohlenberger, 1483.

[12] Ibid, 1463.

[13] https://www.barna.com/research/state-church-2016/ (accessed February 28, 2019).

[14] Kohlenberger, 1480.

[15] Barker, 871.

[16] Ibid, 875.

[17] Ibid.

[18] Ibid.

[19] Kohlenberger, 1400.

[20] Kohlenberger, 1490.

[21] https://www.dictionary.com/browse/acclaim (accessed February 28, 2019).

[22] Kohlenberger, 1430.

[23] Kohlenberger, 1441.

[24] Franklin.

[25] Ibid.

[26] Kohlenberger, 1455.

[27] Keith and Kristyn Getty, Sing! How Worship Transforms Your Life, Family, and Church, Nashville: B&H Publishing Group, 2017.

[28] https://www.hebrew4christians.com (accessed February 28, 2019).

[29] Ibid.

[30] Ibid.

[31] Ibid.

[32] Ibid.

[33] Ibid.

[34] Ibid.

[35] Ibid.

[36] Ibid.

[37] Ibid.

[38] Ibid.

[39] Ibid.

[40] Barker, 46.

[41] https://www.hebrew4christians.com (accessed February 28, 2019).

[42] Ibid.

[43] Ibid.

[44] Ibid.

[45] Ibid.

[46] Ibid.

[47] Ibid.

[48] Ibid.

[49] Ibid.

[50] Ibid.

[51] Ibid.

[52] Franklin.

[53] Ibid.

[54] Kohlenberger, 1407.

[55] Barker, 928.

[56] Ibid.

[57] Kelly Minter, *No Other Gods* (Nashville: Lifeway Press, 2007), 14.

[58] Kohlenberger, 1574.

[59] Franklin.

[60] https://www.space.com/25959-how-many-stars-are-in-the-milky-way.html (accessed February 28, 2019).

[61] https://www.space.com/25303-how-many-galaxies-are-in-the-universe.html (accessed February 28, 2019).

62 Barker, 940.

63 Ibid, 946.

64 Kohlenberger, 1425.

65 Ibid, 1476.

66 Ibid, 1574.

67 Ibid, 1505.

68 Ibid, 1426.

69 Ibid, 1404.

70 Ibid, 1053

71 Barker, 951.

72 Kohlenberger, 1442.

73 https://askabiologist.asu.edu/content/ant-factoids (accessed February 28, 2019).

74 Kohlenberger, 1462.

75 Ibid, 1369.

76 Ibid, 1475.

77 Ibid, 1489.

78 Ibid, 1455.

79 Ibid, 1404.

80 Ibid, 1397.

81 https://greatergood.berkeley.edu/article/item/six_ways_happiness_is_good_for_your_health (accessed February 28, 2019).

82 Kohlenberger, 1406.

83 Barker, 972.

[84] Kohlenberger, 1409.

[85] https://americanaddictioncenters.org/alcoholism-treatment/mental-effects (accessed December 20, 2018).

[86] https://wealthwithpurpose.com/god-money/why-does-the-bible-mention-money-so-often/ (accessed February 28, 2019).

[87] https://www.christianitytoday.com/edstetzer/2014/may/dropouts-and-disciples-how-many-students-are-really-leaving.html (accessed February 28, 2019).

[88] Kohlenberger, 1478.

[89] https://www.biblestudytools.com/commentaries/gills-exposition-of-the-bible/proverbs-25-11.html (accessed February 28, 2019).

[90] Kohlenberger, 1396.

[91] Ibid, 1397.

[92] Gordon D. Fee and Douglas Stuart, *How to Read the Bible for All Its Worth*, (Grand Rapids: Zondervan, 1981,1993, 2004, 2014), 252.

[93] Ortberg, John, *When the Game Is Over, It All Goes Back in the Box*, (Grand Rapids: Zondervan, 2009).

[94] Douglas Stuart, Gordon Conwell Seminary, Lecture 22: Song of Songs, https://www.biblicaltraining.org (accessed February 28, 2019).

[95] Daniel J. Estes, *Handbook on the Wisdom Books and Psalms* (Grand Rapids: Baker Publishing Group, 2005), 405-406.

[96] Barker, 1006.

[97] Ibid.

[98] Estes, 412.

[99] Ibid, 436.

[100] Henrietta C. Mears, *What the Bible Is All About* (Ventura: Regal Books, 1953, 1997), 208.

101 Kohlenberger, 1412.

102 Estes, 20.

103 Barker, 735.

104 Estes, 32.

105 Barker, 736.

106 Estes, 65.

107 Estes, 67.